Encounters with Melai

In *Encounters with Melanie Klein: Selected Papers of Elizabeth Spillius* the author argues that her two professions, anthropology and psycho-analysis, have much in common, and explains how her background in anthropology led her on to a profound involvement in psychoanalysis and her establishment as a leading figure amongst Kleinian analysts.

Spillius describes what she regards as the important features of Kleinian thought and discusses the research she has carried out in Melanie Klein's unpublished Archive, including Klein's views on projective identification.

Spillius's own clinical ideas make up the last part of the book with papers on envy, phantasy, technique, the negative therapeutic reaction and otherness. Her writing has a clarity which is very particular to her; she conveys complicated ideas in a most straightforward manner, well illustrated with pertinent clinical material.

This book represents 50 years of the developing thought and scholarship of a talented and dedicated psychoanalyst.

Elizabeth Spillius originally studied psychology and anthropology and is now a training and supervising analyst of the British Psycho-analytical Society. She is the author of *Tongan Society at the Time of Captain Cook's Visits*, published by the Polynesian Society in Welling-ton, New Zealand and of *Family and Social Network* published by Tavistock-Routledge. She is a member of the Melanie Klein trust and is involved in researching and writing about the development of Kleinian and post-Kleinian thinking. She has edited *Melanie Klein Today Volume 1: Mainly Theory* and *Volume 2: Mainly Practice*, published by Routledge in the New Library of Psychoanalysis series.

Priscilla Roth and **Richard Rusbridger** are training and supervising psychoanalysts of the British Psychoanalytical Society.

THE NEW LIBRARY OF PSYCHOANALYSIS
General Editor   Dana Birksted-Breen

The New Library of Psychoanalysis was launched in 1987 in association with the Institute of Psychoanalysis, London. It took over from the International Psychoanalytical Library which published many of the early translations of the works of Freud and the writings of most of the leading British and Continental psychoanalysts.

The purpose of the New Library of Psychoanalysis is to facilitate a greater and more widespread appreciation of psychoanalysis and to provide a forum for increasing mutual understanding between psychoanalysts and those working in other disciplines such as the social sciences, medicine, philosophy, history, linguistics, literature and the arts. It aims to represent different trends both in British psychoanalysis and in psychoanalysis generally. The New Library of Psychoanalysis is well placed to make available to the English-speaking world psychoanalytic writings from other European countries and to increase the interchange of ideas between British and American psychoanalysts.

The Institute, together with the British Psychoanalytical Society, runs a low-fee psychoanalytic clinic, organizes lectures and scientific events concerned with psychoanalysis and publishes the *International Journal of Psychoanalysis*. It also runs the only UK training course in psychoanalysis which leads to membership of the International Psychoanalytical Association – the body which preserves internationally agreed standards of training, of professional entry, and of professional ethics and practice for psychoanalysis as initiated and developed by Sigmund Freud. Distinguished members of the Institute have included Michael Balint, Wilfred Bion, Ronald Fairbairn, Anna Freud, Ernest Jones, Melanie Klein, John Rickman and Donald Winnicott.

Previous General Editors include David Tuckett, Elizabeth Spillius and Susan Budd. Previous and current Members of the Advisory Board include Christopher Bollas, Ronald Britton, Catalina Bronstein, Donald Campbell, Sara Flanders, Stephen Grosz, John Keene, Eglé Laufer, Juliet Mitchell, Michael Parsons, Rosine Jozef Perelberg, Richard Rusbridger, David Taylor and Mary Target.

ALSO IN THIS SERIES

Impasse and Interpretation Herbert Rosenfeld

Psychoanalysis and Discourse Patrick Mahony

The Suppressed Madness of Sane Men Marion Milner

The Riddle of Freud Estelle Roith

Thinking, Feeling, and Being Ignacio Matte-Blanco

The Theatre of the Dream Salomon Resnik

Melanie Klein Today: Volume 1, Mainly Theory Edited by Elizabeth Bott
Spillius

Melanie Klein Today: Volume 2, Mainly Practice Edited by Elizabeth Bott
Spillius

Psychic Equilibrium and Psychic Change: Selected Papers of Betty Joseph
Edited by Michael Feldman and Elizabeth Bott Spillius

About Children and Children-No-Longer: Collected Papers 1942–80 Paula
Heimann. Edited by Margret Tonnesmann

The Freud-Klein Controversies 1941–45 Edited by Pearl King and
Riccardo Steiner

Dream, Phantasy and Art Hanna Segal

Psychic Experience and Problems of Technique Harold Stewart

Clinical Lectures on Klein and Bion Edited by Robin Anderson

From Fetus to Child Alessandra Piontelli

*A Psychoanalytic Theory of Infantile Experience: Conceptual and Clinical
Reflections* E. Gaddini. Edited by Adam Limentani

The Dream Discourse Today Edited and introduced by Sara Flanders

*The Gender Conundrum: Contemporary Psychoanalytic Perspectives on
Feminitity and Masculinity* Edited and introduced by Dana Breen

Psychic Retreats John Steiner

The Taming of Solitude: Separation Anxiety in Psychoanalysis Jean-Michel
Quinodoz

Unconscious Logic: An Introduction to Matte-Blanco's Bi-logic and its Uses
Eric Rayner

Understanding Mental Objects Meir Perlow

Life, Sex and Death: Selected Writings of William Gillespie Edited and
introduced by Michael Sinason

*What Do Psychoanalysts Want? The Problem of Aims in Psychoanalytic
Therapy* Joseph Sandler and Anna Ursula Dreher

Michael Balint: Object Relations, Pure and Applied Harold Stewart

Hope: A Shield in the Economy of Borderline States Anna Potamianou

Psychoanalysis, Literature and War: Papers 1972–1995 Hanna Segal
Emotional Vertigo: Between Anxiety and Pleasure Danielle Quinodoz
Early Freud and Late Freud Ilse Grubrich-Simitis
A History of Child Psychoanalysis Claudine and Pierre Geissmann
Belief and Imagination: Explorations in Psychoanalysis Ronald Britton
A Mind of One's Own: A Kleinian View of Self and Object Robert A. Caper
Psychoanalytic Understanding of Violence and Suicide Edited by Rosine
    Jozef Perelberg
On Bearing Unbearable States of Mind Ruth Riesenberg-Malcolm
Psychoanalysis on the Move: The Work of Joseph Sandler Edited by Peter
    Fonagy, Arnold M. Cooper and Robert S. Wallerstein
The Dead Mother: The Work of André Green Edited by Gregorio Kohon
The Fabric of Affect in the Psychoanalytic Discourse André Green
The Bi-Personal Field: Experiences of Child Analysis Antonino Ferro
*The Dove that Returns, the Dove that Vanishes: Paradox and Creativity in
    Psychoanalysis* Michael Parsons
*Ordinary People, Extra-ordinary Protections: A Post-Kleinian Approach to
    the Treatment of Primitive Mental States* Judith Mitrani
The Violence of Interpretation: From Pictogram to Statement Piera
    Aulagnier
The Importance of Fathers: A Psychoanalytic Re-Evaluation Judith Trowell
    and Alicia Etchegoyen
Dreams That Turn Over a Page: Paradoxical Dreams in Psychoanalysis
    Jean-Michel Quinodoz
*The Couch and the Silver Screen: Psychoanalytic Reflections on European
    Cinema* Edited and introduced by Andrea Sabbadini
In Pursuit of Psychic Change: The Betty Joseph Workshop Edited by Edith
    Hargreaves and Arturo Varchevker
*The Quiet Revolution in American Psychoanalysis: Selected Papers of
    Arnold M. Cooper* Arnold M. Cooper. Edited and introduced by
    Elizabeth L. Auchincloss
*Seeds of Illness and Seeds of Recovery: The Genesis of Suffering and the Role
    of Psychoanalysis* Antonino Ferro
The Work of Psychic Figurability: Mental States Without Representation
    César Botella and Sára Botella
*Key Ideas for a Contemporary Psychoanalysis: Misrecognition and
    Recognition of the Unconscious* André Green
*The Telescoping of Generations: Listening to the Narcissistic Links Between
    Generations* Haydée Faimberg
Glacial Times: A Journey Through the World of Madness Salomon Resnik

This Art of Psychoanalysis: Dreaming Undreamt Dreams and Interrupted Cries Thomas H. Ogden

Psychoanalysis as Therapy and Storytelling Antonino Ferro

Psychoanalysis and Religion in the 21st Century: Competitors or Collaborators? Edited by David M. Black

Recovery of the Lost Good Object Eric Brenman

The Many Voices of Psychoanalysis Roger Kennedy

Feeling the Words: Neuropsychoanalytic Understanding of Memory and the Unconscious Mauro Mancia

Projected Shadows: Psychoanalytic Reflections on the Representation of Loss in European Cinema Edited by Andrea Sabbadini

Encounters with Melanie Klein: Selected Papers of Elizabeth Spillius Elizabeth Spillius, Edited by Priscilla Roth and Richard Rusbridger

Constructions and the Analytic Field: History, Scenes and Destiny Domenico Chianese

TITLES IN THE NEW LIBRARY OF PSYCHOANALYSIS TEACHING SERIES

Reading Freud: A Chronological Exploration of Freud's Writings Jean-Michel Quinodoz

THE NEW LIBRARY OF PSYCHOANALYSIS

General Editor: Dana Birksted-Breen

Encounters with Melanie Klein

Selected Papers of Elizabeth Spillius

Elizabeth Spillius

Edited and with a Preface by
Priscilla Roth and Richard Rusbridger

Routledge
Taylor & Francis Group
LONDON AND NEW YORK

First published 2007
by Routledge
2 Park Square, Milton Park, Abingdon, Oxon OX14 4RN

Simultaneously published in the USA and Canada
by Routledge
711 Third Avenue, New York, NY 10017, USA

Routledge is an imprint of the Taylor & Francis Group, an informa business

Typeset in Bembo by RefineCatch Limited, Bungay, Suffolk
Cover design by Sandra Heath

Cover photograph of *Queen Sālote of Tonga and a matāpule at a Royal
Kava Ceremony, 1960* by James Spillius

British Library Cataloguing in Publication Data
A catalogue record for this book is available from the British Library

Library of Congress Cataloging-in-Publication Data
Spillius, Elizabeth Bott, 1924–
Encounters with Melanie Klein : selected papers of Elizabeth
Spillius / Elizabeth Spillius.
p. ; cm. — (New library of psychoanalysis)
Includes bibliographical references and index.
ISBN-13: 978–0–415–41998–7 (hardback)
ISBN-10: 0–415–41998–0 (hardback)
ISBN-13: 978–0–415–41999–4 (pbk.)
ISBN-10: 0–415–41999–9 (pbk.)
1. Klein, Melanie. 2. Psychoanalysis. 3. Child analysis.
4. Anthropology. I. Title. II. Series: New library of
psychoanalysis (Unnumbered)
[DNLM: 1. Klein, Melanie. 2. Psychoanalysis—Essays.
3. Anthropology—Essays. WM 460 S756e 2007]
RC506.S665 2007
616.89′17—dc22

2006039502

ISBN 978-0-415-41998-7 (hbk)
ISBN 978-0-415-41999-4 (pbk)

Contents

Preface by the editors   xi
Acknowledgements   xv

General Introduction   1
ELIZABETH SPILLIUS

Part One
From Anthropology to Psychoanalysis

  1 Anthropology and psychoanalysis: a personal concordance   7

  2 Kleinian thought: overview and personal view   25

Part Two
In Melanie Klein's Archive

  Introduction: the Archive   65

  3 Melanie Klein revisited: her unpublished thoughts
    on technique   67

  4 Melanie Klein on the past   87

  5 Projective identification: back to the future   106

Contents

Part Three
Interaction of Ideas and Clinical Work

  6 Clinical reflections on the negative therapeutic reaction   129

  7 Varieties of envious experience   140

  8 Freud and Klein on the concept of phantasy   163

  9 Developments in Kleinian technique   183

10 Recognition of separateness and otherness   199

      References   222

      Index   241

Preface by the editors

Elizabeth Bott Spillius occupies a unique position among contemporary Kleinian psychoanalysts. She is a renowned training and supervising analyst, teaching for many years at the British Society and also in Europe and North and South America. But anyone familiar with the literature of Kleinian psychoanalysis over the last 20 years realizes she is more than that as well – in her capacities as chronicler, archivist, editor and historian, she is Boswell to the Kleinian Dr Johnson. How, in the future, psychoanalysts think about the development of post-Kleinian thought will be profoundly affected by Spillius's description, understanding and organization of these ideas.

Her history and her training have predisposed and prepared her for this role: she grew up in Canada in an academic family with ties to the wild Canadian countryside as well as to university life. She graduated from the University of Toronto and then went to graduate school to study anthropology in Chicago, arriving in London in 1949 to do further work in anthropology at the London School of Economics and the Tavistock Institute of Human Relations. What this has meant is, first of all, that she has never really lost her North American voice – she is direct, unfussy, open-minded and straight-talking. Her writing is at the same time personal and matter of fact.

Secondly, she consistently writes from the dual viewpoints of a psychoanalyst who is also a social scientist: in everything she studies she is by temperament and by training both a participant and an observer. In the first paper in this book, *Anthropology and Psychoanalysis* (Chapter 1) she describes the relationship between these two disciplines, but as one reads through the book, one can see this complex interrelationship running through all her work. *Development* always interests her – her own, that of her patients and the development of her two fields of study. She is interested in how and also why one idea develops out of another, expanding the original or diverging from it. This interest has both anthropological and psychoanalytic aspects as she explores layers of theoretical meaning, unpicking the different roots and the differing paths taken by different writers. The trajectory of her life interests her and leads her to an interest in the trajectory of her patients' lives and that of each analysis she undertakes; her interest in the course of each analysis is also mirrored by her interest in the trajectory of Kleinian psychoanalysis: how it got here from there. It is also interesting that her lifespan parallels the years of a great development and flowering of the Kleinian school of psychoanalysis; her generation of British analysts developed as the Kleinian movement developed.

Her ability to be both participant and observer, both inside and outside what she is studying, manifests itself in a number of ways. In the first place it is clear in her clinical work with her patients, and, of course, this is the position most psychoanalysts wish to occupy. Spillius explicitly describes the way she adheres to a view of technique whereby she allows herself to be fully engaged in her patient's material, subjected to whatever pressures and pulls the material brings, and simultaneously, or from time to time within the session or afterwards, or when it is important that she do so, she emerges from this identification with the patient and/or his objects to observe the process that has been going on. She notes that this technique has its roots in Freud's views of the countertransference, was developed in the work of Racker and Heimann, and, while it has become characteristic of many of her Kleinian colleagues, is not at all a technique adhered to by all contemporary psychoanalysts.

Beginning with her editing of the two-volume *Melanie Klein Today*, Spillius has looked at the work coming out of the Kleinian and contemporary Kleinian school with a similar binocular vision. She is a participant in the rich and growing body of work from Kleinian analysts (her papers here – *Varieties of envious experience* (Chapter 7) and *Recognition of separateness and otherness* (Chapter 10) – demonstrate this) and at the same time she is its chronicler. It is in the rich interplay of these two positions that her work has unique and special value. She has written about being outside as well as in – 'just visiting' – not wanting to be a member of a tribe. And yet she has found her intellectual home among British Kleinians whose work she contributes to, describes, clarifies and enhances. She has developed her own firmly-held point of view, but is endlessly curious about the points of view of others. Her stance is never moralizing; this is consistent with her anthropologist's take on things – she is interested to see how this latest tribe works, whether it's a set of London families, a group of contemporary psychoanalysts or the latest patient on her couch. She's more interested in describing things as they are than in moralizing about them.

Spillius describes differences and defines individual positions within the history of psychoanalysis: her *Freud and Klein on the concept of phantasy* (Chapter 8) and *Melanie Klein revisited* (Chapter 3) from this collection are particularly notable in this regard and she also clarifies distinctions among the works of her contemporaries. In papers such as *Projective identification: back to the future* (Chapter 5) she increases our awareness of differentiation, delineating the subtleties of alternate meanings, and by doing this enhances the structure of the discipline. She categorizes and clarifies, showing an opposition of positions and ideas. In each of these papers she is parsing for individual meaning, comparing one set of ideas with another, juxtaposing and differentiating. She does this with the cool eye of a scholar and, in a scholarly way, she repeatedly returns to the facts as she observes them: we do not know what babies think, she reminds us. These ideas are theories, not 'facts'.

In the first of her papers included in the present book, *Anthropology and psychoanalysis*, she relates the circumstances behind her much admired 1957 work (as Elizabeth Bott) *Family and Social Network* and comments that 'one part of it is important'. She writes:

> I thought that the internal culture and social organisation of a family depended on the particular way they were connected with the people and organisations outside the family. These external contacts formed what I called a 'network', not a group and not a 'community'. Further, I showed that the internal organisation and culture of the family were affected by the way the people and organisations of their external network were linked (or not linked) with one another . . . And the structure of the network was itself affected not only by external economic and demographic factors but also, though to a limited extent, by the choices of the family members themselves. It was not entirely determined from outside.

This seems to be a useful description of families in society, as Spillius understood and demonstrated, and, as well, of her understanding of the place occupied by herself and her contemporary Kleinian colleagues in the larger society of British, and then international, psychoanalysis; we could also see it as a description of her understanding of the continual interplay between inner and outer worlds which forms the basis of the psychoanalytic theory to which she adheres. At the same time it describes the way in which, during the years of her working life, Kleinian psychoanalysts have influenced and been influenced by each other and have influenced and been influenced by the larger psychoanalytic community – their forbears, back to Freud, and their contemporary colleagues from other theoretical positions. This 'network', with its many interacting, mutually enriching strands, comes to life in her work.

Priscilla Roth and Richard Rusbridger

Acknowledgements

I would like to thank most particularly my two editors, Priscilla Roth and Richard Rusbridger, not only for their work in editing the papers and for their Preface, but also for encouraging me to put the papers together in the first place. They have been particularly generous in helping me to decide on suitable principles of selecting and ordering them.

I am also grateful to the Melanie Klein Trust, both for their support as colleagues and for their financial support, especially for my research in the Melanie Klein Archive. I would like to thank Dr Julia Sheppard, Dr Lesley Hall and the staff of the Wellcome Library for the History and Understanding of Medicine and for the generous help they have given me in this research.

To my children and my patients – the greatest thanks of all.

GENERAL INTRODUCTION

Elizabeth Spillius

My encounters with Melanie Klein have taken many forms: reading her books and papers, my two personal analyses, supervision and various other forms of learning from senior colleagues, my own clinical work, discussions with colleagues of my own generation and later with students and supervisees, explorations in the Klein Archive – everything, in fact, except direct exchanges with Klein herself. The closest I came to direct contact with Klein was watching her from a distance at the British Psychoanalytical Society when I first started psychoanalytic training in 1956. After my first year I went away for nearly three years on an anthropological field trip and when I returned in the autumn of 1960 she had just died.

In spite of their indirectness my encounters with Klein have been deeply stimulating and it is because of the thoughts engendered by these contacts that I eventually began to write the papers of the present book.

Becoming an analyst is a slow process: first the training, then the uneasy period of starting to practice. Gradually I began to learn from my patients, especially from several gifted but troubled people who came to analysis soon after I had started in private practice. They helped me to realize that under a spectacular display of symptoms there may be another person with special talents all his own. 'I deaden myself so as to avoid the feeling of dying,' said one of my early patients. 'I am a crustacean, not a vertebrate,' said another. I was impressed by the way they could describe their dilemmas so succinctly. Those patients, and others too, described me as well as themselves.

They showed me that I had been trying to talk to them in psychoanalytic jargon, and their criticism helped me realize that simple thinking and straighter talking would be better for everyone.

I found myself quite intrigued by the formal and informal structure of the British Society, with its complex history, its great proliferation of committees and its three Groups, but one of the first things one learns in anthropology is that it is impossible to make a good study of a group that one is deeply involved in, and so research of that sort was relinquished before it had begun.

Instead of thinking about the Society I started teaching in it, first in small seminars on infant/mother observation which had been initiated by Esther Bick (Bick 1964) and which were later recognized as part of the British training, then on various Freud and Klein courses, and finally on the development of technique in the British Society, a course in which I had the help of many colleagues from all three Groups. All of this teaching helped me to think about ideas and psychoanalytic theory more systematically.

And so I began to feel at home in the world of psychoanalysis and to realize that the sorts of feeling and thinking that were useful in other parts of my life would be useful here too. I had learned in anthropology that one needed to be deeply involved in one's field work while at the same time staying emotionally and intellectually somewhat outside it, and I found that this binocular vision was equally necessary in psychoanalysis – essentially this is a main theme of the first Chapter of this book, 'Anthropology and psychoanalysis: a personal concordance'.

When I started writing papers it was initially because someone asked me to. Towards the end of the 1970s Joseph Sandler, a senior analyst of the Contemporary Freudian Group, asked me to give a paper for a conference on the negative therapeutic reaction, which eventually became what is now Chapter 6. Then I was asked to take part in Melanie Klein's centenary by writing a paper on the development of Kleinian thought (Spillius 1983), which focused especially on the work of contemporary Kleinians and eventually led to my editing *Melanie Klein Today* in 1988. By this time I had been appointed as the editor of the New Library of Psychoanalysis, which made it difficult to do anything but editing for ten years, although I did put together two papers, a more detailed one on Kleinian thought (Chapter 2) and the other on envy (Chapter 7), which I had been thinking about for many years without quite realizing it.

As soon as my stint as editor was over I started exploring the Melanie Klein Archive, which led to the discovery of a new Melanie Klein. The person I found in the Archive was surprisingly different from the stereotypical Klein of the British Society. In the Archive she emerged as a kindly analyst, extremely conscientious about keeping notes, not very good as a lecturer but evidently brilliant as a supervisor, not good at writing – of course we knew that already – but suddenly she would make an intuitive leap into a new idea when one least expected it. Rummaging about in the Archive led to three papers (Chapters 3, 4, and 5) on Klein's technique, her view of the past and on projective identification.

For the last five or six years I have been writing about other matters – phantasy, technique again, and separateness (Chapters 8, 9 and 10) – and I realize once again that I have been thinking about these topics for a long time without being fully aware of it.

One theme of particular interest that has arisen from writing these papers is the relation between theoretical ideas and clinical work. At first sight it looks as if papers arise out of clinical material, but this description is not quite accurate, at least not for the way I experience it. The process starts with a very nebulous idea about something that I have been thinking about without realizing it. This half-formed thought interacts with clinical material in such a way that more clearly articulated thoughts emerge as if arising spontaneously from the clinical material, and then further clinical experiences become enlivened by the theoretical thoughts. Out of this circular process a clearer idea may present itself in a form that can be written about and that may lead to discussion with a few colleagues and sometimes with a friend or two who are not analysts, which gives yet another and very welcome outside view.

Throughout this book, especially when speaking in general terms, I have adopted the traditional use of *he, him* and *his* to include both sexes.

PART ONE

From Anthropology to Psychoanalysis

1

Anthropology and psychoanalysis
A personal concordance[1]

My interest in anthropology began long before I encountered psychoanalysis. In the course of working for an undergraduate degree in general psychology I realized that I was really only interested in social psychology and in a subsidiary course in anthropology. At graduate school in Chicago my interest became even more focused: it was only social anthropology that I wanted to study, not cultural anthropology, linguistics or archaeology, all of which formed essential parts of anthropology as a subject in Canada and the USA in the 1940s.

The central idea of social anthropology that I found, and still find, so intriguing is that society is conceived as a system of interlocking social roles that shape people's behaviour, beliefs and feelings without their being fully aware of it. I first encountered this idea in Emile Durkheim's *Elementary Forms of the Religious Life* (Durkheim 1915). I went on to study the anthropological works of the two leading British anthropologists of the twentieth century, Bronislaw Malinowski and A.R. Radcliffe-Brown, whose ideas had developed, at least in part, from the work of Durkheim.

Malinowski had been virtually marooned in the Trobriand Islands in the Pacific Ocean during the First World War and while there he learned the language and made detailed observations of Trobriand economic, social and religious customs and beliefs. This was in contrast to earlier ethnographers who interviewed people but did not really observe closely what they did or what they thought and felt. Malinowski thought of the totality of Trobriand culture as inter-related and mutually supporting customs whose ultimate function

7

was to satisfy human needs. Hence his sort of anthropology came to be called 'functionalism' (Malinowski 1929).

Malinowski's method of study was called 'participant observation' and it has become the standard research method of anthropology. I had some doubts about the 'need-satisfying' aspect of Malinowski's functionalism. Once one makes that assumption, I thought, one begins to think that because the culture is there it must be satisfying needs, and there is no room in Malinowski's system for cultural change except in the form of intrusion by outside influence.

Radcliffe-Brown used Durkheim's idea of society as a self-maintaining system of interlocking social roles, customs and beliefs in his understanding of a small 'primitive' society in the Andaman Islands. Like Durkheim, Radcliffe-Brown was more interested in the idea of society as a self-maintaining system than in the idea of its satisfying human needs. His approach came to be called 'structuralism' (Radcliffe-Brown 1933, 1952).

At this time, the late 1940s, I became interested not only in the ideas of Durkheim and Radcliffe-Brown but also in the work of the sociologist Max Weber. He emphasized that societies were organized in social systems – that is, interlocking and interdependent social roles – but he thought of the systems as 'ideal-typical'. By this he meant that the social system was an ideal that people did not exactly follow; it was a *guiding* ideology which acted as a blueprint but allowed adaptation to practical necessities without making radical changes in the blueprint. (Much later I thought that one could think of Klein's ideas of the paranoid–schizoid and depressive positions in much the same way.)

By this time it was becoming clear to me that I was not very much interested in the ethnographic descriptive method that was customary in American anthropology in the 1940s or in the need-satisfying approach of Malinowski. What I wanted was to combine the approaches of Radcliffe-Brown and Weber with the research method of Malinowski. A helpful professor at Chicago put me on the right track: following his advice I came to England in 1949 and was delighted to find that the anthropologists I met were working with a combination of the ideas of Malinowski and Radcliffe-Brown.

It was an exciting time. There were only a few social anthropologists in Britain, we all knew each other and everyone had intensively studied a small 'primitive' society, a 'tribe', according to Malinowski's method of 'participant observation', and was analysing the rich data according to Malinowski's 'functionalist' approach or according to the much more social-structural and Durkheim-like approach of Radcliffe-Brown. Many were using some combination of the two approaches, which came to be called 'structural-functionalism'. I was particularly lucky in that I shared an office with Edmund Leach, who was writing up his famous work on the Kachin of Highland Burma (Leach 1954). He was already reaching beyond the thinking of Malinowski and Radcliffe-Brown to the ideas of Claude Lévi-Strauss, who, he said, always got the facts wrong and the theory right. I was happy enough with the research method and ideas of structural-functionalism.

But I realized I had to have a proper tribe. On the second evening after I had arrived in England a terrifying, ancient lady anthropologist with brilliant orange hair accosted me at an anthropological sherry party and demanded, 'Well, young woman, what is your tribe?' I had made a very brief study of the kinship system of an American Indian group in Minnesota, but in England that would never do. 'Kinship algebra,' Leach said dismissively, 'You never found out how it really worked.' So, on the advice of yet another American professor I visited the Tavistock Institute of Human Relations to see what research they were doing, and emerged five hours later with a new sort of tribe. I was to be their anthropological field worker in a study of normal London families, because the Tavistock had just received a large grant of money for an exploratory multidisciplinary study of the urban family.

The next seven years were a sort of heaven. I worked in a supportive team of a psychiatrist who was also a psychoanalyst; a psychoanalyst, Isabel Menzies-Lyth, who was also a social scientist; a psychologist and two social psychologists. All of us were trying to understand the social and psychological variations in the organization and beliefs of 20 London families of similar age, all with young children, but varying widely in social class. My team was very tolerant of my Durkheimian attitudes. My anthropological colleagues, however, did not think much of my tribe. 'Go away and write a novel,' said one of them when I presented my early findings. Even Leach was doubtful. Most of them thought I should be studying a village or a local urban community and were not at all impressed when I said I was comparing 20 little societies. Some said that the differences of familial organization and culture I was describing could all be attributed to social class. I said that was just a descriptive correlation and was no good as an explanation, for existing theories of social class were not proving to be helpful in understanding the data we were accumulating. I decided to describe the social situation that each family was actually living in: their relationships with friends, neighbours, relatives and people at their place of work, and the relationships of these various people to one another, in so far as we could discover it.

Eventually, after much painstaking work and sitting looking at the data and knowing there should be a way of understanding it, an idea floated into my head from nowhere. I remember silently saying to no-one-in-particular, 'I don't know who you are or how you thought of that, but thank you very much!' I felt as if I'd found a real link, albeit on a very small scale. I was especially pleased that an anthropological colleague (Barnes 1954) had thought of a very similar idea when analysing a very different social situation, a Norwegian fishing village. In fact by this time my anthropological colleagues were much more interested in what I was doing and the Tavistock team were pleased too.

I will not describe in detail the argument of *Family and Social Network* (1957), the book I finally wrote about this work, but one part of it is important. I thought that the internal culture and social organization of a family depended on the particular way they were connected with the people and organizations outside the family. These external contacts formed what I called a 'network', not a group and not a 'community'. Further, I showed that the internal organization and culture of the family were affected by the way the people and organizations of their external network were linked (or not linked) with one another. The more connected the network, the stricter was the division of labour between husband and wife. The looser the network, the more 'joint' was the relation between husband and wife. The structure of the network was itself affected not only by external economic and demographic factors but also, though to a limited extent, by the choices of the family members themselves. It was not entirely determined from outside. This study was my expression of the structural-functional approach, but, like Leach and others, I was tacitly recognizing that satisfying though it was, I did not want to go on forever committed to the study of families and other small-scale quasi-closed social systems.

By 1957, when *Family and Social Network* was published, I knew a lot more about psychoanalysis because of working at the Tavistock Institute of Human Relations. I had been in analysis for several years for personal reasons. Several of my Tavistock colleagues were using psychoanalytic ideas in their social projects, and I had helped with some of this work. And I had read Klein, painstakingly and in detail – a revelation. I began to read Freud too, at long last. Neither had quite the emotional impact that Durkheim, Malinowski and Radcliffe-Brown had had years before, but I could see that the theories of Freud and Klein were intended to do justice to facts. Once I'd really grasped the idea of the unconscious I saw that it played the same role in psychoanalysis as society in Durkheim's sociology – another unknown thing that governed one's life without one's realizing it.

I began psychoanalytic training at the British Society in 1956. Although I was a bit put off by the attitude of received wisdom of some of our teachers, I felt that because I was classified as a Kleinian I was in what was at that time a reassuringly small eccentric 'group'[2] and could think what I liked. Sooner or later, however, regardless of group, some seminar leader or other would start explaining to us that primitive people had primitive minds, and I would shrink into myself thinking, 'Oh no, not this again!' It was evident that the anthropological attitude that all people have basically the same sort of mind had not been accepted by all psychoanalysts. In the anthropological view, culture varies, social organization varies, language varies, beliefs vary but, in spite of these differences in content, people's minds work in basically the same way.

Before starting to analyse patients I got married and my husband and I embarked on an anthropological field trip to the Kingdom of Tonga in the south-west Pacific, another formative experience. Intellectually the main development was the introduction of history and myths of history into my anthropological thinking, something that continued in somewhat altered form in my psychoanalytic thinking. When I returned from Tonga I was put under a certain amount of pressure to continue in anthropology, but I thought I would be expected to continue working on families, which I did not want to do, and that network research would probably take a new form that I would not enjoy. (It did.) I was no longer so pleased with structural-functionalism. It was too rigid, too synchronic, too closed. But I was not attracted by Lévi-Strauss's 'structuralism', which was the school of anthropological thought that was gaining ground in Britain, especially in the case of my friend Edmund Leach.

For many years after 1960 I was too busy with family matters and learning clinical psychoanalysis to think about much else, although

I wrote up some of the Tongan material and a study of a mental hospital, and then began to teach and eventually to write about psychoanalysis. I went back to Tonga in 1994 and saw many of my old friends and their children and caught up with general events, but I did not think it would be practicable to drop my psychoanalytic work to take up work in Tonga again and in more detail. Both anthropology and psychoanalysis are 'greedy' disciplines. If one is going to do either, one has to work in it empirically, read the relevant literature, keep in touch with colleagues, take part in its respective institutions. And by this time I was becoming increasingly out of touch with the burgeoning developments in anthropology in both Britain and the USA.

I realized that I had come to think of the two fields as parallel, not reducible to each other but using the same basic methods of thinking. Without quite realizing it, I began to think that the study of an individual through psychoanalytic sessions was much like the study of a small society by the structural-functional method, although of course the content of a social system is very different from the content of a personality system. And although the consulting-room setting of psychoanalysis is apparently very different from the field research setting of social anthropology, the exploring attitude of mind of the psychoanalyst is similar to that of the anthropologist.

By the late 1960s I realized I could not continue doing anthropological research; it was too hard to combine it with having children and with psychoanalytic work in the consulting room. I knew that if I had had Leach's facility for scanning many societies and pulling out a crucial structural element I could probably have written something interesting linking the two disciplines. But I also knew that temperamentally I prefer to know everything about nothing rather than to know nothing about everything, and I knew that I could not know everything about everything as I often felt Leach did. I decided that for the time being I would settle down to learning how to be a psychoanalyst, which takes many years.

It was a long time before I began to think again about my two disciplines, the things they had in common, the things that were different. I want now to discuss the results of my musings: first, the basic aims and fundamental differences between anthropology and psychoanalysis; second, their research settings; third, problems of causation; and fourth, anthropological ideas in the consulting room.

Aims and differences between the two disciplines

Both disciplines aim to study human nature, especially the human mind, but they study different expressions of it: anthropology studies its expression in social behaviours and cultural practices and beliefs; psychoanalysis, or at least my sort of psychoanalysis, studies its expression particularly in the analyst-patient relationship. In both disciplines there is tension between deductive and inductive methods of thinking – a reaching after understandings that do justice to the details of particular situations while simultaneously looking at these situations in a wider context.

The two disciplines differ in that psychoanalysis usually has a therapeutic as well as a scientific aim and anthropology typically does not. When I began clinical work in psychoanalysis I found the therapeutic aim extremely intimidating. I thought I would never be able to cure anyone of anything. It was a relief some time later to discover that Freud himself thought that the wish to cure was not a good basis for psychoanalytic work. The therapeutic aim of psychoanalysis is necessary for psychoanalysis to occur at all, but it greatly complicates the psychoanalyst's involvement, making him financially and narcissistically involved in therapeutic success as well as in 'scientific' and aesthetic understanding. The difference of therapeutic aim also means that the two disciplines are typically embedded in different institutions: anthropology in universities and psychoanalysis mainly in privately-organized institutes. This is one of the social factors that makes it difficult to be equally involved in both disciplines at the same time.

The research setting: on being inside and outside

Anthropology began in social and political philosophy with the comparison of known civilizations with the findings of gentleman travellers about remote and 'primitive' societies. Psychoanalysis, on the other hand, grew out of the study of neurotics according to the medical model of the doctor-patient relationship. In both cases there was at first a sharp distinction between 'us' the professionals and 'them' the primitives or the neurotics.

In time this sort of hierarchical attitude has been modified in both disciplines. In anthropology, Malinowski's 'participant observation' relied on direct observation of behaviour rather than, or as well as, on statements of informants. Participant observation has its counterpart in psychoanalysis as its practitioners have come to realize that their immediate subject matter is not only the patient but also the analyst-patient relationship. Hence the analyst is inevitably a participant as well as an observer.

In anthropology, Malinowski's participant observation has been modified still further. In modern anthropology, as Leach puts it '. . . the investigator soon discovers that those he is investigating have become his personal friends and fellow anthropologists' (Leach 1977: 362).

Psychoanalysts also know that they are the same sort of human creature as their subjects of study. There have been times when a psychoanalyst and his patient have become more totally committed to symmetrical involvement with each other – Ferenczi's 'mutual analysis', for example, although he concluded in the end that it was not workable (Ferenczi 1985). And at least in my sort of psychoanalysis it is now accepted that there is a basic asymmetry in the therapeutic relationship.

Why should anthropology and psychoanalysis differ in this respect? I think it is because of the difference in their respective aims. The anthropologist aims to understand his informants' social behaviour and its implicit though not dynamically unconscious meanings, and usually there is no expectation of change. Further, neither informant nor anthropologist is focused on the relationship with each other as a central aspect of the investigation, which makes it comparatively easy for anthropologist and informant to become friends and colleagues without changing the aim of the enterprise, which, for both, is to understand social not individual behaviour and beliefs.

In psychoanalysis the relationship between analyst and patient cannot reach the easy familiarity that is sometimes – depending on the prevailing social and political situation – reached between anthropologist and informant. The therapeutic aim of psychoanalysis means that the relationship normally takes the form of the patient seeking help from the psychoanalyst. Study of the relationship between analyst and patient is central because it is largely through the understanding of this relationship that both analyst and patient can understand more about the patient. It is a means to the end of the patient understanding himself better, meaning to understand not only his conscious but also his dynamically unconscious mind in such a fashion that change in his beliefs and behaviour may become possible. The involvement of patient and analyst is basically asymmetrical and complementary, even though feelings of understanding and empathy may occur − or at times be felt not to occur − during the process of analysis.

There is another respect in which the emotional/intellectual 'set' of the psychoanalyst is both similar to but different from that of the anthropologist. Both find that they have to be 'in' the field situation in order to understand it, but on the other hand both have to be 'outside' the situation in order to have enough alternative perspective to be able to think about it conceptually. In anthropology this is comparatively easy. The anthropologist has the feeling of 'going native' at least some of the time, especially while in the field situation, and the outside perspective tends to come into its own later, when he has left the field and is writing up his material. In psychoanalysis it is more difficult to be inside and outside the analytic situation because one has to do both in the session and at nearly the same time. I think, following a suggestion of Michael Feldman, that what happens is that there is a fluctuation, often very rapid, between being almost completely drawn into the immediate emotional situation with the patient and then withdrawing a little to see the situation from the perspective of one's profession and one's colleagues. When emotion runs high in the session, however, the analyst is likely to find that he cannot think very clearly until the session is over. I believe that this greater entanglement occurs not only because the psychoanalyst is more deeply involved emotionally than the anthropologist but also because he tries to be conscious of his involvement at the same time. The anthropologist is not obliged to understand his own unconscious as a means to understanding his field data.

Beliefs about method and causation

Both anthropologists and psychoanalysts have quite a lot of trouble with the concepts of time, the past and causation. Causal explanations have tended to be historical, based to a considerable extent on the view that what comes first causes what comes later. 'How did this society get this way?' asks the anthropologist. 'How did the patient get the way he is now?' asks the psychoanalyst. However, questions about the past take the investigator outside his immediate research setting, outside what can be directly studied in the small society if he is an anthropologist and outside the session if he is a psychoanalyst.

From times of antiquity there have been philosophical speculations about the nature of man, of society and its historical processes, speculations designed to explain the present and to predict the future. From today's perspective some of these speculations seem plausible, some ludicrous, but all are bound to be conjectural because any immediate field of empirical study is limited and cannot give answers to questions of general and historical causality.

Something similar has happened in psychoanalysis. The immediate situation of study, the session, cannot answer all questions, and psychoanalytic theories have tended to be phrased in terms of speculations about the development of infants and small children. These speculations are bound to be conjectural for, although the behaviour of infants can be observed, one cannot know what they think. Freud, Anna Freud, Winnicott and Mahler all assume, for example, that very young infants exist at first in a state of mental fusion and confusion with their mothers, a state sometimes described as 'symbiosis'. Klein, on the contrary, assumes that very young infants distinguish between self and not-self from birth, although not very realistically. Detailed psychological observations and experiments suggest that Klein is more likely to be right about this than the others, but there is still no way of being sure (see Stern 1985: 10). And empirical research is unfortunately probably never going to be able to tell us what infants think, which is really what psychoanalysts would most like to know.

Once anthropologists began to study particular societies they dropped their speculative history and devoted themselves to synchronic analyses of whatever group they had chosen to study. This they thought of as the scientific approach based on the expectation that all behaviour can be rationally understood in terms of cause and effect linkages of which the social actors are unaware. This is the view of Durkheim and of the structural-functionalists I have described above. It is also, much of the time, the view of Freud, in that he expects that a patient's behaviours and beliefs can be rationally understood in terms of cause and effect linkages of which the patient is unaware.

Once anthropologists gave up their focus on speculative history, they developed a method of studying what the people in a society did in various social situations; they also listened to what their informants said about their personal experiences, present and past, and about the history of their society. Some of this history, especially in societies without writing, shades into myth and much of the anthropologist's work is concerned with making a meaningful synthesis of current social, economic, religious and aesthetic behaviour with his informants' accounts of their history, myths and religious beliefs.

But comparative and sometimes historical anthropology has returned, though in a rather different form. Occasionally, written historical records are available which makes possible diachronic study through time as well as the usual sort of synchronic analysis of a society at one time. This was to some extent true of the work I did in Tonga. Sometimes, cross-cultural comparisons are made using a correlational method similar to certain sorts of psychological research. But cross-cultural comparisons are also made using another method that assumes, as Leach puts it, that 'underlying all the seemingly chaotic permutations in the empirical data, there are grammatical rules which allow us to distinguish sense from non-sense' (1977: 372). This is the structuralist point of view of Lévi-Strauss, agreed with to a considerable extent not only by Leach but also by some other anthropologists and to some extent by some psychoanalysts, especially those of the French school who follow, or partly follow, Lacan.

For the most part, Anglo-Saxon psychoanalysts are would-be scientists looking for causes but dealing with a mixture of limited observations carried out in sessions combined with much more conjectural speculations. Psychoanalysts tend to assume that what happens to the individual when he is an infant and a small child has an important causal effect on the development of his character and on the way he acts in the present. It is very difficult to know, however, whether patients remember their past accurately; and even if patients have remembered their past accurately, it is very difficult to know what the effects of this past might be, and it is also very difficult to know what the effect of the patient's *beliefs* about the past might be. At least some of what a patient says about his past acts as a sort of personal myth which makes sense of his experience and gives it meaning even though the analyst may not be in a position to know whether what the patient says is literally true. It is part of the analyst's task to try to discover what sort of psychic truth this mixture of memories and beliefs has for the patient.

Analysts vary considerably in the importance they attach to what the patient says about his past, but I think there has been a gradual and increasing focus on what can be immediately studied in the consulting room, especially on the understanding of the conscious and unconscious aspects of the analyst–patient relationship. In this respect psychoanalysts are like anthropologists in that there is increasing focus on the situation that can be immediately studied and less focus, or a different sort of focus, on what is said about situations that cannot be directly observed in the consulting room. As in anthropology, the analyst compares what he experiences in the immediate setting with what he hears about the patient's other relationships, both past and present, and gradually works out a synthesis relating what is expressed in behaviour, what is described as fact and what takes the form of the patient's personal explanatory myths and theories about himself and his world.

In the awkward situation created by the fact that psychoanalysts tend to believe that the past has a causative effect on the present but cannot know exactly what the past was, they have tended to be susceptible to the nature/nurture controversy. In its crudest form this controversy involves what may be thought of as a 'culture of blame': blame of the 'environment' (parents) or blame of the 'child', or, rather, of the child's 'constitution'. Most psychoanalysts pay at least lip service to the idea that the final result in the form of the patient in the session must be a product of both nature *and* nurture, but in the absence of immediate opportunities to study the question directly in the analytic situation, emotional prejudice and feelings of certainty easily replace hypothesis and tentativeness.

When I was first a psychoanalytic student I found the naivety of this sort of thinking surprising and I was equally troubled by the way psychoanalysts of all schools described theories of infantile thought almost as if they were fact, when according to my way of thinking they were hypothetical models. This was a conceptual approach I had learned in anthropology almost without realizing it. It was a relief somewhat later to realize that at least Bion thought in terms of models.

Some psychoanalysts have turned to developmental psychology, infant research, attachment theory and brain research to answer the tantalizing questions about causation, but although the generalizations derived from such studies are of considerable interest and can sometimes be applied to clinical situations, and although they have influenced the thinking of many analysts, they rely on data that usually do not immediately arise from the research situation of the analytic session. In relation to psychoanalysis they are *applied* rather than arising directly from the session.

There is another issue concerning causality and determinism about which I have found that at least some anthropologists and some psychoanalysts have adopted similar attitudes. This concerns one's attitude towards the various theories that have already been developed for understanding situations similar to the one the investigator is studying. In both anthropological and psychoanalytic situations I have found it important to keep existing theories in mind but not to try to make them fit new data. I have already described the way I thought existing theories of social class did not do much to further a deeper understanding of the organization and culture of urban families. Similarly, when studying rank and authority in the Kingdom of Tonga I had to disregard certain theories which could have been *made* to fit but which did not *quite* fit, and which would have distracted me from grasping more important principles that illuminated the working of the system more adequately. In the same way, when studying envy I had to keep Klein's seminal work on this topic in mind but without assuming that it would exactly fit my data. But being too much influenced by existing theories is not the only problem. One may be so determined to be original that one may disregard existing theories even when they are relevant.

Bion is very much aware of this problem. He describes the need in a session to avoid 'memory' (e.g. known theories and what one already knows about one's patient) and 'desire' (the wish to cure, to be creative oneself, or whatever) if one is to allow the potential understandings of the events of the session to emerge (Bion 1967b). I think it is the fear that no potential understanding, no new thought, will emerge at all that sends the psychoanalyst scrabbling about in his mind for causes. Without quite realizing it, I think I have adopted a method in psychoanalysis similar to the one I used in anthropology. I start with what appears to be happening in the immediate situation of the analytic relationship, but with memories of other situations inevitably present (in spite of Bion), if possible in the back not the front of my mind. I find myself making tentative, lateral comparisons which may or may not lead to some sort of new link. The outcome is unpredictable.

In summary, I think there has been a tendency in both anthropology and psychoanalysis to focus increasingly on the situation that can be immediately observed, and to work to develop a synthesis that relates the understandings derived from such study to other beliefs and behaviours which informants and patients talk about but which cannot be directly studied.

Anthropological attitudes and ideas in the consulting room

I have already mentioned the idea that psychoanalytic theories about infantile development should be viewed as models rather than as fact or even theories. And I have briefly described how I have come to think of the study of each patient as rather similar to the study of a small society by the structural-functional method.

But now in addition I want to describe two ways in which I have found myself looking at patients' actual material from a perspective more explicitly learned in anthropology. One example concerns patients' attitudes towards time and the past, another concerns what Leach calls the 'wilderness'. These are analogical comparisons rather than applications of content.

In societies without written records of the past, the research situation is somewhat similar to the analytic patient's memory of his past. In both cases I assume that actual events in the past have affected the present, but there is no way of studying these historical events directly. The anthropologist's approach is to study the current situation and to look at remembered history together with myths for similarities and dissonances with the current situation. This approach is usually combined with studying the particular conceptions of time that the people one is studying actually use.

In the analytic situation I have found it useful to adopt a similar attitude, that is, to keep an open mind about the patient's past and to look at the patient's uses of his past and at congruencies and dissonances between the remembered past and current experiences in the session. I do not mean that the actual events of the past are unimportant or that the patient is necessarily wrong (or right) about what happened, only that these are questions whose historical accuracy cannot be directly studied in the session. And so anthropology has helped me towards a more tentative view of time and causation. Many if not most psychoanalysts have come to similar views without having been anthropologists. Hence, for example, the concept of *Nachträglichkeit* in Freud, *après-coup* in French psychoanalysis and 'retrospective phantasising' in Jung's analytical psychology (1956, 1961). And hence too the view about the past that is current in Kleinian and other schools of thought in psychoanalysis – namely, that the patient's present behaviour is an expression at least in part of his past as it lives in his internal world now, and his view of the past is partly a statement about his present (see Sandler and Sandler 1983, 1984, 1987, 1994; Birksted-Breen 2003).

A second useful point of view from anthropology is Leach's idea of the 'wilderness'. He developed this idea from observing certain patterns that differed in content but were similar in structure in aspects of religious and social belief systems in widely different societies and situations: certain beliefs of the Kachin of northern Burma; a head feast in 1947 in Sarawak; the investiture of himself as a knight in 1975 in England; the layout of an English parish church; the symbolism of fish in early Christianity; many Biblical myths and many different sorts of festival and ceremony (Leach 1955/1961, 1981, 1986; Hugh-Jones and Laidlaw 2001.)

The basic structure consists of a binary pair, the sacred and the profane, each of which exists only by virtue of its opposition to the other. One can find further examples: this world/the other world; everyday/holiday; everyday/special; ordinary/extraordinary etc. Sometimes the basic duality of the binary opposites may be modified by the introduction of degrees of distance between the binary pair.

Leach regards the 'wilderness' as a territory or time in which the binary opposites overlap; the wilderness belongs to this world and to the other world, to both and to neither; its properties are different from both and similar to both, depending on one's perspective. In this respect the wilderness is somewhat similar to certain aspects of Winnicott's idea of transitional objects and transitional space (1953). It can also be linked to Britton's ideas about PS n + 1, that is, the post-depressive paranoid-schizoid position (Britton 1998b). This is an idea Britton develops from the work of Bion in which there is a recognition that the integration of a particular form of depressive position may become rigid and stultifying and needs to be shaken up by a move to a new form of paranoid-schizoid position which Britton calls 'PS(n + 1)'. Out of the apparent un-connectedness of this new form of the paranoid-schizoid position a new and more appropriate form of the depressive position may arise.

Access to the wilderness usually involves what van Gennep calls 'rites of passage', in which an individual undergoes a symbolic 'death' of one status ('rite of separation'), spends some time in a 'special', 'marginal' or 'liminal' status and is then 're-born' into ordinary secular society with a new status ('rite of aggregation') (see van Gennep 1908/9; Douglas 1966, especially Ch. 6; Turner 1969).

I have found these ideas useful in thinking about the psychoanalytic situation. Leach himself notes this. He says:

> I have heard it argued that the beginning and the end of an analysis are of more importance than the process of analysis as such. Moreover, both for analyst and for patient, the beginning and end of every analytical session must present a problem of how to move from an ordinary relationship to an extraordinary relationship and back again.
>
> (1986: 131)

I have found it useful to think of the session as a 'special place', or 'extraordinary place' where both analyst and patient make an effort, through free association and free-floating attention, to allow the unknown, the unforeseen, to happen. The session itself is the wilderness, the place between, the place that has attributes both of everyday life and of the 'other world', the unknown, unconscious inner world which analyst and patient are trying to reach and to understand. The setting expresses this double identity. The couch, for example, has attributes of the 'ordinary' secular world, but its use in the analytic setting makes it 'out of place', certainly out of its 'usual' place. It is ambiguous and 'special'.

The 'way in' and the 'way out' of the session/wilderness are always somewhat fraught, as Leach noted. There is no agreed social procedure for such arrivals and departures, but each analytic pair tends to devise a ritual that both expresses and partly copes with the awkwardness of these transitions, usually with slight alterations to note the specialness of longer breaks and, even more, to mark the ending of analysis.

In conclusion

I have described certain affinities between anthropology and psychoanalysis as I have experienced them. Both disciplines try to understand the human mind, though each studies different expressions of it: social behaviour and belief systems in anthropology, individual behaviour and belief systems in psychoanalysis.

At the level of content, psychoanalysis and anthropology are very different and attempts to link them causally are in my view superficial and reductionist. Concordance comes on a more generalized and abstract level.

There are four areas of analogical similarity that I have found useful.

The first is the idea of the patterning of a patient's mind being somewhat analogous to the organization of a small society, and the relationship between patient and analyst being somewhat similar to the relationship between 'tribe' and anthropologist.

The second is the attitude of mind towards research, in which the analyst and the anthropologist need to be emotionally and intellectually both inside and outside the situation that is being studied. Only in this way can a new understanding be reached, but insight is not guaranteed. The anthropologist or psychoanalyst puts himself in the hands of his research reality and endures its uncertainties as best he can. This is the attitude and the experience Bion describes as 'faith' (1970: 35).

The third area is the use of time in causal explanations, in which one takes the informant's or the patient's ideas about the past as an expression of aspects of the present which one can observe in the field situation or in the psychoanalytic session, as well as the more usual procedure of regarding the present as determined by the past.

The fourth area of concordance is the idea of the session as the wilderness, the place between, the marginal, liminal place between 'this world' and the 'other world', between the outside world and the world of the psyche, having attributes of both worlds and of neither.

Notes

1   A slightly different version of this chapter was published in 2005 in *Community, continuity and change in the study of Britain: a Festschrift for Ronnie Frankenberg, The Sociological Review*, 55: 658–67.
2   At that time, and still today to a considerable extent, the British Psychoanalytical Society was divided into three 'Groups': Kleinian, Independent and Contemporary Freudian. These groupings had developed during or shortly after the Controversial Discussions in the 1940s (King and Steiner 1991). The Groups were originally defined in terms of variations in psychoanalytic ideas but have also acted as 'political' entities. In the 1950s the Klein Group was the smallest but has

gradually increased in size up until 2005 when it became slightly larger than the Independent group. The Contemporary Freudian group is about half the size of the other two.

2

Kleinian thought
Overview and personal view[1]

Developments in Klein's thinking

All her life, in spite of the controversies and furore raging around her, Klein thought of her work as following in the footsteps of Freud, as an extension of his work. In my view too, there is a consistent allegiance throughout Klein's work to what she regarded as the essential spirit of Freud's approach and technique. But she was an innovator. She regarded the play of a child as the counterpart to the free association of adults. In her play technique Klein was fully prepared to enact many (though not all) of the roles suggested to her by the child in order to arrive at an understanding of the child's motives and feelings. She was critical in 1927 of Anna Freud for introducing educational elements into child analysis and for emphasizing the positive transference and not interpreting the negative transference (Klein 1927a). Klein's descriptions of her technique with adults years later in 1943 (King and Steiner 1991: 635–8) and in 1952 ('The origins of transference', 1952a) are basically very similar to her technique as she described it in 1927, and she clearly thought that both were closely based on Freud. (Anna Freud, however, thought otherwise; see King and Steiner 1991: 629–34.)

Of crucial importance in Klein's work is that it began in the study and treatment of children. She was not the first analyst to treat children, having been preceded by Freud and the father of Little Hans and by Hug-Hellmuth; Anna Freud had started analytic work with older children at about the same time as Klein, though along rather different lines. But Klein invented an analytic way of using the technique

25

of play, which gave even very young children under 3 years of age a suitable medium for expressing their thoughts and feelings, a medium which could easily be combined with their developing capacity to express themselves in words. The invention of this new technique uncovered new data and slowly gave Klein an unshakeable conviction in the reality of the clinical facts she was discovering. In time it led her to new theoretical developments as well: the central importance of unconscious phantasy; the implications of the very aggressive as well as loving phantasies that she found in the play of small children and which she assumed were part of the unconscious of adults as well; the central role of anxiety in both normal and pathological development; the importance of reparation; the idea of internal objects and the internal world; the existence of a very sadistic early superego. Eventually her work with both children and adults led her to conceive of the ideas of the paranoid-schizoid and depressive positions, both as part of a developmental sequence and, especially in the view of her later colleagues, as states of mind.

Up until 1935, which I think of as the first period of her work, she was basically working within the theoretical framework of Freud and Abraham, though she made many changes in it, some of them inadvertent. After 1935, with the two papers on the depressive position (1935, 1940), the paper on the paranoid-schizoid position (1946), and *Envy and Gratitude* (1957), she developed a new theory of her own. (For a general introduction to the work of Klein, see Segal 1964a. See also Hinshelwood 1991, Meltzer 1978, Caper 1988 and Likierman 2004). Petot (1990 and 1991) gives a detailed textual analysis of the development of Klein's thought. Greenberg and Mitchell (1983) discuss her position as an object-relations/drive-structure theorist. Glover (1945), Bibring (1947), Zetzel (1956, 1958), Kernberg (1969) and Yorke (1971) present critical reviews.)

The first period of Klein's work, 1921–35

The work of this period is innovative, complex and piecemeal. Klein was discovering new data and working out new conceptualizations of it so quickly that her formulations were bound to be inconsistent, especially as she was holding fast at the same time to the libidinal phases theory of Freud and Abraham (Freud 1905b; Abraham 1924). I will summarize her work during this period under a number of

conceptual headings, which, in keeping with her explosion of findings and ideas at this time are somewhat unconnected with one
another. Further, some are descriptions of her findings and ideas,
whereas others are my own inferences about her approach. Some of
the ideas of this early period were retained throughout all her work,
others were dropped or reformulated. (For a chronological account of
this early period, see especially the editor's notes in *The Writings of
Melanie Klein*, 1975, and Petot 1990.)

Freud's drives and Klein's drives

During this early period Klein seems not to have seen any difference
between her conception of drives and Freud's. But imperceptibly she
was making an important conceptual shift. Where Freud thinks of
drives as biological forces which become almost fortuitously attached
to objects through post-natal experiences, for Klein drives are inherently attached to objects. During this period she had not yet wholly
rejected the idea of primary narcissism (which she does later, 1952a),
but she was moving in that direction. Even in the early years hers is an
object relations theory. Further, she conceives of the individual's own
body not as the source of biological drives but as the medium by
which the psychological drives of love and hate – mostly hate was
explored in these early years – are expressed (Greenberg and Mitchell
1983). Hence Klein's approach is simultaneously a drive theory and
an object relations theory, though her 'drives' are becoming increasingly psychological rather than biological, and the role of anxiety in
affecting their expression becomes increasingly important as her work
develops.

Phantasy

Klein hardly mentions phantasy conceptually and gives little sign of
realizing that she was using the concept differently from Freud. Freud
uses the term in different ways, but in his central usage phantasy
is resorted to when an instinct is frustrated (Freud 1911; see also
Chapter 8). For Klein, unconscious phantasy accompanies gratification as well as frustration but, further, it is the basic stuff of all mental
processes; it is the mental representation of instincts. This view was

not formally stated conceptually, however, until Susan Isaacs's paper 'The nature and function of phantasy', first given in 1943 during the Controversial Discussions (King and Steiner 1991) and later published (1952). It is Klein's view that phantasizing is an innate capacity, and that the content of phantasies, although influenced by experiences with external objects, is not entirely dependent on them. She thinks that hate is innate; later she would stress that love too is innate.

Throughout this early period it is implicit that Klein believes that the infant also has innate unconscious knowledge, however hazy, of objects – breast, mother, penis, womb, intercourse, birth, babies – although she does not state this unequivocally until much later (but see 1927b: 175–6).

Internal objects and the inner world

Klein vastly develops the concept of the 'inner' world of internal objects, once again, in this early period, without much conceptual emphasis. In her early clinical work with children she was powerfully struck by the fact that the internal imagos of parents were very much more ferocious than the actual parents appeared to be. Gradually she developed a conception of internal objects and the inner world as built up through the mechanisms of introjection and projection which she believed operate from the beginning of life. Thus the inner world is not a replica of the external world; experiences of the external world help to shape the inner world, and the inner world affects the individual's perception of the external world. Unlike Freud, she does not restrict the idea of 'internal object' or superego to the single internalization of parental figures after the passing of the Oedipus complex (see Hinshelwood 1991 and Greenberg and Mitchell 1983 for detailed descriptions of internal objects).

The early superego and the Oedipus complex

Klein thinks that the children she treated showed clear signs of an early and very sadistic superego (as well as a more developed conscience) which did not correspond to their real parents and which Klein thinks is based on their own sadistic phantasies. (Freud acknowledged this statement of Klein's in *Civilization and its Discontents*, 1930:

28

130.) Klein dates the Oedipus complex progressively earlier and earlier, linking it to weaning (1927a) but later to the depressive position (1935, 1940, 1945, 1952c). At times, like Freud, Klein links the development of the superego to the Oedipus complex but by 1932 and 1933 she was thinking of superego development and the development of the Oedipus complex as separate though related processes.

Sadism and psychotic anxiety

In her very first papers Klein emphasized libidinal drives and their expression in unconscious phantasy in every activity (see especially Petot's discussion, 1990). Klein here means 'libidinal' not in the general sense of 'loving' or 'life-giving', but in the sense of sexuality, involving a somewhat ruthless pursuit in phantasy of sexual aims. Soon afterwards she began, with characteristic enthusiasm, to explore a new terrain, that of aggression and destructiveness, which at this point she almost always called sadism. Until Freud's *Beyond the Pleasure Principle* (1920) and even later, aggression was generally neglected in psychoanalysis as a phenomenon in its own right; it was usually spoken of as a component of the libidinal instinct. In this early period and indeed throughout her work Klein thinks that the mother's breast, her body and the parental intercourse are the main targets for the projection in phantasy of destructive impulses. This means that the breast, the mother and the parental intercourse come to be felt as cruel persecutors, and they are then aggressively attacked. During this early period Klein develops the concept of the 'combined object' – the phantasy of a hostile mother containing a hostile penis. Sadistic phantasies arouse intense anxiety, which Klein feels can be the basis of childhood psychosis and of adult mental illness. She develops, in this connection, a new conception of obsessional neurosis as a defence against early psychotic anxiety instead of regarding it as a regression to a fixation point in the anal phase of libidinal development (see especially 1932b: 149–75).

Klein's concentration on sadism must certainly have been affected by the change in Freud's theory of instincts outlined in *Beyond the Pleasure Principle* (1920) and by Abraham's work on oral and anal sadism (1924), but I think the main reason for her stress on it came from her clinical work with children, for she found that the children she analysed had extremely ruthless sadistic phantasies about which they characteristically felt very guilty. She then extends her ideas backwards to construct a theory of sadism in infancy, and she thinks of sadism as an important root of the epistemophilic instinct, the wish to know. Towards the end of this phase of her work she begins to distinguish descriptively between anxiety and guilt. But she makes little use of the idea of love during this early period. And in spite of her emphasis on sadism, it is not until *The Psychoanalysis of Children* (1932a) that she begins to use Freud's idea of the death instinct, and to mention the conflict between life instinct and death instinct. Even so, she does not really use the idea of the conflict conceptually until the later phase of her work.

The epistemophilic instinct and symbolism

In her very earliest papers Klein talks about the wish to know, the epistemophilic instinct, as rooted in libido and expressed in all the child's activities. Gradually she comes to think of sadism as a crucial element in the urge to know. She thinks the infant feels the mother's body to be the source of all good (and bad) things, including the father's penis, and in phantasy the child attacks the mother's body both out of frustration and in order to get possession of her riches. Such phantasized sadistic attacks arouse anxiety, which can be a spur to development. Combined with phantasies of projecting sadism into the mother, anxiety about attacks on her body means that her body is felt to become dangerous. The child is then constantly impelled to find new and less dangerous objects, to make new equations, a process which forms the basis of symbolism and the development of interest in new objects. Klein makes it clear too that such equations are what gives life to children's play, and that the same processes are the basis of transference. If anxiety about attacking the mother's body becomes excessive, it leads to inhibition, neurosis and, in very severe cases, to psychosis, as in the case of 'Dick' discussed in 'The importance of symbol-formation in the development of the ego' (1930).

The development of the boy and the girl

Here Klein puts forward new ideas of development, emphasizing the importance of the phantasized sadistic attacks on the mother's body described above, with their accompanying fear of retaliation and the formation of a severe superego. She thinks that both boys and girls go through a 'feminine phase' in which, out of frustration by the mother and fear of her retaliation for their attacks on her, they turn away from the mother to seek satisfaction from the father and his penis; the phantasied relation with the mother during this phase is one of identification in which the child 'becomes' the mother in order to take her place with the father (1928), a forerunner of at least one form of Klein's later idea of projective identification (1946). In girls this phase is the basis of future femininity, in boys it is normally overcome as Oedipal desires increase. Klein thinks the girl has a lasting fear of damage to the inside of her body because of the sadistic attacks she has made on her mother, and that this is for girls the counterpart of castration anxiety in boys. In *The Psychoanalysis of Children* (1932a) Klein further discusses the complexities of the development of the boy and the girl, stressing, like some other female analysts of the period, the girl's awareness of her vagina. In the later phase of her work Klein revised some of her early views on sexual development (1945). Klein's views on sexual development have interested certain analysts and some feminists, but so far none of her British colleagues has taken up her work in this area.

Phases

In her theoretical formulations of this period Klein stuck to the idea of the phases of the libido outlined by Freud (1905b) and to the further divisions within them propounded by Abraham (1924), but it is beginning to be apparent that she thinks that anal and phallic phantasies may occur alongside oral ones. One gets the impression that in her clinical observations she largely disregarded the phases, which creates a certain discordance between her theory and her clinical reports.

The effect of external parents

In spite of developing an object-relational theory rather than a solely biological-drive theory, Klein does not stress conceptually the actual external parents' personalities and behaviour as part of her theoretical system. She frequently mentions the importance of parents, and her clinical work shows that she related children's behaviour and phantasies to the behaviour and character of the actual parents (see especially Part 1 of *The Psychoanalysis of Children* and *Narrative of a Child Analysis*, 1961), but in her theory, especially in the early period, she tends to stress the role of parents as 'correctives' to the anxieties arising from the child's inherently sadistic phantasies. In the later period of her work she explicitly states the importance of the environment (1935: 285, 1952c: 94, 98, 1955b: 141 n3, 1957: 175, 185 n2, 229–30, 1959: 248–9, 1963: 312). But it is clear even in the later period that Klein thinks that, even though the character and behaviour of parents is extremely important in shaping the child's development, the child's constitution is also an extremely important factor and the child is a very active agent. This view of Klein's has frequently been mistaken to mean that she thinks the parents (the 'environment') are unimportant, and she has been much criticized for it.

Klein's approach to Freud's theories

Klein appears not to have been explicitly interested in the more abstract aspects of Freud's theories. The idea of the System Unconscious with its own special logic of the primary process does not seem to have caught her imagination; she left it to her colleagues to point out that many of the qualities of the System Unconscious are worked into her concept of unconscious phantasy. She does not distinguish between ideas and feelings that are descriptively unconscious (Freud's System Preconscious) from those that are dynamically unconscious (Freud's System Unconscious). Perhaps because her early work was not rooted in the topographical model, she does not make a point of the fact that Freud's development of the structural approach in place of the earlier topographical model meant a major change in his basic model of the mind. Her theoretical ideas begin from the structural model of Freud's *The Ego and the Id* (1923), though she uses his terms somewhat differently and her use of the structural model differed from his because she incorporated her ideas about object relations as an integral part of it. The superego, as described above, is for her earlier and more complex than for Freud. Her idea of the 'id' is not so rooted in biology as Freud's. In the case of the ego, Klein never really distinguishes between the ego and the self, and throughout her work she uses the terms interchangeably, though of course Freud often did this too. Klein does not seem to have realized how important in Freud's thinking was the change from conceiving of anxiety as dammed-up libido to thinking of anxiety as a signal. Even in the early period of her work she was beginning to think of anxiety as a response to destructive forces within the personality.

Klein's new theory: the paranoid-schizoid and depressive positions, 1935–60

The work Klein had done up until 1932, piecemeal and incomplete, was followed by a great leap of imagination which brought her previous work into a new and more integrated synthesis. This was not occasioned by a new method such as the play technique, as her earlier work had been; it involved the forming of new thoughts about already-known clinical facts and partly worked-out concepts. It is a remarkable achievement of theoretical formulation, perhaps surprising and even mysterious in that Klein was never preoccupied with theory-building as a primary aim. 'I would like to draw attention,' she said of herself, 'to the fact that I have always been primarily a clinician.' (I discuss this further in Ch. 3.)

The new theory consists of the delineation of two sets of anxieties, defences, and object relations which Klein calls the 'paranoid-schizoid position' and the 'depressive position'. It has not been easy for other analysts to understand, and many, especially in the USA, have not considered it important or plausible enough to be worth the effort. In Britain, much of Europe and in South America, however, the theory has had considerable influence, and it is the theory of this later period that has been the basis for most of the developments worked out by Klein's contemporary and later colleagues.

The theory is expounded in three main papers and one book: 'A contribution to the psychogenesis of manic-depressive states' (1935); 'Mourning and its relation to manic-depressive states' (1940); 'Notes on some schizoid mechanisms' (1946); and *Envy and Gratitude* (1957). A concise statement of the theory is given in 'Some theoretical conclusions regarding the emotional life of the infant' (1952c), though of course without including specific emphasis on the concept of envy which she did not include until her book *Envy and Gratitude* in 1957.

The new theory makes two main changes in the conceptions I have described above as typical of the first period of Klein's thought. I believe that these changes are both necessary for the formation of the new theory but also, somewhat paradoxically, are a consequence of it.

First, Klein reformulates her earlier descriptions of sadism and aggression in terms of an interaction of life and death instincts as expressed in love and hate. In her view of the death instinct Klein follows Freud quite closely, especially when she is making formal theoretical definitions of it; in clinical contexts she often speaks of 'destructive instincts' or 'aggressive instincts' and sometimes 'self-destructive instincts' without explaining each time the way in which such instincts are derived from the death instinct. In keeping with her view that instincts are inherently attached to objects, Klein's formulation of the death instinct is more clinically directed and less biological and philosophical than Freud's. Where Freud thinks that the unconscious contains no idea of death or annihilation (Freud 1923: 57, 1926: 129), Klein thinks that '. . . there is in the unconscious a fear of annihilation of life' (1948: 116). For Klein, this fear of annihilation is the primary anxiety, more basic than birth anxiety, separation anxiety or castration anxiety. Where Freud attributes the deflection of the death instinct to 'the organism', Klein attributes it to the ego (1957: 190–1, 1958: 237). Klein thinks that part of the death instinct is projected into the primal object, the breast, which thereby becomes a persecutor, while part is retained within the personality; some of this remaining internal death instinct is turned against the persecuting object as aggression (Klein 1946: 4–5, 1958: 238n). Like Freud (1923: 54) she thinks that some of the internal death instinct is bound by libido, but she also thinks that some of it remains unfused and continues to be an active source of anxiety to the individual about being annihilated from within.

Accompanying her reformulation of sadism and aggression in terms of their derivation from the death instinct, Klein increases her use of the idea of love, libido and the conception of the good object as the core of normal ego development. Klein had noted the interplay of love and hate in the late 1920s and early 1930s, but at that time she did not make much conceptual use of it. In the later period this interplay becomes central to her new conceptions of the paranoid–schizoid and depressive positions.

The second major change after 1935 is that Klein reduces her adherence to Freud's and Abraham's conception of instinctual phases in favour of a theory of development based on changing modes of internal (and external) object relations. She continues to think that oral expressions of love and hate come first, but she thinks that they overlap with, rather than are sequentially followed by, anal, urethral, phallic and genital modes of expression. Instead of 'phase', in her new theory she speaks of 'position', that is, an organization of typical anxieties, defence mechanisms and object relations. Klein thinks that in infancy the paranoid-schizoid position is the first of the two positions to be attained, and is then followed by the depressive position, but she uses the word 'position' rather than 'phase' to emphasize that throughout childhood and indeed also in later life there can be fluctuation between the two positions (1952b). Positions, as she conceives of them, are thus not phases which one passes through and leaves behind: 'I chose the term "position" in regard to the paranoid and depressive phases because these groupings of anxieties and defences, although arising first during the earliest stages, are not restricted to them but occur and recur during the first years of childhood and under certain circumstances in later life' (1952c: 93).

Klein's concept of position made it possible for some of her colleagues, especially Bion, to loosen the connection with literal developments in infancy still further, to the point where the positions are conceived as 'states of mind' regardless of the chronological age at which they are experienced. This emphasis has helped many analysts to look for moment-to-moment shifts in a session from integration and depressive anxiety towards fragmentation and sometimes persecution, rather than looking only for major shifts of character and orientation.

The paranoid-schizoid position

At first Klein used the term 'paranoid position'; later she added the word 'schizoid' in recognition of Fairbairn's work (Fairbairn 1941, 1944) on splitting of the ego and its relation to schizoid states.

Klein thinks that the normal paranoid-schizoid position occurs in the first three months of infancy and is characterized by persecutory anxiety – that is, fear of annihilation from within – and, because the feared malignancy is in phantasy projected outwards, from without as

35

well. She assumes that the infant experiences sensations as 'caused' by malevolent or benevolent objects. Thus hunger in her view is likely not to be just an experience of 'no-food-is-here' but to be something like 'that object is starving me to death', or 'something terrible is attacking me'. A feeling of comfort would be attributed to the benign motive of a good object. It is clear that Klein thinks infants distinguish between self and object, between me and not-me, from birth, though the distinction is based on perceptions shaped by phantasy and by phantasized attributions of motive, and are thus, presumably, very different from the perceptions that would be made by an adult observer. Of course, any phrasing of such early perceptions in words is misleading. Susan Isaacs assumes that these very early events are first experienced as sensations, then gradually draw upon plastic images – visual, auditory, kinaesthetic, touch, smell, taste – before becoming linked up with words (Isaacs 1952).

The concern in this very early period is for oneself, not yet for one's object. Klein assumes that anxiety about being annihilated from within is dealt with by splitting and projection. The infant splits his good from his bad feelings and in phantasy projects both into objects felt to be external, 'not me', so that both the ego (self) and object are split. The infant thus lives in a world in which he and some of his objects are extremely good whereas other objects and other aspects are extremely bad. Emotions are labile; good rapidly changes into bad and bad into good, and there is no recognition of the fact that the good and the bad object are the same person. The infant thus lives in a world of 'part' objects, in the sense that what would to an outside observer be one object is to the infant at least two (good and bad). Further, Klein assumes that the first object is a part object, the breast, but in Klein's view this 'breast' is not just a purveyor of food, a satisfier of instinct; it is the source of love, of life itself. She tacitly assumes that in early infancy anatomical part-objects are normally perceived and treated as if they were whole objects and that whole objects may be treated as if they were parts. Full recognition of the identity of objects as wholes and of oneself as a whole in her view comes later, in the depressive position.

Klein uses the term 'projective identification' to describe a complex set of processes by which parts of the self, both good and bad, are split off in phantasy and projected into an object to which the individual reacts as if the object were the self or the part of the self that has been projected into it. The individual who projects in this way will then in phantasy introject the object as coloured by what he has projected into it. It is through such constant interplay that the inner world of self and internal objects is built up. Splitting, projection and introjection are the characteristic mental mechanisms of the paranoid-schizoid position, accompanied by idealization, denigration and denial. Omnipotence of thought is characteristic of the paranoid-schizoid position. Klein notes that when projection is excessive, objects and the self become fragmented, but in her 1946 paper she does not explain why projection should be excessive in some individuals and much less pronounced in others.

Klein thinks that failure to work through the persecutory anxiety and the tendency to split of the paranoid-schizoid position are basic preconditions for paranoid and schizophrenic illness.

In later work Klein makes important additions. In *Envy and Gratitude* (1957) she states that a more than usually marked degree of primary envy, which she regards as a constitutional factor, leads to a pathological paranoid-schizoid position. Because envy attacks the *good* object, it arouses a premature experience of depressive anxiety about damage to the good object, and interferes with the primal differentiation between good and bad in the object and in the self. Hence it is likely to result in confusion and in very severe cases to confusional states (see Rosenfeld 1950). Such a breakdown of normal splitting leads to difficulty in achieving and working through the paranoid-schizoid position and in proceeding to a normal experience of the depressive position (Roth 2001).

In a late paper (1958) Klein suggests that the bad objects of the paranoid-schizoid position are not the most terrifying objects; the most terrifying figures are split off into an area of the deep unconscious which remains apart from the normal developmental processes that give rise to the superego. She does not, however, fully work out this idea or integrate it with her other work.

The depressive position

Klein believes that at about 3 to 6 months the infant's object relations change from relation to a part-object to relation to a whole object. Although she does not explicitly say so, Klein seems to base this dating on the well-known observation that at some time between 3 and 6 months infants begin to look more 'human' and to behave in a much more integrated way. Klein supplements this sort of casual observation with more systematic observations by Middlemore (1941). Klein made her own observations of infants (1952d) but these are examples based largely on her theoretical formulations rather than raw data from which her formulations were derived.

In Klein's view of the depressive position the good and the bad mother are seen to be the same person; the infant begins to feel that the good mother he loves has been damaged by the attacks he has made and continues to make on the bad mother, for they are one and the same. This realization is extremely painful and gives rise to what Klein calls 'depressive anxiety', as distinct from the persecutory anxiety of the paranoid-schizoid position. It consists of a mixture of concern for the object, fear of its being damaged beyond repair, guilt and a sense of responsibility for the damage one has done. The individual is afraid of losing his object and has a strong urge to repair the damage. The actual state of the external object is extremely important; if the mother appears to be damaged, the child's guilt and despair are increased. If she appears well, or at least able to empathize with her child's problems about her state, the child's fear of his destructiveness is decreased and trust in his reparative wishes is increased. The idea of reparation, already introduced in 'Infantile anxiety situations reflected in a work of art and in the creative impulse' (1929b), now becomes a key concept. The pain of the new integration is sometimes so great that it leads to defences characteristic of the depressive position such as manic and obsessional reparation, denial, triumph and contempt. If these defences fail, the individual may retreat temporarily or for longer periods to the defences characteristic of the paranoid-schizoid position.

The favourable outcome of the depressive position is the secure internalization of the good object, which in Klein's view becomes the 'core of the ego', the basis of security and self-respect. The individual's future mental health and capacity to love depend on this internalization. Failure to achieve it constitutes the psychic basis of manic–depressive illness.

In her 1940 paper Klein also adds normal mourning to the phenomena of the depressive position. Mourning in later life reactivates the depressive position of infancy and indeed leads for a time to a feeling of losing all internal goodness. Mourning that is successfully worked through leads to a deeper and stronger establishment of the good internal object.

In her new theory Klein makes a crucial and most interesting link between the Oedipus complex, Freud's 'nuclear complex of the neuroses' and the depressive position. She maintains that the onset of the depressive position coincides with the beginning of the Oedipus complex, and says that the sorrow about feared loss of good objects in the depressive position is the source of the most painful Oedipal conflicts, for attacks on one's Oedipal rival are simultaneously attacks on one's loved object (Klein 1940: 345, 1952d: 110, 1957: 196, 1958: 239).

In later papers Klein makes additions to some of her early findings; among several others she notes that the dreaded combined object of her earlier work is modified, in the depressive position, by a conception of internal and external parents in a happy relation with each other (1952d). She revises her earlier views of the Oedipus complex (1945). She notes too that transitory experiences of depressive anxiety and guilt can occur in relation to part objects in the paranoid-schizoid position (1948, 1960).

The delineation of the paranoid-schizoid and depressive positions, combined with the role of early envy in exacerbating the difficulties of the paranoid-schizoid position, comprise Klein's final theoretical statement, integrating most of her earlier ideas into a new constellation. The concepts of the paranoid-schizoid position and the depressive position have proved to be exceedingly rich, so much so that their expressions and implications are still being explored.

Developments by Klein's colleagues in Britain

Many developments of Klein's ideas have been made by 'post-Kleinian' or 'contemporary Kleinian' analysts. The term 'post-Kleinian' has come into general use, but I prefer Roy Schafer's term 'contemporary Kleinian' because the term 'post-Kleinian' seems to me to carry a slight suggestion that the current generation of Kleinian analysts have left Klein's ideas behind, which is not the case (Schafer 1997).

A central feature of Kleinian analysis in Britain since the 1950s has been a decline in the amount of psychoanalysis of children by Kleinian analysts, although child psychotherapy has developed rapidly as a profession. Analysts who continue to work with children are especially interested in trying to bring together developments in child analysis with technical developments that have been worked out with adults.

Interest shifted first from work with children to work with psychotic patients, especially evident in the papers of Bion, Rosenfeld, Segal and Sohn, particularly in the 1950s. Work with such patients has continued, though fewer papers have been written about psychotic patients since the 1950s, and the number of papers involving border-line and narcissistic patients has increased. Many developments have occurred through continued work with these and other types of patient: refinements in the concept of projective identification; development of new theories of symbolism and thinking; new ideas about the paranoid-schizoid and depressive positions; and developments in technique. (My discussion of these topics is closely based on the introductions I have already written to the various sections of *Melanie Klein Today*, 1988.)

Studies of psychosis

Many of the analysts who undertook work with psychotic patients developed a conviction that the thinking of such patients could be intelligible and accessible. They found Klein's ideas about the anxieties and defences of the paranoid-schizoid position to be profoundly useful in understanding the way very disturbed infantile object relations inhabit the inner world of the psychotic patient, and they found too that these relations could be understood as they were lived out in the relationship with the analyst. This work led Segal and Bion to develop ideas about the process of thinking, and Rosenfeld to productive studies of many topics including confusional states, homosexuality in relation to paranoia, narcissism and borderline states (Rosenfeld 1965, 1987).

Projective identification

Although Klein defined the term 'projective identification' almost casually and was apparently always somewhat doubtful about its value because of the ease with which it could be misused (Segal 1982), the term has gradually become the most popular of her concepts. It is the only one that has been widely accepted and discussed by psychoanalysts generally, even though this discussion is sometimes incompatible with Klein's conception.

As I have described elsewhere (Spillius 1988: 81–6, 1992) there has been much discussion about whether the term should be used to refer only to instances where the recipient is emotionally affected by the projection. In my view such a restriction would be most unwise, for it would greatly limit the usefulness of the concept and is in any case totally contrary to the way Klein herself used it. I think the term is best kept as a general concept broad enough to include both cases in which the recipient is emotionally affected and those in which he is not. It might be useful, however, to have distinguishing adjectives to describe various subtypes of projective identification; 'evocatory' might be used to describe the sort where the recipient is put under pressure to have the feelings appropriate to the projector's phantasy.

Most of the other questions that have developed in the use of the concept are best answered in the same way, that is, by using the concept as a general term within which various subtypes can be differentiated. The many motives for projective identification – to control the object, to acquire its attributes, to evacuate a bad quality, to protect a good quality, to avoid separation (Rosenfeld 1971a) – are all most usefully kept under the general umbrella.

It is perhaps unfortunate that Bion did not develop a special term for the behaviour the individual uses to induce the other person to behave in accordance with his phantasies of projective identification. Especially when analysing psychotic patients Bion spoke to them in very concrete language because that was the way his patients thought; thus he would say, for example, 'You are pushing your fear of murdering me into my insides' (1955: 224). This led for a time to a fashion, especially among relatively inexperienced analysts, of speaking *conceptually* of phantasies actually being concretely put into the analyst's mind. Such usage has been sharply criticised by Sandler (1987a), who uses the useful terms 'actualization' and 'role responsiveness' to describe the processes by which individuals behave so as to get their object to feel and behave in a way that will satisfy the projector's unconscious wish (1976a, 1976b; Sandler and Sandler 1978). The current practice among British Kleinian analysts, partly because of the criticisms of Sandler and others, and especially because of the work of Betty Joseph (1989), is to distinguish conceptually between projective identification as a phantasy and the behaviour unconsciously used by the individual to get his object to behave in accordance with it.

41

Another change in thinking about projective identification is that the term used to be used almost entirely to characterize a very pathological, primitive defence. It continues to be used in that way when the patient being described is functioning mainly at the level of the paranoid-schizoid position, but it is also used to describe less pathological attributions of self and internal objects to external objects, attributions that are the basis of empathy and characteristic of the depressive position. This distinction between 'normal' and pathological projective identification has occurred largely through the work of Bion (1959, 1962a, 1962b, 1963).

Work on symbolism and thinking

Two of Klein's ideas have been important starting points for later work on thinking. The first is her theory of symbols (1930) and the second is the idea of projective identification, discussed above.

In a seminal paper on symbol formation developed from Klein's ideas about symbolism, Hanna Segal distinguishes between symbol formation in the paranoid-schizoid position, which she calls 'symbolic equation', and symbol formation in the depressive position, which she calls 'symbolism proper' (Segal 1957). In symbolic equations the symbol is confused with the object to the point of *being* the object; her example is a psychotic man who could not play the violin because it meant masturbating in public. In such a state of mind the ego is confused with the object through projective identification; it is the ego which creates the symbol, therefore the symbol is also confused with the object. In the depressive position, where there is greater awareness of differentiation and separateness between ego and object and recognition of ambivalence towards the object, the symbol, a creation of the ego, is recognized as separate from the object. It *represents* the object instead of being *equated* with it, and it becomes available for use to displace aggression and libido away from the original objects to others, as Klein described in her symbolism paper (1930).

Bion uses the idea of projective identification in developing a theory of thinking that has had a profound effect on the conceptual and technical repertoire of many analysts (Bion 1962b, 1963, 1965, 1967a). In this body of work Bion suggests three models for understanding the process of thinking.

The first model is similar to Segal's idea of an unconscious phantasy being used as a hypothesis for testing against reality (Segal 1964a). In Bion's formulation of it, a 'preconception', of, for example, a breast, is mated with a realization, that is, an actual breast, which gives rise to a conception, which is a form of thought. He thinks of the preconception as part of the individual's inherent mental equipment, an idea that has affinity with Freud's inherited phantasies (Freud 1916–17), with Klein's notion that the infant has an innate idea of the mother and the breast (Klein 1952d and 1959), and the developmental psychologists' idea of predesigning (Stern 1985).

In the second model a preconception encounters a negative realization, a frustration, that is, no breast available for satisfaction. What happens next depends on the hypothetical infant's capacity to stand frustration. Klein had pointed out that in earliest experience an absent, frustrating object is felt to be a bad object. Bion took this idea further. If the infant's capacity for enduring frustration is strong, the 'no-breast' perception/experience is transformed into a thought, which helps to endure the frustration and makes it possible to use the 'no-breast' thought for thinking, that is, to make contact with, and stand, persecution. Gradually this capacity evolves into an ability to imagine that the bad feeling of being frustrated is actually occurring because there is a good object which is absent and which may or may not return. If, however, capacity for frustration is low, the 'no-breast' experience does not develop into the thought of a 'good breast absent' but exists as a 'bad breast present'; it is felt to be a bad concrete object which must be got rid of by evacuation, that is, by omnipotent projection. If this process becomes entrenched, true symbols and thinking cannot develop.

The third model has come to be called the formulation of the container and the contained (Bion 1962b; see also O'Shaughnessy 1981a). In this model the infant has some sort of sensory perception, need or feeling which to him feels bad and which he wants to get rid of. He behaves in a way 'reasonably calculated to arouse in the mother feelings of which the infant wishes to be rid' (Bion 1962a). The projective identification in itself is an omnipotent phantasy, but it also leads to behaviour that arouses the same sort of feeling in the mother. If the mother is reasonably well-balanced and capable of what Bion calls 'reverie', she can accept and transform the feelings into a tolerable form which the infant can reintroject. This process of transformation Bion calls 'alpha function'. If all goes reasonably well, the infant reintrojects not only the particular bad thing transformed into something tolerable, but also, in time, the function itself, and thus has the embryonic means within his own mind for tolerating frustration and for thinking. Symbolization, a 'contact barrier' between conscious and unconscious, dream thoughts, concepts of space and time can develop.

The process can, of course, go wrong, either because of the mother's incapacity for reverie or the infant's envy and intolerance of the mother being able to do what he cannot. If the object cannot or will not contain projections – and here the real properties experienced in the external object are extremely important – the individual resorts to increasingly forceful projective identification. Reintrojection is effected with similar force. Through such forceful reintrojection the individual develops within himself an internal object that will not accept projections, that is felt to strip the individual greedily of all the goodness he takes in, that is omniscient, moralizing, uninterested in truth and reality-testing. The individual identifies with this wilfully misunderstanding internal object and the stage may be set for psychosis.

Of all Bion's ideas, the notions of container and contained and alpha function have been the most widely accepted and more or less well understood. Their adoption has led to a less pejorative attitude towards patients' use of projective identification and to a better conceptualization of the distinction between normal and pathological projective identification. The container/contained model of the development of thinking has lessened the divide between emotion and cognition. Further, to Bion, the external object is an integral part of the system. As described above, Klein has often been accused, wrongly I think, of paying no attention to the environment (see p. 29.) Bion shows not only *that* the environment is important, which Klein also stated, but *how* it is important. The importance of the environment had been stressed by many other British analysts especially Fairbairn (1941, 1944), Bowlby (1944, 1951) and Winnicott (1945, 1952, 1956a, 1956b), before Bion's formulation of the container/contained model of thinking (see also Rodman 1987: 89–93, 144–6; Rayner 1991). The distinctive feature of Bion's construction is that it uses the ideas of projection and introjection to formulate a conception of the internal dynamic involved in the mutual interaction of the container and the contained. He puts a particular emphasis on mental understanding: mental understanding by the other, in his view, is what makes it possible for the individual to develop mental understanding in himself and thus to move towards having a mind of his own and an awareness of the minds of others. Further, he focuses attention not only on the effect of the container on the contained, but also of the contained on the container. His is an 'internal' notion, very much concerned with the modification of thoughts and feelings by thinking. It is a model that he describes rather than an empirical description; it can be applied not only to a mother giving meaning to an infant's fear, or to an envious infant developing an envious superego (the particular mother/baby examples Bion describes) but to many other forms of interaction, including of course the analytic process.

In *Learning from experience* (1962a) and in 'A theory of thinking' (1962b), and indeed in much of his later work, Bion did not do as much as he might have to link his three models of thinking. It is surely repeated experiences of alternations between positive and negative realizations that encourages the development of thoughts and thinking. And the return of an absent mother gives rise to a particularly important instance, repeated many times in childhood (and in analysis), of a mother taking in and transforming, or failing to transform, the bad–breast–present experience.

In subsequent work (1962b) Bion further elaborates the model of container/contained and thinking as an emotional experience of getting to know oneself or another person, which he designates as 'K', in distinction from the more usual psychoanalytic preoccupations with love (L) and hate (H). He also describes the evasion of knowing and truth, which he calls 'minus K'. He says that K is as essential for psychic health as food is for physical well-being. In other words, K is synonymous with Klein's epistemophilic instinct, though in a more elaborated form.

Bion also develops the idea of fluctuation between the paranoid-schizoid and depressive positions, which he represents by the sign Ps<---->D, as a factor in the development of thinking (1963). This movement back and forth from the paranoid–schizoid to the depressive position was originally pointed out by Klein herself, but Bion focuses on the dimension of dispersal/disintegration (Ps) on the one hand and integration (D) on the other, ignoring for the time being the other elements of the paranoid–schizoid and depressive constellations as described by Klein. Further, Bion's formulation draws attention to the positive aspects of the paranoid–schizoid chaos, to the need to be able to face the possibility of a catastrophic feeling of disintegration and meaninglessness. If one cannot tolerate the dispersal and threatened meaninglessness of the paranoid–schizoid position, one may of course break down; or one may push towards integration prematurely or try to hold on to a particular state of integration and meaning past its time (see also Eigen 1985). Britton also addresses this problem (2001).

Bion's work on thinking is used by many analysts and is still being developed and explored, particularly in Britain by O'Shaughnessy (1981a, 1992a) and Britton (1989, 1992b, 1998a).

Elsewhere (Spillius 1988 Vol. 1: 158, 1989: 107–9) I have briefly described Esther Bick's theory that there is in infantile development a phase of 'unintegration' and 'adhesive identification' which precedes the processes of projection and introjection so crucial to Klein's theory of the paranoid–schizoid and depressive positions and to Bion's theories of thinking (Bick 1968, 1986; see also Anzieu 1989). Although many of Bick's students have used some of her ideas in clinical work, only Meltzer (Meltzer *et al.* 1975), Tustin (1972, 1981, 1990) and Ogden (1990) have attempted to incorporate her ideas into their conceptual systems.

The positions and the concept of pathological organization

The depressive position has continued to be a central conception, though changes have occurred in ideas about it, sometimes through careful clinical and conceptual analysis (Steiner 1992a) and sometimes without people realizing they were occurring. In her own descriptions Klein stresses the integration of anatomical part objects – breast, face, hands, voice, smell – to form the whole object; she also stresses the integration of the goodness and badness of the object and of the subject's own love and hate. These features have been retained, but use of the idea of the depressive position in the study of borderline, psychotic and very envious patients has led to a gradual and increasing emphasis on recognition of the object's separateness and independence as another hallmark of the depressive position. Jean–Michel Quinodoz (1991) has written specifically on this topic and its connection with loneliness.

Studies of thinking and artistic endeavour have also shown the very close, indeed, intrinsic relationship that exists between the depressive position, symbolic thought and creativity (Segal 1952, 1957, 1991).

A third aspect of the depressive position that has received even more stress than Klein gave to it is the intrinsic connection between the Oedipus complex and the depressive position (Britton 1989, 1992a; O'Shaughnessy 1989). As described above, Klein herself drew attention to this connection; I believe that the increased stress on the intrinsic nature of the connection between the Oedipus complex and the depressive position has come about because of the focus on recognition of the object's separateness as a crucial aspect of the depressive position. Once another person is perceived to be separate, they are felt to have a life of their own which the subject does not control; the relationship with a third object is the essence of one's primary objects' 'life of their own'.

Further explorations of psychosis, addiction, sexual perversion, perverse character structure and especially studies of narcissism and borderline states have led to refinements in the understanding of the paranoid–schizoid position and the relation between the paranoid–schizoid and depressive positions. Klein herself made a distinction between the normal paranoid–schizoid position (1946) and the pathological developments that occur when primary envy is very strong (1957). Bion took this further, outlining, especially in the container/contained model of thinking, the processes that can lead to pathology in the paranoid–schizoid position. In his model he mentions two factors: deficiencies in the mother's capacity for reverie and overwhelming envy in the infant. He implies that other factors in the hypothetical infant may be involved, but envy is the only one he discusses. Gradually the idea of an 'organization' of interlocking defences has been evolved to order the clinical phenomena encountered, especially those involved in narcissistic and borderline states. Many authors have contributed to the development of the concept, and the word 'organization' has been in use for some time, first as 'defensive organization' (Riviere 1936; O'Shaughnessy 1981b), also as 'narcissistic organization' (Rosenfeld 1971a; Sohn 1985) and more recently by John Steiner as 'pathological organization' (Steiner 1982, 1987, 1992a). In addition, a great many other analysts have used the idea without using the term (Spillius 1988 vol. 1: 195–202); obviously they have influenced one another though evidently without being explicitly aware at the time of having a common theme.

There are two main strands of thought in the idea of the pathological organization. The first is the dominance of a 'bad' aspect of the self over the rest of the personality. Many authors point out a perverse, addictive element in this bondage, indicating that it involves sado-masochism, not just aggressiveness. The second strand is the idea of the development of a structured pattern of impulses, anxieties and defences which root the personality somewhere between the paranoid-schizoid and depressive positions. This pattern allows the individual to maintain a balance, precarious but strongly defended, in which he is protected by the defences of the paranoid-schizoid position from feelings of threatened chaos, that is, he does not become frankly psychotic, and yet he does not progress to a point where he can confront and try to work through the problems of the depressive position with their intrinsic pain as well as their potential for creativity. There may be shifting about and even at times the appearance of growth, but an organization of this sort is really profoundly resistant to change. The defences appear to work together to make a rigid system which does not develop the flexibility characteristic of the defences of the depressive position, and efforts by the individual to make reparation, so characteristic of the depressive position, are usually too narcissistic to bring lasting resolution. There is considerable variation in the psychopathology of pathological organizations, but the analyses of these patients tend to get stuck: either being very long, only partially successful or sometimes interminable. The various authors are concerned with the question of whether the destructiveness of these organizations is primary or defensive. Often it is both, and indeed it is implicit in the work of many of the authors that the organizations they discuss are compromise formations, that is, they are simultaneously expressions of inherent destructiveness and systems of defence against it.

On technique

Strong feelings are experienced about the technique as well as the ideas of Klein and her colleagues. Analysts who are sympathetic to her point of view find the technique rigorously psychoanalytic. Those who are unsympathetic find it unempathically rigid.

Basic features of Klein's technique

As Segal (1967) notes the basic features of Kleinian technique are closely derived from Freud (1911–15): rigorous maintenance of the psychoanalytic setting so as to keep the transference as pure and uncontaminated as possible; an expectation of sessions five times a week; emphasis on the transference as the central focus of analyst-patient interaction; a belief that the transference situation is active from the very beginning of the analysis; an attitude of active receptivity rather than passivity and silence; interpretation of anxiety and defence together rather than either on its own; emphasis on interpretation, especially the transference interpretation, as the agent of therapeutic change. There is also an emphasis on the totality of transference. The concept is wider than the expression in the session towards the analyst of attitudes towards specific persons and/or incidents of the historical past. Rather, the term is used to mean the expression in the analytic situation of the forces and relationships of the internal world. The internal world itself is regarded as the result of an ongoing process of development, the product of continuing interaction between unconscious phantasy, defences and experiences with external reality both in the past and in the present. The emphasis of Klein and her successors on the pervasiveness of transference is derived from Klein's use of the concept of unconscious phantasy. She conceives of unconscious phantasy as underlying all thought, rational as well as irrational, rather than there being a special category of thought and feeling which is rational and appropriate and therefore does not need analysing, and a second kind of thought and feeling which is irrational and unreasonable and therefore expresses transference and needs analysing.

Klein and her successors believe that when patients regress, analytic care should continue to take the form of a stable analytic setting containing a correct interpretive process; the analyst should not attempt to recreate or alter infantile experiences in the consulting room through non-interpretive activities. Even in the development of the play technique with children Klein adhered to these principles, except that play as well as talk was the medium of expression. Similarly, in work with psychotic patients, some changes enforced by the patient have been contained without loss of overall method.

Developments in technique

Certain changes of emphasis have taken place in Kleinian technique in the last 30 years or so, partly through belonging to a psychoanalytic society in which there are other points of view, and partly through constant exploration, through being prepared to discard existing accepted procedure. Developments in technique and in ideas have gone along together, each influencing the other. Most of these changes have developed piecemeal and without anyone being very much aware of them at the time; they have been 'in the air' rather than the product of conscious striving.

The interpretation of destructiveness

Both Klein and her colleagues have often been accused of over-emphasizing the negative. Certainly Klein was very much aware of destructiveness and of the anxiety it arouses, which was one of her earliest areas of research, but she also stressed, both in theory and practice, the importance of love, the patient's concern for his objects, of guilt, and of reparation. Further, especially in her later published work, she conveys a strong feeling of support to the patient when negative feelings were being uncovered; this is especially clear in *Envy and Gratitude* (1957). It is my impression that she was experienced by her patients not as an adversary but as an ally in their struggles to accept feelings they hated in themselves and were therefore trying to deny and obliterate. I think it is this attitude that gave the feeling of 'balance' that Segal (1982) says was so important in her experience of Klein as an analyst. Certainly that sort of balance is something that present Kleinian analysts are consciously striving for. In this respect some of the authors of early clinical papers in the 1950s and 1960s, many of them given to the British Society but not published, took a step backwards from the work of Klein herself, especially from her later work. This was also a period when stated 'belief in the death instinct' was tacitly used, in my opinion, as a sort of banner differentiating Kleinians from the other Groups of the British Society. (Perhaps the other Groups used their opposition to the idea of the death instinct in similar fashion.) Since that time there has been a change, not in the emphasis on destructiveness and self-destructiveness, which has continued to be considered of central importance both clinically and theoretically, but in the way destructiveness is analysed, with less confrontation and more awareness of subtleties of conflict among different parts of the personality over them. This change has been influenced not only by the work of Bion but also by Rosenfeld's continued stress on the communicative aspect of projective identification and by Joseph's emphasis on the need for the analyst to become aware of the subtleties of the patient's internal conflict over destructiveness and thus to avoid joining the patient in sado-masochistic acting out.

Although the actual term 'death instinct' is now probably used less frequently than it was 30 years ago, there is basic agreement on its importance. There are two emphases, not mutually exclusive. One idea is that individuals with a particularly strong tendency towards inherent destructiveness and self-destructiveness tend to attack or to turn away from potentially life-giving relationships, wishing to obliterate any awareness of desire that would impinge on their static and apparently self-sufficient state. Another idea, closely related, emphasizes what Rosenfeld, following Freud, calls 'the silent pull of the death instinct', which promises a Nirvana-like state of freedom from desire, disturbance and dependence (Rosenfeld 1987). Both Joseph and Segal also stress the conflict among different parts of the personality over the voluptuous lure of withdrawing into despair, masochism and perversion.

There are differences in the extent to which analysts believe that marked tendencies to attack positive relationships and/or to withdraw into self-sufficiency are innate or acquired, inherent or defensive. In my view this is a false opposition. From the perspective of treating a particular patient, I think it is impossible to tell what is innate, what has been acquired through interaction with others, and what is the continuing product of that interaction. What one *can* tell is how deep-rooted the patient's negative tendencies are in the present analytic situation, but this does not tell one whether the deep-rootedness is innate or acquired. And, of course, it is part of the analyst's job to tease out how much his own behaviour may exacerbate his patient's negative tendencies. It is equally important for the analyst to avoid an attitude of blame, whether blame of the patient's innate tendencies, or of the character of the patient's objects, for an attitude of blame, whatever its target, disturbs the analyst's active but impartial curiosity.

The language of interpretation

Klein developed her very concrete, vivid language of part objects and bodily functions in work with small children for whom it was meaningful and appropriate. Extrapolating backwards, she assumed that infants feel and think in the same way and, further, that this is the language of thinking and feeling in everyone's unconscious. Work since Klein's day has amply demonstrated that vivid bodily-based phantasies often become conscious in the analysis of adults, especially readily in the case of psychotic and borderline patients. No one who has read Klein's accounts of her work with children or the clinical reports of her more talented students and colleagues can fail to be impressed by their clinical imagination and their grasp of unconscious phantasy. In less skilled hands, however, this approach loses its freshness and becomes routinized. Some of her more youthful and enthusiastic followers made and still sometimes make interpretations in terms of verbal and behavioural content seen in a rigidly symbolic form which now seem likely to be detrimental to the recognition of alive moments of emotional contact. Such interpretations are based not on the analyst's receptiveness to the patient but on his wish to find in the patient's material evidence for his already formed conceptions. 'Memory' and 'desire', in Bion's terms, replace hypothesis and receptivity (1967b). This prejudiced attitude can of course operate with any set of analytic concepts.

A number of analysts, perhaps especially Donald Meltzer, find it appropriate to interpret unconscious phantasy directly in part-object bodily language, but the general tendency nowadays is to talk to the patient, especially the non-psychotic patient, less in terms of anatomical structures (breast, penis) and more in terms of psychological functions (seeing, hearing, thinking, evacuating etc.). Together with the increasing emphasis on function, concentration on the patient's immediate experience in the transference often leads to discovery of deeper layers of meaning, some of which may be seen to be based on infantile bodily experience. Talking about unconscious phantasy in bodily and part-object terms too soon is likely to lead to analyst and patient talking about the patient as if he were a third person (Riesenberg-Malcolm 1981; Joseph 1989). But there is a danger also that if the analyst concentrates too exclusively on the immediate present, the here and now, he will lose sight of the infantile levels of experience and phantasy that the immediate expression in the here and now is based on, that the baby will get thrown out with the bathwater so to speak. Both levels of expression need to be listened for together and linked with experience. And, indeed, several colleagues have said that they think the concepts of the inner world and unconscious phantasy are in danger of becoming so attenuated in contemporary Kleinian analysis that much of the clinical richness of Melanie Klein's approach may be lost.

Transference, countertransference and projective identification

Transference is now regarded as based on projective identification, using that term in the widest sense as I have suggested above. According to Segal, Klein frequently used the concept of projective identification in her own work, but phrased her interpretations about it as statements about the patient's wishes, perceptions and defences. Her emphasis was primarily on the patient's material, not on the analyst's feelings, which, she thought, were only aroused in a way that interfered with the analytic work if the analyst was not functioning properly.

There is much evidence in the Melanie Klein Archive, which I discuss in Chapter 3, to show that Klein did not think that the analyst's emotional response to the patient was a valid source of information about the patient. Klein's view is illustrated in the now classic story about a young analyst who told her he felt confused and therefore interpreted to his patient that the patient had projected confusion into him, to which she replied, 'No, dear, you *are* confused' (Segal 1982). This example, however, is a case of a wrong or inadequate use of the idea of projective identification; the analyst was not seeing his own problem and was blaming his deficiencies on the patient. Bion, however, made use of exactly the same process but based on an accurate grasp of the way his patients were attempting to arouse in him feelings that they could not tolerate in themselves but which they unconsciously wished to express, and which could be understood by the analyst as communication. Bion, Rosenfeld and now most contemporary Kleinians are explicitly prepared to use their own feelings as a source of information about the patient.

Klein was uneasy not only about possible misuse of the concept of projective identification but also about the closely related issue of widening the concept of countertransference, as described by Heimann (1950), to mean use of the analyst's feelings as a source of

53

information about the patient. She followed Freud's definition in which countertransference is regarded as strongly influenced by the analyst's pathology (Freud 1910), and so she did not like the idea of using it as a source of information about the patient. She was very much aware of a tendency, especially in inexperienced analysts attempting to use their feelings constructively, to become over-preoccupied with monitoring their own feelings as their primary clue to what was going on in the session, to the detriment of their direct contact with their patient's material. Nearly all Kleinian analysts, however, now use the concept of countertransference in the wider sense, that is, as a state of mind at least partly induced in the analyst as a result of verbal and non-verbal action by the patient, thus giving effect to the patient's phantasy of projective identification (see Spillius 1988 vol. 2: 11–13). As Money-Kyrle says: 'The analyst experiences the affect as being his own response to something. The effort involved is in differentiating the patient's contribution from his own' (1956: 342 n10; see also Sandler 1976b: 46).

Bion usually uses the literal word 'countertransference' in the restricted sense to mean the analyst's unconscious pathological feelings, his 'transference' towards the patient, which indicates a need for more analysis for the analyst. This is of course confusing, since Bion constantly uses the *idea* of countertransference in the widened sense. In practice, however, the two types of countertransference are not invariably separable, since arousing pathology-in-the-analyst is often the means by which the patient effects his projective identification.

It has become increasingly apparent that far more is involved in transference and countertransference than explicit verbal communication, that there is a constant non-verbal interaction, sometimes gross, sometimes very subtle, in which the patient acts on the analyst's mind. Many analysts have discussed the importance of what the patient does in contrast to the content of what he says, but Betty Joseph has particularly emphasized this contrast as a starting point for her understanding of the way patients very early in their lives and in the analytic situation adapt to their objects and attempt to control them through projective identification (Joseph 1989). The patient is constantly but unconsciously 'nudging' the analyst to behave in accordance with his unconscious phantasies and expectations, a more colloquial term for what Sandler describes as 'actualization' (1976a, 1976b; Sandler and Sandler 1978).

Joseph's approach builds on and extends the usual psychoanalytic

view that the patient relives and repeats in the transference his infantile experiences, his particular patterns of anxiety and defence, the
conflicts between different parts of his personality. Her method particularly stresses the repetition of infantile defences, the attempt to
draw the analyst into behaviour that will evade painful emotional
experiences by attempting to maintain or restore a lifelong system of
psychic equilibrium.

Her method of work has aroused the interest of many analysts. All
agree with the importance of emotional contact, but many feel that
one can make more comprehensive, holistic interpretations and more
immediate links with the patient's history without losing emotional
contact in the immediate analytic situation. Some feel the method to
be too limiting and restrictive, but no one doubts that she has
developed a new and very important emphasis in Kleinian technique.

Reconstruction and the 'here-and-now'

Finally, in recent years there has been much discussion among
Kleinian analysts of the way past experience emerges in the analytic
situation, especially of whether and when the patient's account of the
historical past should be explicitly linked with interpretations of the
transference/countertransference situation in the session. There is a
considerable range of views which do not fall into neatly demarcated
sets.

Reconstruction, remembering and repeating have always been
considered important ever since Freud first drew attention to them,
but I think the renewed interest in the topic has come about at least
partly because of the emphasis of Joseph and her colleagues on acting-
in, that is, on 'repeating' as the central process that analysts should
address themselves to. The hope is that through thoroughgoing analysis of 'repeating', 'remembering' will occur, not only in the form of
remembering forgotten historical events but in the sense of making
conscious anxieties, defences and internal object relationships that are
being kept unconscious in the present.

According to one view, this is all that is necessary. If explicit links
are to be made with actual events of the past, which can in any case
usually be known only through the filter of the patient's projections,
the patient will make these links for himself. Reconstruction by the
analyst in the form of making explicit links with the historical past is
both unnecessary and misleading, for making such links is likely to

distract the patient from the emotional impact of the session, and it is in the session itself that the relevant aspects of the past are most immediately experienced.

Many analysts, however, think that explicit linking with the historical past is a crucial part of the psychoanalytic process which enriches the meaningfulness of the psychoanalytic experience and gives the patient a sense of the continuity of his experience (Brenman 1980). There is some disagreement over when and how explicit linking with the past should be done. There is one set of analysts who think that although the first objective should be to clarify and make conscious the past in the present through analysis of the patient's 'repeating', his acting-in, one can then make links with the patient's current view of his historical past (Riesenberg-Malcolm 1986; Joseph 1989). Common to these authors is a view that talk about the past is more distant than experience in the immediacy of the here and now of the transference/countertransference situation, but all agree that it can be extremely useful provided it is not used defensively.

Segal, however, does not agree that interpretations about the past are necessarily more intellectual and distant than interpretations about the immediate analyst-patient interaction. In this she is joined by Rosenfeld, who thinks that useful reconstructive interpretations and observations can be brought in whenever they seem relevant and are indeed thought of as an essential component in the analysis of transference (Rosenfeld 1987).

But in some of his later work Rosenfeld goes further. In the case of traumatized patients he thinks that interpretations in the immediate transference/countertransference situation are likely to be positively harmful because the patient experiences them as the analyst repeating the behaviour of a self-centred primary object, always demanding to be the centre of the patient's attention and concern (Rosenfeld 1986). He thinks the analyst should concentrate, at least initially, on a sympathetic elucidation of the traumatic events of the past in all their ramifications. Critics of Rosenfeld's view think that the problem of repeating the behaviour of a self-centred parent can be dealt with by interpretation rather than by behaving differently from the parent, and are further concerned that concentrating mainly on elucidation of past traumas may lead to splitting between an idealized analyst and denigrated primary objects, and to a belief by the analyst that he can know what the external reality of the historical past actually was.

Thus after many years of very little explicit discussion of technical issues, it now seems likely that these and similar exchanges will lead to more explicit statements of a growing range of views.

Personal thoughts on the hypothetical infant

In the lectures Klein gave in England in 1925, which eventually became Part 1 of *The Psychoanalysis of Children* (1932a), she reports detailed clinical material, and such theory as she uses and develops is restricted to the ideas she needs in order to make sense of her particular clinical observations. In Part 2 of *The Psychoanalysis of Children*, originally given as lectures in 1927, and in many of the more theoretical of her early papers, Klein writes not about actual clinical material with children but about a hypothetical infant. She extrapolates backwards, assuming that infants think in much the same way as the children she analysed and assuming too that there is psychic continuity from infancy to early childhood to latency to puberty, adolescence and adulthood. When discussing infants she does not bring much supporting evidence from infant observation (but see 1952d), and indeed it is often difficult to know how and why she arrives at her system of dating.

In the development of her theory of the paranoid–schizoid and depressive positions this process of speculative theorizing about developments in infancy is carried further. As described above, however, the positions are now increasingly thought of as states of mind, with decreased emphasis on their place in a conjectural sequence of infantile development. The positions cannot be 'proved' by infant observation or experiment since they are concerned with modes of thought and feeling, and it is even more difficult to gain direct access to infantile thinking and feeling than to the conscious and unconscious thoughts and feelings of older children and adults.

In constructing a hypothetical infant, Klein is not alone. Freud, Abraham, Winnicott, Mahler, indeed virtually all analysts are very free in constructing hypothetical accounts of the mental development of infants. I believe that these accounts are mainly derived from what happens in clinical work with patients, adults and children, supplemented by some rather unsystematic observation of infants and by general reasoning and ideas of what is plausible. In other words, the theories are derived from one set of data but expounded as if they were based on a different set. It is as if the analyst had asked himself,

'What reconstructed thoughts and feelings of infants would be consistent with what I observe clinically and with my thoughts about it?' Ideas about what is plausible are likely to be strongly influenced by whatever theory of psychology is current at the time. (In connection with the rival theories of the Controversial Discussions, Riccardo Steiner (1991) presents a most interesting account of the various scientists and authors who influenced the Viennese into believing that very young infants could not phantasize and think and, in contrast, the thinkers and scientists who influenced Susan Isaacs in the opposite direction.)

Coming from another discipline which had already moved from a belief in hypothetical phases to the view that theories should be designed to make sense of specific ethnographic facts, I found it surprising that psychoanalysts of all schools of thought phrased so much of their theory in terms of hypothetical conjectures about infant development when it seemed obvious that these assertions and conjectures could not be directly investigated with infants. This preoccupation with infantile thought was particularly striking in the Controversial Discussions in which much of the scientific part of the controversy consisted of arguments over highly speculative constructions of infantile experience. I find Isaacs's paper on phantasy plausible partly because she presented considerable observational evidence and made good use of the idea of genetic continuity, and partly, of course, because I am very familiar with her point of view. But the real usefulness of Melanie Klein's concept of phantasy emerges not from its conjectured role in infantile thought but in the meaningfulness and enrichment it gives to clinical work with patients. The relation of concepts to actual clinical data, however, was not the principal focus of the Controversial Discussions.

I am not at all against making conjectural hypotheses – psychoanalysis would be immeasurably poorer if Freud, Abraham, Klein and others had not had the courage and imagination to do so. And it is hardly surprising that the hypotheses should have taken the form of speculations about infant thought. But trouble starts when such speculations are treated as fact. In the Controversial Discussions each side tended to act as if what Freud said must be a 'correct' theory and then to shift from regarding it as a correct theory into regarding it as fact. Since Freud said many things and each side hunted for statements that supported their own point of view, it is hardly surprising that they did not come to any agreement, or even to a better understanding of each other. Such emotional attachment to conjectural theories puts one in danger of clinging to a theory that is not as useful as it should be because one thinks it is literally 'true'.

Freud describes the appropriately tentative attitude one should adopt towards one's hypotheses in the first paragraph of 'Instincts and their vicissitudes' in 1915. Indeed it was one of the great strengths of both Freud and Klein that they were prepared to drop one set of speculative hypotheses in favour of another that fitted clinical material better or that made more sense of existing observations and theory. This sort of development has been continued by Klein's colleagues, though on a smaller scale, and with more attention to clinical work and less to phrasing theory in terms of speculative reconstructions of infancy.

Meanwhile, in recent years there has been a vast increase in studies of infancy both by psychoanalytic infant observation and by observations and experiments made by developmental psychologists. And it is worth noting that experimental research on very young infants has substantiated some of Klein's more 'cognitive' conjectures, especially her assumption that very young infants are able to make rudimentary distinctions between self and object. Daniel Stern (1985: 10) puts it as follows:

> Infants begin to experience a sense of an emergent self from birth. They are predesigned to be aware of self-organising processes. They never experience a period of total self/other undifferentiation. There is no confusion between self and other in the beginning or at any point during infancy. They are also predesigned to be selectively responsive to external social events and never experience an autistic-like phase.

I find it interesting that Kleinian analysts have not drawn particular attention to this bit of confirmation of their approach. Presumably this lack of interest has occurred because their interest has shifted away from making conjectures about hypothetical phases of infancy.

In my view the experiments and observations of developmental psychologists are best at testing cognitive discriminations and sequences of behavioural interaction. They are not, or not yet, so good at telling us about infants' thinking and feeling and other such matters of especial relevance to psychoanalytic theory. Most of the concepts of developmental psychologists are not formulated in a way that would discover such matters, and perhaps such formulation is not possible. I surmise that it is for this reason that many psychoanalysts are only peripherally interested in the experiments of developmental psychologists. André Green, for example, thinks that infant observations and experiments do not tell the psychoanalyst what he needs to know, and that in any case the observer is likely to see only what his preformed theory encourages him to see (Green 1990). My own view is that psychoanalytic theory should at least be consistent with the findings of developmental psychology, although it cannot be reduced to them. And, reciprocally, I think that developmental research would be enriched by making more use of psychoanalytic concepts of development, however conjectural.

It seems to me that two new trends of psychoanalytic thinking have been developing recently. Both depart from the highly conjectural theories of infantile development and phases current at the time of the Controversial Discussions. One trend is closely associated with (though not limited by) empirical developmental psychology; an example is the observational and therapeutic study by George Moran and his colleagues at the Anna Freud Centre of the development of the individual's theory of mind (Fonagy 1991). A second trend is the development of a theory of mental models, and this is the trend of much recent Kleinian thinking. Following the initiative of Bion, interest in the precise dating of the paranoid-schizoid and depressive positions in infancy has ceased to be a preoccupation. It is implicit in most papers that the author is thinking of the positions as mental models, if viewed from the analyst's perspective, or as states of mind if viewed from the point of view of the patient's experience.

Change of emphasis from the infant-development aspect to the states-of-mind aspect is much more pronounced in some analysts than others. Analysts who have a particular talent for seeing the expression of infantile experience in the analytic relationship are more likely to think within the infant-development framework and to use reconstructive interpretations. Analysts who stay more explicitly in the here-and-now are more likely to use the positions as current and fluctuating states of mind. But overall, compared to the thinking and clinical practice of 30 or 40 years ago, it seems to me that the general trend for both the reconstructive and the here-and-now analysts is towards a greater use of the positions as models.

An overview

Klein's early work, then, was a great period of empirical clinical discovery which included findings at variance with some of Freud's views and findings, although Klein always regarded her work as firmly based on that of Freud. Then came her later period of theory-building with its delineation of the paranoid–schizoid and depressive positions, a new understanding of anxiety and new ideas about the importance of envy and gratitude in primary experiences of object relations.

I have described some central developments by contemporary Kleinians: studies of psychosis; theories of symbolism and thinking; projective identification; transference and countertransference together with developments in technique; the relation of 'present' to 'past'; and developments in the conception of the paranoid–schizoid and depressive positions, including the use of these conceptions as models.

I think of this work by contemporary Kleinians as a development of Klein's thought rather than a fundamental change. In my view there are only two respects, one major, one minor, in which contemporary Kleinian thought differs from that of Klein herself. The major difference concerns the use of countertransference as at least a partial source of information about the patient. The minor difference is a change of language, a greater caution about describing thoughts in terms of body parts.

Looking at the Kleinian development overall, I think two features stand out. First, in theoretical orientation it is both an object-relations and a drive-structure theory. Second, the clinical attitude: it is an approach that has special regard for psychic reality and for the individual's 'need to know' in Klein's and Bion's sense – and sometimes to evade 'knowing'. There are now many variations of interest and orientation in Kleinian thinking, but all have in common an interest in exploring the roots of current object relations in the internal world and at least to some extent in the remembered past experience of the individual, and all are involved in studying the expression of the object relations of the internal world in modified forms in the relationship of analyst and patient.

Acknowledgements

Many colleagues have made helpful suggestions about this chapter, most particularly Ronald Britton, Michael Feldman, Peter Fonagy, Betty Joseph, Ruth Riesenberg-Malcolm, Edna O'Shaughnessy, Eric Rayner, Richard Rusbridger, Priscilla Roth, Helen Schoenhals and John Steiner.

Note

1 Under the title 'Developments in Kleinian thought: overview and personal view', a slightly different version of this chapter was published as a paper in *Psychoanalytic Inquiry*, 1994, 14(3): 324–63.

PART TWO

In Melanie Klein's Archive

Introduction
The Archive

In the following three chapters I focus particularly on Kleinian ideas about technique, the use of the past and projective identification. I will use material from the Melanie Klein Archive as well as from the published writings of Klein and several contemporary Kleinians.

In her will Klein left her notes and papers to the Melanie Klein Trust, and in 1984 these documents were given to the Contemporary Medical Archives Centre of the Wellcome Library for the History and Understanding of Medicine. There are 29 boxes each containing 800 to 1000 pages of papers, some in German, some in English, some handwritten, some typed. The papers had already been catalogued in 1961 and this 1961 catalogue was used as a guideline by Dr Lesley Hall, Senior Assistant Archivist at the Wellcome Library, who corrected certain anomalies and added further material when it was donated. Most of the Archive has now been microfilmed. The Archive is available to bona fide scholars who contact the Contemporary Medical Archives Centre at the Wellcome Institute, but it is not always possible to see the original documents because some of them are very fragile.

There are 12 boxes of clinical notes and 9 boxes of lectures and notes about psychoanalytic technique and theory. So it is clear that Klein, unlike Freud, thought that her unpublished notes were worth preserving. It seems likely that she destroyed most of her letters concerning professional matters, because there are very few letters from and to colleagues, although there are many family letters. Klein dates her clinical notes, but most of her notes on theory and technique are undated. Most of the clinical notes stop in about 1950. Her notes on theory and technique appear to continue until the late 1950s, although it is difficult to be sure of this because most of them are undated. However, there is one set of notes on projective identification which, unusually for Klein, is given a date, which is 1958. I could not find any explanation in the Archive for Klein's different treatment with respect to dating of her clinical and conceptual notes.

The material of the Archive is classified into six sections:

A Personal and biographical
B Case material, child and adult
C Manuscripts
D Notes
E The Controversial Discussions within the British Psycho-analytical Society, 1939–44
F Family papers

I will quote extensively from the Archive, using mainly material from the B, C and D categories. Within each category there are numerous files, each with its own number and varying greatly in size from just a few pages to as many as 200. All the Klein files are prefaced by PP/KLE, but since this notation is the same for all the files I refer to, I will cite the material only by letter and number. It is not possible to give exact page numbers within each file because most of them were not numbered systematically.

3

Melanie Klein revisited
Her unpublished thoughts on technique

Klein published only three papers on technique, 'Symposium on child analysis' in 1927, 'The origins of transference' in 1952 and 'The psycho-analytic play technique' in 1955, but she left a set of unpublished lectures on technique and over 1500 pages of notes especially devoted to technical problems. She intended to write a book on technique, but did not do so. She was also going to write books on schizoid mechanisms, loneliness and mental development – too many topics, perhaps, for her to focus on any single one of them.

It is important to remember that although Klein eventually developed a new, influential and controversial theory, she was basically a clinician. She was fascinated by clinical material even to the point of losing herself in its details. I know too from discussions with James Gammill, whose work with a small child patient Klein supervised from 1957 to 1959, that she had a remarkable memory for clinical material, her own as well as his (Gammill 1989 and personal communication). Winnicott makes the same point (1965). I am told that in arguments about theory with colleagues Klein tended to resort to convincing clinical examples. She was sometimes accused of confusing concepts and data, which I imagine she found puzzling and unfair.

My view that Klein was basically a clinician was also her view of herself. In an unpublished note she says:

I would like to draw attention to the fact that I have always been primarily a clinician. It has never happened that I arrived at a concept theoretically and then allowed this concept to guide my clinical work. It has always been the other way round. From time to time going over my psychoanalytic experience and observations, I have arrived at certain concepts . . .

(D17)

I also think that she liked clinical material for its own sake. The Archive shows that she sometimes presented long descriptions of patients' material in her lectures and technical seminars, including far more detail than she would have needed to prove a point. At first I found this rather surprising. So great is Klein's reputation in the British Society for having strong, even dogmatic views, that I had expected that she would be tempted to start with her view and would then have tried to make her patients' material fit it. One tends to feel something like this when reading the *Narrative of a Child Analysis* (Klein 1961). But Klein's supposed dogmatism is much less evident in the material of the Archive than one might expect. Indeed, one of the most exciting parts of the Archive concerns a sea change in Klein's approach in the 1940s when, through her clinical work, she began to see the importance of splitting, projection, fragmentation and reintegration. At this time, new data and new ideas tumbled over each other in such profusion that it is perhaps surprising that she got her schizoid mechanisms paper (Klein 1946) to be as orderly as it is – and even so it is not an easy paper. Making links between clinical material and conceptual formulation was always something of a problem for Klein, and her most innovative papers are not easy reading. Nor, unlike Freud, was literary style her forte. As Riccardo Steiner says, her thinking and writing were 'intuitive, turgid and at times too condensed' (2004).

In the present chapter I will focus on Klein's technique with adult patients. Her technique with children is important too, of course, but she has published a paper on it (Klein 1955a) and has published much material that illustrates it (1932a, 1932b, 1961).

Klein's unpublished lectures on technique, C52 and C53

In the Archive there are two complete and very similar sets of lectures on Klein's technique with adults (C52 and C53). It is difficult to be sure of the exact dates of these lectures because, as I described in the Introduction to Part Two, Klein only gives dates for her clinical notes; her lectures, manuscripts and technical and theoretical notes are usually undated. We know from the records of the British Psychoanalytical Society that Klein gave a course of formal lectures on technique in 1936 and again in 1945–6. But we also know from the British Society's records and from Klein's own notes that she gave many seminars in which she spoke about technique. Klein also gave formal lectures on child analysis – these being what she was chiefly renowned for – which she gave year after year from 1947 until her death in 1960. Many points of technique were covered in these lectures and in both her child and adult seminars. She taught something in every term in every year from 1945 until 1960, and she held private seminars too.

It is likely that the lectures of C52 were given in 1936, for a letter from Edward Glover dated 19.1.1936 is to be found in an adjacent file, C54. His letter asks for the titles and dates of the lectures Klein is to give, and the titles she gives in reply tally more or less with the titles of lectures listed in C52. It is also possible, however, that the lectures of C52 and C53 were worked-over versions given later, or perhaps intended for publication. C52 is unusually neat, tidy and uncorrected. Versions of several of these lectures of C52 and C53 are to be found in other places in the Archive.[1]

Throughout the work for this chapter I have had two questions in mind. Does this unpublished material add to what we know about Klein's technique from her published work? And does her technique as revealed in the Archive as well as in her published work differ from current Kleinian technique?

After first describing the formal lectures I will summarize some of the special points about technique from Klein's voluminous notes. I will then give a session of material from her clinical notes. These clinical notes, detailed although not verbatim, give a feeling of how she thought and worked clinically. Finally I will briefly discuss the ways in which Klein's ideas about technique differ from those of her present colleagues.

Tucked away amongst her notes on technique is a perspicacious little comment:

Note re teaching technique. The difficulty for developing technique which has always existed – people always have great difficulties in speaking about their own technique. It is a very secret thing, and the reason for that secrecy.

(C54)

Unfortunately the note stops there and her ideas about the reasons for the secrecy are not described. Certainly she did not keep her own technique secret. Neither did Ella Freeman Sharpe, whose lectures on technique in 1930–1 Klein draws attention to (C52) (Sharpe 1930–1; Whelan 2000).

I have wondered why Klein's lectures are written out in full the way they are. Did she actually read them aloud? Did she speak to them? Not many analysts now remember what her lectures were like. But Isabel Menzies-Lyth, a senior Kleinian analyst, now retired, has told me that for the most part Klein read her lectures aloud although occasionally she spoke more spontaneously about particular points. Isabel thought that Klein's lectures were not very well organized, and that the experience of listening to Klein lecture was very different from being supervised by her, which Isabel, like others, felt to be a very enriching experience. There is a brief note in the Archive in which Klein herself gives a bit of an idea of her mode of presentation and it sounds consistent with Isabel's description. Klein says:[2]

Note for Seminar File   11.5.50.

A successful seminar was on transference from the beginning; accordingly, approach to first interviews or first session. Material for that from my old lectures on technique, Number Two, instances. Further points were transference in connection with situation. I read from page 5 onwards, expanded on page 10 re phantasy situations and real experiences, and the end of page 12 and so on transference displaced onto other people in repetition of primary defences. On page 15 about unconscious thread between one hour and former sessions.

(B99)

There are six lectures on technique in the Archive, with the following titles (C52, C53 and C54):

1   Guiding principles
2   Aspects of the transference situation
3   On interpretation
4   On interpretation
5   The analysis of experiences
6   This title appears to have got torn off the list Klein sent to Glover, but the lecture is concerned with the analyst's approach

to patients' complaints and grievances especially about their objects and past experiences

In the first lecture Klein describes the '*analytic attitude*', a combination of eagerness and patience in which the analyst is both detached from but also absorbed by the patient, humble but confident. Above all, the analyst should have 'a deep and true respect for the workings of the human mind and the human personality in general'. She describes Freud's discoveries of the unconscious and of transference and goes on to outline their origin in the love and hate of the infant and small child for the mother and her breast, the first object. She describes the painful recognition by the infant that his feelings of love and of hate are directed to the same person, and she shows how these positive and negative feelings come to be felt towards the father, siblings and other objects, especially the analyst. Our understanding of transference and the unconscious, she says, is what distinguishes psychoanalysis from other forms of therapy. She says that positive transference was mainly stressed at first, then there was an over-emphasis on negative transference, but the important thing is not the strength of either set of feelings but the deep and complex connection between them.

The remaining lectures are a further exemplification of the complex themes of this first lecture. In the second lecture she explores the theme of *transference* further, describing what she means by the 'transference situation' and its links with the past in both its realistic and phantasy aspects. She gives an example of the first interview with patient B in which he thought Klein spoke rather like his mother, who kept him too dependent, and then he wondered if seeing Klein would make him late for his next appointment. In her comment on this material Klein moved rather gently from his anxiety about whether he would be able to get away on time from his meeting with her to his next appointment, then to his mother having made him too dependent so that it was good to get away from her. And from there she described how he seemed to feel that analysis might make him too dependent on Klein, and that he felt she would keep him in analysis against his will. He agreed and added that he had wanted to get away from the session and also that he hadn't wanted to be ana-lysed by a woman but had not wanted to say so. And so the analysis began. Soon much deeper anxieties emerged about his worry over being too dependent. Later Klein describes a session in which B stressed his positive feelings for Klein while hiding his mistrust and hostility, and she says that both feelings are always there though one or other may be denied or displaced onto other people. She describes her finding that some aspect of transference is always evident at the beginning of analysis. She gives several examples, too, of patients displacing their attitudes towards the analyst to other external people. She ends this lecture by saying that there is always some sort of continuity between one session and the next, and that within each session there is a thread running throughout.

Interpretation is the theme of Lectures 3 and 4. Klein repeats some of what she said about the analytic attitude, including the analyst's inevitable countertransference. She says that patients must not mean too little or too much to their analyst, and that the analyst will be better at his work if he has a wide range of imagos derived from his own past and present object relations. She does not describe the analyst's countertransference as a useful source of information about the patient, which, as we shall see later, was a view that Klein never adopted even though it has become an important view in contemporary Kleinian analysis.

In Lecture 3 Klein describes clinical material from a child, 'John', who in his play was being a lion eating up the sleeping Klein, which she interpreted as his fear that Klein would eat him up because of his wish, as the lion, to eat her. She linked his feelings for Klein to his feelings about his mother. John became more anxious temporarily – because his defences had been put out of action, Klein says – but then he felt better and feelings of love and confidence in Klein increased.

In Lecture 4 Klein explains the development of *internal objects* through their constant projection and reintrojection. She gives very detailed material about patient B again, but this time he is further along in his analysis and is much annoyed because Klein changed the time of his session and he now meets patients he dislikes.

Lecture 5, 'The analysis of experiences', is concerned with *experiences of external reality*. Klein is especially concerned to show that however 'real' the experiences are, they are also affected by phantasies and, similarly, phantasies are affected by real experiences. She gives an example of a man traumatized by being his mother's favourite until his sister was born. Something similar happened in analysis when he realized that Klein had a child patient, which led the patient to get very angry, threatening to break off analysis and refusing to lie down. He began having very strange and perverse dreams, which led Klein to interpret that he felt his mother and sister had poisoned him because he had poisoned them. This led to further distressing dreams and to clarification of a phantasy of his having inside him a mother with the patient inside her. Eventually he developed a more positive attitude towards Klein's child patient, to Klein herself and to his sister, though with considerable guilt about the sexual play he had indulged in with his sister when they were children. I found this material very interesting, and so, I believe, did Klein. I think this was one of the times when she was so deeply intrigued by her patient's material that she went beyond what was needed to explain her technical approach to her students and she got very much involved in the material for its own sake.

Finally, there is Lecture 6 which is concerned with the analysis of patients' *grievances*, although Klein does not use that word. Her view is that one cannot know to what extent a patient's complaints are justified, and that, although the analyst should be fully sympathetic to the depth of the patient's feelings, he should not take the further step of agreeing or disagreeing with the patient about the content of his grievances. Further, the analyst should realize that the complaints also refer to the analyst. Even a patient full of grievance, she says, unconsciously appreciates that the analyst keeps to the proper analytic work.

In this last lecture Klein quotes Strachey on the way little bits of 'cure' occur when the patient can compare the analyst's actual behaviour with the archaic imago the patient has projected onto him (Strachey 1934). Like Strachey, Klein thinks interpretations should address the 'point of urgency'.

Klein ends Lecture 6 with several points which she mentions again over the years in her somewhat scattered notes on technique. I quote from the last pages of Klein's Lecture 6:

> No experience, past or present, can be considered by itself, that is, isolated, since it is always interwoven with the person's phantasy life and his unconscious conflicts, and while he is in analysis, with the transference situation. But then we need to be fully aware of the extreme variety and manifoldness of the transference situation, and of the circuitous ways the patient can use to disguise and to divert it . . .

> From what I have said just now I hope it has become clear that I do not mean that the analytic procedure is carried out by interpretations only, nor that the analyst should interpret all the time. For one thing, he must give the patient

plenty of opportunity to express his thoughts and feelings, while at the same time he is gathering the material he is going to interpret. In the normal course, he should not interrupt the patient but let him run on for a while . . .

I have made much in this course of lectures of the analyst's capacity to face the unconscious as it is, to pursue his work in the search for truth, and so on. All this is closely linked up with the insight which it is so important to make clear in the patient, but which, first of all, must be operative to a sufficient extent in the analyst . . . Speaking broadly of types of mental make-up, and not in the clinical sense, I may say that, from my observation, people of a depressive type seem to possess more of this insight than do others.

(C52)

The lectures of C53 are substantially the same as those of C52 although there is one important addition. Klein makes a strong statement to the effect that Freud's closest followers have not properly used the technical implications of his new ideas of the 1920s about the death instinct (Freud 1920, 1924), the superego (1923) and anxiety (1926). She criticizes Ferenczi and Rank for their book *The Development of Psychoanalysis* (1924) which, she says, stresses the old principle of catharsis; she criticizes Alexander for his belief that the analyst should try to convert the superego to ego (D53). Elsewhere in the Archive she criticizes Hartmann, Loewenstein and Kris for not using Freud's concept of the death instinct and destructiveness (D7), Anna Freud for assuming that small children have only a very weak superego (D16), and psychoanalysts generally for not really using Freud's great discoveries in their own technique (D16).

Klein's technique notes

These technique notes (as distinct from 'lectures') are mainly to be found in files D3 to D17, although the C category has some important files too: C47, C48, C67, C76 and most of all, C72. I will refer to them collectively as the 'technique notes'. Each file usually contains many entries. Some are only a few lines long, some are many pages. They cover many topics, and in no particular logical or temporal order, although there is a strain of consistency of clinical and theoretical thinking that runs throughout.

In these technique notes Klein refers to herself as 'K' rather than using the personal pronoun, as if taking an outsider's view of herself. Some entries sound as if she were giving herself instructions for a presentation or a paper. Occasionally she puts question marks in the notes, as if asking a colleague for an opinion, though I think these questions were probably addressed to herself.

Certain themes crop up again and again. *Transference* is by far the most frequently discussed topic. It is transference, Klein says, that distinguishes psychoanalysis from other forms of therapy (D7, D10). An understanding of the transference is the way to the unconscious – almost the royal road, she seems to be saying. The following quotation is one of the many ways she puts it:

> From the beginning, make it clear that the fuller understanding of transference and the understanding of the deeper layers of the unconscious are bound up with each other.
>
> (D10)

She says that she does not make transference interpretations insistently, but that she does mention the transference at least once in every session (C72). She emphasizes the way people unconsciously repeat the experiences and phantasies of infancy and childhood in their relationship with the analyst, as in other current relationships. She says:

> In these cases [neurotics and psychotics] there is also a restricted number of specific situations which are repeated over and over again. But also with normal individuals who have good all-round relations and whose lives do not seem to be dominated by the urge to repeat certain situations, one discovers in analysis that though they have a wider range they are also to some extent bound to patterns of figures, situations and behaviour derived from early childhood, which influences their relations to people and their experiences in life.
>
> (D10)

This theme of repetition crops up again and in considerable detail (D7). In several entries she points out that transference feelings to the analyst may be displaced to some other figure (D5, D7, D11), a point she also makes in her published paper 'The origins of transference' (1952a). She reiterates her view that transference begins to operate in

75

the first session – a point of disagreement with Anna Freud – and gives many examples (D5, D7, D11).

It is essential, Klein says, for the analyst to have a feeling for both the positive and the negative transference (D3, D7, D17, D26). She thinks both forms are always present, though one or other may be masked by the other, but the hidden one will be expressed through displacement to some other person or activity. She makes a point of disagreeing with Freud over his statement in 'Analysis terminable and interminable' that he could not analyse the negative transference of a patient (actually Ferenczi) because the patient did not express it (Freud 1937).

In the technique notes Klein expresses particularly strongly her firmly held view that analysts should link the transference to the patient's experiences in the past (D3, D7, D16, D17), a topic which I discuss in greater detail in Chapter 4. She was clearly aware that many analysts were emphasizing the 'here and now' and she regretted that links with the past were being correspondingly 'left out'. I think too that Klein, although she does not explicitly say so, thinks of the past in two senses: the first is the *remembered past*, that is, the particular patient's own unique and mainly conscious view of his past – his parents' and siblings' characters, the major events, including traumas. The second is the *unconscious past*, the typical pattern of infantile phantasies, emotions, object relations: the brief primal relation *à deux*, as Klein puts it, between mother and baby with its love and hate constantly developed by projection and introjection; the love for the primal object, the breast, and the hate for it; the intense curiosity about the mother's body and the belief that inside it are the father's penises and the babies; the attack on the mother's body; the paranoid-schizoid position, with its splitting and lack of integration of different aspects of objects and the self; attempts at reparation; love and hate for the mother and the father; the gradual development of the capacity to conceive of whole objects; the primal scene; the combined object; the Oedipus complex; the development of the depressive position; the mixed feelings not only for parents but also for siblings and others. Borrowing a term from Max Weber, I think of this as Klein's *'ideal-typical' model* of infancy (Weber 1947). Klein constructed this ideal-typical model by inferences drawn from clinical explorations of dreams, transference experiences of adult and child patients, and the gradual accumulation of intensive clinical experiences and formulations about them.

There are individual variations, but the overall pattern is, she assumes, 'typical'.

Although there are more entries on transference than on any other topic in the technique notes, there are many other entries as well. *Anxiety* is mentioned so frequently that it would be impossible to list all the references to it. Klein's attitude to anxiety is such a fundamental part of her approach that she says something about it on nearly every page. Her goal is to find the most urgent point of anxiety and to help the patient by interpretation to make it explicit, which, she says, at first often increases the anxiety, but eventually leads to its resolution. She describes the character an interpretation should have if it is to deal with anxiety effectively: it should be a transference interpretation, specific, timely and connected with the layer of the mind which has come into play at the moment (D3). This is a point to which she was alerted in her earliest work with children and she adhered to it right to the end. Another basic attitude towards anxiety that she frequently repeats is that anxiety and the defences against it should be interpreted together (D9, D14). She also describes her interest in patients who show very little sign of anxiety (D15).

Contrary to popular opinion, and in spite of her reputation for 'deep interpretations', Klein did not advocate sudden jumps from the surface to the depths. Instead she advocates '*balance*': balance between interpretation and listening (D3); between ego and id (D3, D17); between rigour and flexibility (D15); between the transference situation, the remembered past and the 'unconscious' past; between waiting on the one hand and relieving anxiety as soon as possible on the other (D7).[3] 'There is so much besides interpretation which the analyst does', Klein says (D7), and she has a long entry on the 'inadequacy of short symbolic interpretations' (D14). The entries on balance are very close to what Klein says about the 'analytic attitude' in her first technique lecture and again in the technique notes (see D5, D7).

Klein's views on *countertransference* are very different from the current view initiated by Paula Heimann (1950) and others, that countertransference can be a valuable source of information about the patient. Klein's view on the topic is close to Freud's. She thought of countertransference as an undesirable emotional response to the patient, a response in which the analyst was too much involved, too overwhelmed by the patient, or too antagonistic to him. The analyst's stability, she thought, should protect him from countertransference.

Klein's discussion on countertransference with young colleagues

In 1958 a small group of six young, recently qualified analysts held a tape-recorded meeting with Klein in which, at her request, they gave her a list of questions on technique which she answered. The file that records this long discussion almost verbatim is called C72. My name for it is 'Discussion with young colleagues'. There is also an edited version of this discussion in D17. The discussion was amiable but became quite heated on the topic of countertransference. Klein was first asked to comment on whether countertransference would be of value in understanding silent patients. She replied at length:

> Yes, well, if I start with that then I have altogether to say [a] little more about countertransference which has seen extremes of fashion in recent years. And [on] one occasion I have been called counter-countertransference. Now, it isn't so. You know, of course that the patient is bound to stir certain feelings in the analyst and that this varies according to the patient's attitude, according to the patient, though there are of course feelings at work in the analyst which he has to become aware of. I have never found that the countertransference has helped me to understand my patient better. If I may put it like this, I have found that it helped me to understand myself better.
>
> . . . At the moment when one feels that anxiety is disturbing one, I think probably it is again a matter of experience, one would really on the spot come to the conclusion what went on in oneself. Therefore I cannot really find a genuine account that countertransference, though unavoidable, is to be a guide towards understanding the patient, because I cannot see the logic of that; because it obviously has to do with the state of mind of the analyst, whether he is less or more liable to be put out, to be annoyed, to be disappointed, to get anxious, to dislike somebody strongly, or to like somebody strongly. I mean it has so much to do with the analyst that I really feel that my own experience – and that goes back a very long time – that I had felt that – is rather to find out within myself when I made the mistake. I always think it was because I had not enough got hold of myself, I would say. I'm not saying that I didn't make mistakes, of course I did make mistakes. But I was very much inclined to study those mistakes and really to find out what led me to that mistake. And then I really found it was a difficulty [in] myself.
>
> (C72)

Klein continues for quite a time in this vein and then says:

What are the uses of countertransference in analysis? Where countertransference is unavoidable, it should be controlled, studied and used by the analyst for his own benefit, I would say, and not for the benefit of the patient, I don't believe in it. Any other questions about that?

One of participants asks Klein:

How closely akin are countertransference and the empathy you were earlier mentioning as being a *sine qua non* of a good analyst?

She replies:

There is a great deal in what you are saying now, because to be able really to accept that now I see very mean traits in the patient, that he is really out to get everything out of him [I think she means 'me'] what he can, that his attitude is really one in which he gets out of [people] what he can, then turns away, and even perhaps maligns them. We get such characters to be treated as patients and what Dr L has just said has a great deal to do with that, and that is empathy with the patient . . . If we see such character traits just worked out against ourselves and instead of feeling, 'Now, I can't bear this patient and that proves that he is that and that and that' – Now, instead of that, if I really feel, 'Well, I want to study him, if he is so greedy, if he is so envious, that is part of his psychology, that is why he came to me which is what I want to understand.' There is there another element, not only empathy, and that is the *wish to know* [emphasis added]. Now, the wish to know, I think, is a very important thing in being an analyst, the wish to explore the mind whatever the mind is like . . . Shall I get very annoyed [at the patient's envy, greed etc.] or shall I then think, 'Why has he got that attitude?'

(C72)

Neither Klein nor her six colleagues could leave the topic alone. They went on arguing in the interval (apparently a long one), this time about a psychotic patient Klein had briefly treated when she was in Berlin. She had been quite frightened. One of the young analysts suggested that perhaps the patient was frightened and that he wanted to make Klein as frightened as he was, and hoped she would deal with it better than he had. I thought this was rather a good suggestion, but Klein did not agree with it at all. The editor of the discussion sums up what Klein said as follows:

I don't really believe that it was because he put me in an anxious position that I could understand him better. I feel that he put me in an anxious position because he was so tall, because I noticed there was something entirely different to any case I had dealt with before, and that this was a fact that I realised might lead to danger. But that did not help me to understand him better, what helped me was that I remembered for instance how persecuted he was by his uncle and how terrified. I interpreted to him that he was afraid I would put him back in the asylum . . . Now it was not really because I felt he could be dangerous that I gave that interpretation, it was because I understood something about his psychology.

(D17)

Finally, Klein tried to end the discussion by saying:

I think I have answered it [their question about countertransference]. Whether I answered it satisfactorily or not is quite another matter, and I am afraid I left some of you with the feeling that I didn't make myself clear and that you don't agree with me. But that doesn't matter. I have given you at least my point of view as well as I could.

(C72)

But even then they could not stay off the topic for long. They had a discussion about 'linking' – Bion had read his 1959 paper 'Attacks on linking' to the Society in 1957 – and then they talked about projective identification, which led once more to the question of countertransference. Their differences remained unresolved.

One can but sympathize with both parties in this discussion. The young analysts were espousing the wider view of countertransference that was beginning to become generally accepted in modern Kleinian thinking. But Klein was 'right' too: she did not want analysts to be carried away by their transference to the patient and to regard this aspect of their own character as valid data about the patient.

As one might expect from her views on countertransference, Klein does not use the concept of *projective identification* in exactly the way it is generally used by contemporary Kleinian analysts today. Even though she is usually thought to have 'invented' the concept in her paper 'Notes on some schizoid mechanisms' (Klein 1946), she makes comparatively little use of it in her published work. In the Archive Klein gives considerably more clinical illustration and conceptual discussion of projective identification than she devotes to the topic in her published papers; I will discuss these contributions in Chapter 5.

Klein mentions many other topics of interest in the technique notes: her idea of the differences between her approach and that of Anna Freud; 'deep' interpretation; reassurance; resistance; the importance of not getting drawn into patients' complaints and grievances; envy; an intriguing series of entries under the heading 'on making use of apparently not very significant material'; 'when to ask for a dream'; dissociation; the manic position; memories in feelings – a particularly poignant entry; the negative therapeutic reaction; 'on the interpretation of very frightening material'; internal objects; and aggression.

A final comment about the last item, *aggression*. Feelings of aggression are mentioned frequently throughout the notes, as are feelings of love. But Klein mentions her attitude to the interpretation of aggression only once, in the discussion with young colleagues. She says:

> . . . there was a time when I felt very badly because my work on bringing out the problem of aggression [led to the result] that there was nothing but aggression. [I] was quite despairing. Whatever I heard in seminars, in the Society, it all was aggression, aggression, aggression. . . . the point is that aggression can only be tolerated [when it is] modified, mitigated, if we are able to bring out the capacity for love.
>
> (C72)

We know from James Gammill (1989) that Klein felt the same way about some of her students' indiscriminate use of her concept of envy. I wonder what she would make of the fact that her contemporary Kleinian successors, nearly 50 years later, are accused of much the same sort of thing. Would she take us to task? Or would she think these are stereotypes used for other than clinical purposes?

Klein's notes on a session with a male patient in 1947

I want to end this account of Klein's thoughts on technique as revealed in the Klein Archive by giving a brief excerpt that shows the way Klein was working in 1947. The war and the Controversial Discussions were over; she was beginning to have a group of young colleagues who were interested in her work; her paper 'Notes on some schizoid mechanisms' had been published not long before the session I report.

An illustration of the schizoid mechanisms

First material: Frustration. Having had to leave without breakfast. Kept waiting on my door-step because the first bell was not heard. Complained about the cold which makes him feel 'depersonalised'. Wonders about the reason for such a feeling. In-between an association to the dream of last night which had been forgotten. The association has something to do with a white bowl. Cold brings up memories of the War (though it has always stirred in him particular feelings). Looking out to the landscape covered with snow: white, still, with the need to watch every movement which meant danger. The intentness of the look, together with this particular feeling which cold produced, makes him think that there was nothing there of him any more, that everything had become eyes looking out. The week-end break enters as a special frustration at this particular stage. The night before he had had a very affectionate feeling about me, and the anxiety that this changes over the week-end contributes very much to the difficulty. Quite recently the conflict that together with great feelings of gratitude, friendly, loving feelings etc. grievance against me exists has been brought out under great difficulties. He is fighting obviously hard against this combination of feelings in this particular hour. Back to the breakfast situation, he feels that this was really quite unimportant in comparison to much comfort and other things he otherwise enjoys in his home situation.

The same he felt when I drew his attention to it about the frustrations in analysis and felt ashamed and angry about himself because of his resentment. He added that there is something about coming back after that which makes it so difficult. The picture of an affectionate child coming back to mother and then everything is different. Now I had interpreted the internal situation in connection with this feeling of depersonalisation regarding cold, that everything inside was dead and frozen and had reminded him of material in which he had very strongly felt that it was internal. A situation in a trench in which there was no noise, no sound to be heard, and a complete state of apathy and fatigue. The only thing in which he felt any interest and which he watched was a bit of grass on top of the trench and a clump of earth which were slightly moving. On this occasion the material had shown most convincingly to him that this was an internal situation and that he watched the death of his objects inside, only these two moving objects representing what was still alive in him. When I referred now to this internal situation he said: that is true, but it is not only the thing here, there is something more important. And he came back again to the eyes looking so intently that nothing was left of him but eyes. He thought of a ferret and a rat, in digging themselves into something. I suggested that when leaving me he felt that one part of himself was digging himself into me in a ferret- or rat-like way and that everything was so changed when he wanted to come back in an affectionate way because this part of himself left in me had in the mean-time done havoc inside me, controlled me, etc. To this he agreed with great conviction and said: but it is not only you who will then be so injured. When I come back, I am afraid to meet the bad me in your room.

Again went back to the eyes and to the ferret. The ferret has pink eyes, and that reminds him of crying. I pointed out that while the ferret and the rat, biting and tearing up etc, represent the destructive part of himself left inside me, the crying also shows the lonely and anxious child. He had maintained that it was not I (K) who was the main thing here but his bad 'me' which he was afraid to meet again, but I could remind him by material of a former dream in which I had so completely changed and was so indifferent and hostile towards him and had indicated how much of my time he had already taken and that I dismissed him – that it was me too who was changed by the ferret and rat. This had been the most difficult part of the whole material, and it is an interesting point that here the attempt was, if he had to meet his bad 'me', that at least I should not have been changed into a bad object – one of his greatest difficulties to acknowledge.

(B98)

Differences between Klein's technique and contemporary Kleinian technique

The most striking differences between Klein's views on technique and the views of current Kleinians are to be found in the use of the concepts of projection and countertransference. Even in 1958 I believe that Klein was somewhat out of step, not only with the young colleagues, but also with other more established colleagues: Heimann (1950), Racker (1953, 1957, 1958, 1968), and Money-Kyrle (1956). Heimann's paper had already aroused considerable interest and adherence in the British Society; in it she defined countertransference in a widened sense and advocated its use as a source of information about the patient. Racker had published several papers in Spanish in Argentina in the 1940s advocating the use of countertransference in the widened sense as a source of understanding of the patient and of the analyst-patient relationship, and these papers were published in English language journals in the 1950s and were attracting consider-able attention in both Britain and the USA. Money-Kyrle's 1956 paper 'Normal counter-transference and some of its deviations' addressed the difficult question of how, when assessing countertransference, to distinguish between the contribution of the patient and that of the analyst.

Bion's attitude towards countertransference appears to have been somewhat contradictory. When he mentions the actual, literal term, he usually uses it in the sense defined by Freud (1910) and Klein, as the analyst's transference to the patient, which is largely unconscious (Bion 1962a: 23–4; 1963; 1975, as published in 1994: 6, 1978 as published in 1994: 248). At the same time Bion constantly uses the idea of countertransference, though usually not the actual word, in the widened sense advocated by Paula Heimann and Racker. His papers of the 1950s collected in his book *Second Thoughts* in 1967 give an idea of how he was using this idea, particularly in understanding the analyst's response to the patient's projections. One of his most explicit statements about the effect of the patient's projections on the analyst occurs in his early paper 'Group dynamics: a review', (Bion 1952, reprinted in *Experiences in Groups*, 1961) and here, uncharacteristically, he actually uses the term countertransference in a way that is close to the widened usage of Heimann and Racker. He says: 'Now the experience of counter-transference appears to me to have quite a distinct quality that should enable the analyst to differentiate the occasion when he is the object of a projective identification from the occasion when he is not' (1961: 149). He continues gradually developing this insight in the papers of the 1950s, eventually coming to the formulation of the container/contained in *Learning from Experience* in 1962, although he does not use the specific term 'countertransference' as an essential aspect of that formulation.

I believe the work of Heimann, Racker, Money-Kyrle, Bion and others has led to some change of clinical focus. Nowadays we expect to be influenced by patients' projections and to be able to use our responses to such projections to help us to understand our patients better. At the same time, most of us recognize that, as Klein pointedly said, the 'wish to know' is exceedingly important in psychoanalysis, and most analysts agree that it is better for the analyst's wish to know to be directed at the patient rather than narcissistically at the analyst. In her argument with the young colleagues the point Klein did not agree with was the idea that the analyst's wish to know could be directed at himself not only narcissistically but in the service of the analytic task.

We have become aware of being observers not just of the patient but of the analytic relationship, including not only the patient's involvement but also our own. We are subjectively involved, but we also try to observe our involvement as best we can and to think about the effects it is probably having, just as we observe and think about the patient and his involvement. These two attitudes of 'subjective' involvement and 'objective' observation alternate throughout the session, often uncomfortably, and it is partly through the relation between them that understanding may emerge. Klein, like Freud, saw the analyst as having a simpler task. The analyst was to observe the patient, and only the patient's side of involvement in the analyst-patient relationship; the analyst was supposed to guard against his own involvement, not to use it.

However, in spite of Klein's view that countertransference should not be used as a source of information about the patient, I think it is possible, though it is only a conjecture and would need more evidence, that implicitly she was using her emotional reactions to her patients, especially her reactions to their projections, to understand them better. In the session I have quoted above Klein does not describe what she was feeling, but it would not be surprising if she had felt mildly attacked, and this might have helped her to formulate her interpretation of the defensive basis of the patient's guilt and self-attack.

Another difference between Klein's technique and that of some contemporary Kleinian analysts concerns transference and the past, which I discuss more fully in Chapter 4. Klein thought that transference interpretations were 'feelers' to the past, both the particular past of the individual patient and the 'unconscious' past which I have called Klein's 'ideal-typical model' of the infant. On this topic of the past, as I discuss elsewhere (Spillius 1988 vol. 2: 13–16, 1994a: 353–5; Chapter 2 above), there is now considerable variation among Kleinian analysts. Some start with the experience of the patient's inner world as expressed in the immediacy of the analyst-patient relationship and then make links later with the remembered or assumed past. Some tend to stay in the immediate present. Some readily bring in links with the past at any time.

What I suspect has also changed is that we do not follow all the details of Klein's ideal-typical model of infancy in quite the way she did. We are more likely to think in terms of her later model of infantile development, that is, of fluctuations between the fragmentation of the paranoid–schizoid position and the integration of the depressive position, thus using Klein's final model of psychic development. This change is linked to the change of language, that is, to the tendency now not to phrase interpretations in terms of anatomical part objects.

But in reading the clinical and technique notes of the Archive I have found myself much impressed and moved by Klein's use of her ideal–typical model, by her conscientiousness in making notes, by her immense curiosity about her patients and her respect for them, and by her constant working at developing ideas based on her clinical experience. Indeed, in the Archive I found a remarkable woman: sensitive, courageous, endlessly curious, occasionally stubborn to the point of prejudice – a great clinician and, in spite of herself, a great theorist.

Notes

1   These other listings and versions will be found in C47, which includes part of Lecture 3, Lecture 4, Lecture 5 and Lecture 6; C48 contains Lecture 1 and Lecture 3, although this is possibly a child analysis lecture; D3 contains Lecture 2, although it contains the child material about lions formerly used in Lecture 3; D7 contains Lecture 1, somewhat revised.

2   All quotations in sansserif font are from the Archive. If I think a word should have been omitted I put it in round brackets (   ). If I have added something, I put it in square brackets [   ].

3   The main entries on 'balance' are in D3, D7, D14, D15 and D17.

---------------------- 4 ----------------------

Melanie Klein on the past

It is generally believed that contemporary Kleinian analysts interest
themselves in a patient's past mainly in so far as it is expressed in the
immediate analyst-patient relationship, a view which is particularly
associated with Betty Joseph's work but which is shared by many
other contemporary Kleinian analysts. It therefore comes as something of a surprise to discover that Klein, especially in her writings in
the Archive, pays close attention to what the patient actually says
about his past as well as to the way he expresses it in the transference.
She also thinks, however, that a person's unconscious phantasies are an
important part of his thinking and feeling and influence his memories
so that the relation between experiences and thoughts about the past
and the present are never simple or straightforward.

Of Klein's published papers, 'The origins of transference' is the one
that tackles the relation between past and present most directly (Klein
1952a). In it Klein says 'I hold that transference originates in the same
processes which in the earliest stages determine object-relations' (p.
53), which is the basis of her belief that full exploration of the conscious and unconscious aspects of the transference will reveal the past
experiences and unconscious phantasies of the patient. She also makes
a rather condensed statement about the transference *situation*, which
she says consists of many situations transferred from the past into
the present (1952a: 55); she calls this putting together of many past
situations the '*total situation*'. She goes on to say:

> It is only by linking again and again . . . later experiences with
> earlier ones and *vice versa*, it is only by consistently exploring their
> interplay, that present and past can come together in the patient's
> mind. This is one aspect of the process of integration which, as the

analysis progresses, encompasses the whole of the patient's mental life.

(1952a: 56)

Thus integration of the patient's past and his present was an important therapeutic aim for Klein.

It is clear that Klein does not confine her ideas of the past to a patient's conscious memories. She includes his unconscious phantasies. And she goes further, because by the time she wrote 'The origins of transference' in 1952 she had come to believe that the past of all patients involved a more or less typical sequence of conscious and unconscious developments. Her picture of this typical sequence was based on her ideas about her extensive experience with both child and adult patients and by 1952 – in fact by 1946 in 'Notes on some schizoid mechanisms' – it had assumed the shape of a new theory of development. In Chapter 3 I referred to what I think are Klein's two views of the past as the patient's *'conscious view'* and Klein's *'ideal-typical model'* of infant development. Klein describes this typical developmental sequence in some detail in her paper 'The origins of transference'.

The first form of anxiety, Klein thinks, is caused by the working of the death instinct within, which gives rise to a fear of annihilation, the primordial cause of persecutory anxiety (Klein 1952a). She spells out what she thinks happens next in more detail in a later paper, 'On the development of mental functioning' where she says, 'The primal process of projection is the means of deflecting the death instinct outwards' (1958: 238). In a footnote she adds: 'In my view two processes are involved in that particular mechanism of deflection. Part of the death instinct is projected into the object, the object thereby becoming a persecutor; while that part of the death instinct which is retained in the ego causes aggression to be turned against that persecutory object' (1958: 238 n1).

In 'The origins of transference' Klein says that the persecutory feelings aroused by the death instinct within the infant are intensified by painful external experiences and partly alleviated by comforting experiences (1952a). She goes on to describe the typical development through the paranoid–schizoid position (1946) to the depressive position (1935, 1940), although she does not use these terms in 'The origins of transference'. (This developmental sequence is described in an even more condensed form in another of Klein's 1952 papers, 'The mutual influences in the development of ego and id', 1952b.)

Thus Klein's idea of a patient's past includes what the particular patient has said about his past and his more immediate unconscious phantasies about it, but it also includes Klein's organized conception of what a patient's typical past is likely to have been, which I have called her 'ideal-typical' view of the past. And the patient will live out his past in the transference, because, as Klein says in 'The origins of transference', 'transference originates in the same processes which in the earliest stages determine object-relations' (1952a: 53).

In the Archive Klein discusses the ramifications of the past and the present in considerably greater detail than she describes it in 'The origins of transference'. She was evidently intending to write a book on technique and another on infant development, and her discussions about the past and the present are described in the context of these two central ideas. Her plans for these and other books were not realized, however, so that we are limited to her somewhat unorganized but nevertheless intriguing occasional entries in the Archive. A further difficulty, as I described in Chapter 3 is that most of the entries are undated – usually Klein only gives dates for her notes of actual clinical sessions, not for her thoughts about ideas.

I will quote from the Archive in some detail, but of course it is important to remember that these notes were not intended to be published in this unedited form, and that they were made largely in preparation for teaching students.

The following quotation from the Archive gives an idea of the way Klein thought about the patient's past (the underlining is Klein's).

One of the rules of technique applicable both to child and adult analysis: <u>transference interpretations are in a sense feelers towards early situations.</u> They must however be fully dealing with the actual situation and the feelings aroused in this situation, which implies the whole present reality into which so many of the transference feelings are deflected. In <u>taking the transference situation back to the past</u>, there are <u>certain general situations in childhood to which we may tack them on</u> and which we can be sure that they are always attached to. Enumerate such general situations of jealousy, frustration, rivalry, diffidence, lack of confidence in comparison with adults, night situations, afraid or unwilling to go to bed, left alone by grown-ups, etc.

Even such tacking on must have some basis in the situation we are just exploring. It can never just be guess-work. Give instances for that.

To which situation are we going back from the transference situation? Quite early ones or others from later stages of life? That depends entirely on the material. There are certain situations coming up in the transference which so closely and intensely point to quite early situations, such as the breast situation for instance, that one can make a suggestion in this direction. Try to give instances for that. There is however no rule to which stage of development the transference situation should take us back. There is material in which the early situation becomes at once prominent and we might have to follow this up again and again until the picture of childhood and of later life with adults fills itself in. As little as we can make up our minds that we are analysing first genital feelings and only step by step go back to oral ones – as was supposed to be a general rule in analysis in former time and is still maintained by some analysts – as little can we decide about a definite order in which to go back to the past. It is true we may find that with the child as well as with the adult we may get greater resistance to reconstructing intermediary steps let us say in the child's life the present relation to the parents than even the early situations in which these important feelings were evolved. It must come in an analysis which wants to achieve fully its purpose.

Another important point here is the balance between interpretations referring to the transference and space and time allowed for the reconstruction and expression in the patient of past situations.

But we must not forget that there is also something like a flight from the transference situation into the past. That is different between adults and children, because of course the child still has got his parents as such important figures in his present life. But it is even true to some extent of the child. Adults at certain times may be quite willing to feel again guilt, etc. in relation to the past but shy from re-experiencing this in the transference situation. Explain why. At other times the past, when it is revived in full strength, becomes so overwhelming that there is a constant flight or turning to the transference situation. The measure lies with where the greatest emphasis on anxiety and guilt is at the moment, and that is what must guide us. One instance: Richard. There were various points at which he did not mind aggression towards the early mother, when she was the Hitler mother, but could hardly bear any aggression towards me.

(D7)

As usual, there is no date for this entry, though clearly it must have been after 1941 when Klein analysed 'Richard'.

At another place in the Archive, D3, Klein talks again about transference and the past, and here she makes it even clearer that by 'the past' she means not only what the patient remembers but also what she calls 'quite early situations' – 'oral desires and anxieties' – meaning what I have called above her conception of the ideal-typical development of the individual through the paranoid–schizoid and depressive positions. This is what she says – and, as before, the underlining in this quotation is Klein's:

How do transference interpretations make their way into the past of the patient? For we must not forget that it is only part of a transference interpretation that we connect it with the analyst and the analytic situation; and that the other half is that we take it back to earlier situations. Which situations are we attempting to revive in the patient when we give a transference interpretation? I think no rule can be made about that because it entirely depends on the context of the material presented. Sometimes we find the links with quite recent situations starting with actual situations at the moment and only gradually do we make our way back to what must always be in our mind, the earliest situations and how they developed. That is to say fundamentally to the early oral desires and anxieties.

Sometimes we can gather – and that may happen quite early on in analysis – that the material and the attitude of the patient, the intensity of his feelings at the moment, suggest links with quite early situations. And then we should not allow ourselves to apply any rule [. . .] we must wait with the analysis of such situations. To give you an instance: the oral desires and anxiety may appear so clearly and so intensely in the material that our impression is that to suggest early situations of frustration, relation to mother's breast and other early situations of frustration is quite justified. And usually we shall find that the responses to such an interpretation opens the way to further material which takes us to all sorts of intermediate steps and even to quite recent situations. We are also making use in transference interpretations of the knowledge that certain general situations in childhood can be assumed. The way in which a patient may at the moment express his grievance, his frustration, sometimes in an entirely irrational way, allows us to draw his attention to the fact that such situations (like being sent out of the room, not being wanted any more, having to go to bed when the adults are still up, etc.) are revived. Jealousy about other patients can then be explained in the family setting. Though we do keep in mind that the content

91

of our interpretation should be <u>specific</u> we may <u>start transference</u> interpretations with certain patients with the reference to such <u>general</u> situations experienced in childhood.

Note: Be careful in qualifying these general interpretations and compare them with the need for specific ones.

To mention one more of the many essential points which could be discussed in this connection: I have stressed in this lecture – and as you will see I shall do so throughout this whole course – the <u>importance and value of interpretation.</u> However, the art of interpretation is only part of our work. We must keep in mind that another very essential part of our work is to give full attention to the associations of the patient, to allow him to express his feelings, thoughts, fully; to pay full attention to this, to understanding fully the defences, and altogether to be <u>as interested in his ego as we are in his unconscious.</u> This implies that our interest could not and should not only be directed towards what we are going to interpret, because this should be based on the picture which we allow to emerge at his own pace. We have to keep a balance between the need of the patient to produce his material, to express his feelings and give full rope to that need. And we are thus confronted with the necessity to keep a balance between the time we are giving in an analytic session to this part of the work (which is in fact the fundament on which we base our interpretations) and the interpretations themselves.

(D3)

I find myself touched by the last part of this entry, for in it Klein makes clear one of the qualities that I think makes her not just an important theorist but also a concerned analyst: she is interested in the patient for his own sake, not just because she can use his material for her theories.

In another part of the Archive, D17, Klein makes a particularly strong statement about the importance of explicit linking of the transference with the patient's past. Once again, it is impossible to date this entry, but I think it probably comes from the late 1950s:

Notes on technique
It cannot sufficiently be stress[ed] and conveyed to the patient that transference phenomena are linked with the past. In recent years the importance of transference to be gathered from the unconscious, as well as from conscious material, has been recognised, but the old concept that transference means

a repetition from the past seems to have correspondingly diminished. One hears again and again the expression of the 'here and now' which, though not out of place, is often used to lay the whole emphasis on what the patient experiences towards the analyst and leaves out the links with the past. Freud's discovery that the feelings towards him were transference from the past – one of the fundamental discoveries in psychoanalysis – retains its full value. Both for teaching purposes and in the analysis as such we must beware that analysing the relations of the patient to the analyst both from conscious and unconscious material does not serve its purpose if we are not able, step by step, to link it with the earliest emotions and relations. One of the many mistakes which is made by enthusiastic beginners is to misuse the rule that the present transference situation should be linked with the past by trying straight on to go to the earliest breast relation. To quote an instance: After my querying why the candidate had not made transference interpret-ation in the full sense, somebody else suggested 'One should, shouldn't one, line [link?] that with the breast disappointment?' Now the instance in ques-tion was that the patient was deeply disappointed by having been allotted to a younger analyst (actually a student), whereas she of course wanted to be analysed by the senior analyst by whom she had been first interviewed. In her material the deep disappointment with the father had come out quite clearly. She had loved and admired him, but later on discovered that he was not what she had thought him to be (he had taken to drink) and then she started relations with boy friends, which were quite unsatisfactory to her. Later on, she found a more mature man, whom again she idealised and badly wanted to marry. The candidate had made no connection whatever between the disappointment that he, as a junior person, had become her analyst, with the fact that the idealised father, after disappointing, had been replaced by unsatisfactory boy friends, and that the more mature man again appears as the wished for object. The right interpretation would have been to link the disappointment about the choice of analyst with the disap-pointment of not being able to have the ideal father, and that the choice of young boy friends was unsatisfactory because they could not replace the ideal father, whereas the more mature man seed [seemed?] to revive the old idealised relation to the father.

This illustrates one of the steps by which the link with the past can be estab-lished. (Give more instances of those gradual links). We see here the Scylla of not linking at all with the past, and the Charybdis of linking it straight away with the breast relation.

(D17)

Another central view of Klein concerning transference is what she calls '*the total situation*', a term she uses not only in the technique notes of the Archive but also in her published paper 'The origins of transference' (1952a). What she was apparently trying to convey by this term was that the analyst does not usually represent only one person or one aspect of a person; she does not speak, for example, of the 'mother transference' or the 'father transference'. Instead she thinks that many aspects of an important object are represented in the analytic relationship, and that many and complex object relations are re-enacted in the analytic setting. By 'total situation' she means that a whole set of complex internal object relationships involving many experiences and phantasies will be lived out in the transference. In the Archive she explains this in more detail:

What is a total situation?

Actually experienced and mixed with phantasy. Never a relation to one person but to a whole set and then external and internal. I have already referred to the fact that in analysing any experience we have to keep in mind that experiences from the beginning of life are coloured by the infant's emotions and phantasies. This is particularly true of the young child but persists in some measure throughout life. Another essential aspect of a situation reappearing in the transference can be found in the fact that the relation to the analyst is not only the relation to one person but involves other people as well . . . To return here to my summary of earliest development: I have mentioned that the relation to the mother or her breast as the primary object soon entails relations to the father or other people in the infant's surroundings, but to this correspond the infant's phantasies of the mother containing the penis of the father and babies. It may well be that the relation to the mother and her breast as independent from her being bound up with other objects is very short. We have every reason to assume that such a phase, a relation fully and actually *à deux* does exist, and it is the basis, I think, of all object relations . . . Accordingly, it is from a very early stage onwards that the relation to the mother is bound up with the relation to other objects, and similarly the relation to the father is bound up with that to the mother and again to other people, particularly brothers and sisters. In addition processes of introjection lead from the beginning of post-natal life to objects established within the self which very soon include the father's penis and the father and other objects, particularly brothers and sisters (or expected brothers and sisters). All these objects enter into the individual's experiences and object relations, and reappear in transference experiences. The analyst, therefore, does not on the whole deal with a relation *à deux* for this applies only in so far as the analysis goes back to the very earliest stages of life . . . To summarise: the total situation which we try to explore in analysis, taking it back to its origin, includes the patient's relation to his inner world, therefore between phantasy and reality experiences, his object relations external and internal.

(D7)

But Klein can hardly bear to leave out the clinical material. She concludes this entry by saying:

Should I give here the instances X and Y as illustrations of what I have described, remarking that even that is not the total situation which I have described here, but can easily be related to its foundations (the King in the background, the rejection by the bus-conductor who will not stop)?

(D7)

I will illustrate Klein's attitudes towards transference and the past by describing a particular session with a woman patient in 1942. In this case the Archive contains not only Klein's account of the particular session but also her notes of a discussion of it which she held with students two months later, in October 1942. The session itself is described in the Archive as follows:

Patient G, August 1942

Instance. A woman patient has been to see *Macbeth*. She is struck by the way in wh. she experiences this play. She finds that she had very seldom felt so strongly identified with the hero and also experienced her feelings of guilt in this identification. There are a few other things she noticed. One, in leaving the theatre, she suddenly felt quite close to the people who were going out, as if she was somehow linked up with them, had come closer to other people. There are many associations relating to her present and past life in connection with her incapacity to overcome her hatred and to forgive things wh. have been done to her in the past. She realises that she never forgave anything; but what had become clear now to her is that her hatred was really murderous. In the same hour and even preceding these associations about *Macbeth*, she spoke with great friendliness about another woman whom she thinks very kind and friendly, doing genuinely kind things for other people, and recently she had also shown great appreciation of another woman for similar reasons. Following on her associations about

95

Macbeth, she says that it is striking that at the same time when she can definitely feel great changes in herself and progress in the analysis, she should also have such great doubts about K. and her work, wondering sometimes if K. really did not do harm, as people suggest K. might actually [be] driving people mad. It suddenly occurs to her that K. might really be like Lady Macbeth, and that though Macbeth was definitely a psychotic type, he might have remained all right and nothing of this disaster happened if she had not prompted him and made him more mad.

K. takes up this analogy, and suggests that according to this the patient and K. in her mind are married, and she the patient represents the man; K. reminds her of material about homosexual desires to K. She [K] points out that not only are we then in a love relation, but we are allied against the father, represented here by the King. If this is so, the situation was to her particularly emotionally loaded because it showed her the fulfilment of her homosexual desires in connection with K., but realised as a wish situation in wh. she allied herself with K. against somebody who would now stand for K's husband, or some man closely connected with K. – in the past an alliance with her mother against her father, whom she wanted to kill.

The patient is deeply impressed by this interp. and said she had never considered it from this aspect, and now recognises that the depth of her guilt is related to this particular situation wh. in a way is new to her and the result of recent work about her homosexuality. She associates something, and while she tells it says it must be a confirmation. On the escalator she saw a man who was sick. He obviously felt very unwell, as if he was in danger of having a stroke. He was supported and looked after by a man friend who took great care of him, and there was no particular reason at all why the patient should have the feeling, wh. she definitely had, that she was called upon to look after the sick man and that she should do something about it. It had all gone out of her head, but came back to her after K.'s interp. She then refers to a phobia of hers, and that is of seeing anybody sick, and to her impression that if she saw a man standing in a certain position she always assumed that he would vomit, though nothing of that actually substantiated. She described position.

The particular point wh. brought out all the emotions here was that K. did not leave it at the guilt connected with the homosexual relation with K. but followed up this analogy, given through the identification with Macbeth into the details and into this particular alliance against a third person. Also fear of madness here wh. was attributed to Lady Macbeth, and in the present situation was expressed in the fear of the analyst driving her mad, was bound up with the fact that the wish to kill one's father and to be allied with one's mother in such an undertaking is equal to madness. The murder wish itself is felt as madness.

(B99)

The discussion with students about this session with Patient G is described in the Archive as follows:

Seminar 8.10.42.

I. The importance of stressing and reviving situations in interpretation in connection with my way of analysing transference situation

II. Technique

In this connection also the compound of various emotions appears, i.e. not love alone but hate as well, etc. This was illustrated by an instance (Woman patient G, Notes, August 1942). First of all of course this applies to transference situation. It is not the relation to the analyst as one person only, but in the background the analyst's relations with other people and particular brands of emotional situations appear. In this case, going back to childhood material, which is not included in the material presented in the notes, we could see that this situation of distrust, or rather of fear of being murderous and plotting with the mother against the father, reappeared in various connections in her life: alliance with sisters against brother – every homosexual relationship was coloured in this way, and I think this was the main reason why she had not become a stable and manifest homosexual. Putting it simply, the child, in his early life, is never concerned only with the relation to father or mother but with both, and with other people in the family life. The importance of interpretation in this light is that it also brings out the variety of emotions and not only one i.e. I illustrated this by pointing out that I might have satisfied myself in this particular case by stressing, in the material referring to *Macbeth* performance, that the patient's comparing K. with Lady Macbeth includes that she was Macbeth and that we were the couple, in which she played the male role. That was sufficiently supported by earlier material, and I could have left it at that and explored her fears of me in this connection (Lady Macbeth driving him [Macbeth/the patient] mad). But in taking up this whole situation I got much further. A few questions put to me: Do I follow up an analogy included in the material in all its details? Do I feel that every detail of the analogy would apply? In comparison, Freud, analysing in his Dream Interpretation, goes on to bits of the material, does not pursue one analogy or one situation so fully.

Reply: That if one keeps in mind a particular situation, which had, in this case, and obviously in others as well, already presented itself to the analyst formerly, even if one did not follow up completely the analogy expressed in this case but took bits of the material, one would probably get back to this particular dominant situation. My impression in this case was that to consider the situation and to follow this up first was the more necessary, and it was proved by the subsequent associations. Enlarge on the reply to this question and consider it more closely as regards the question of keeping in mind the *situation* [italics added] when interpreting and not only the relation to one person whom the analyst predominantly represents; remember the variety of internal and external *situations* [italics added] and the fact that in the early mind one person by itself probably never actually exists? The mother containing the father, etc.

(This point *of situation* [italics added] is to be made one of the angles by which I want to approach technique in my book.)

I took up the possibility of my not having interpreted this situation fully, having left it at the homosexual relation, which no doubt would in itself be quite fruitful, but incomplete.

Another question: That patient already at the theatre had this great experience and feelings, felt this greater closeness and contact with other people, and this was before the interpretation.

Reply: That this material had been becoming more and more clear, and was obviously nearer to the surface at the theatre performance.

Referring to this particular case, the question was also discussed: why is it that the patient became aware of the strength of her murderous feelings, of the fact that she had never forgiven [anyone] for any frustration, and yet at the same time felt so close to people who left the theatre and spoke so warmly of the kindness of another woman.

[I omit several paragraphs at this point, and then continue]

Of course in the play it is true that Lady Macbeth instigates it, but that is why the comparison was chosen. The projection here was that the instigation came from the mother. She would instigate murder of father, and the lessening of these feelings of projection implies a better relation to mother. All this is very contradictory, because so many trends are going on at the same time. The material showed that she was accusing me of that, and all these projections were at work. Yet at the same time there was already the setting in all these other trends wh. I have described.

Notes added later

Stressed importance of situations in connection with the transference, as a repetition and revival of patterns of situations in the past. Transference situation not only a relation of patient to father or mother, but much wider and complicated situations including other people and particular constellations. That was exemplified by the material of woman patient in connection with Macbeth (Seminar file, also Technique). This should be added to the second course of lectures in which much of this is pointed out.

(D16)

I have described these notes about the Lady Macbeth material in such detail not only because they show Klein linking her patient's material to her past but also because they show her working out her idea of 'situations' and their complexity, which ten years later she put into her paper 'The origins of transference', although without giving examples. This material also shows particularly clearly how Klein used her patient's attitudes towards her analyst, her particular transferences on this occasion, as a form of repetition of the 'situations' of her patient's past.

I want also to describe a session of my own work in which a patient's experience of a painful past event was powerfully enacted between us.

Mrs Z [1]

Mrs Z, aged 37 at the time of the session I shall describe, had had a difficult separation from her parents when she was a small child between 2 and 3 years of age. Because of her parents' occupation, this sort of separation was repeated several times in Mrs Z's early childhood.

The session I shall describe occurred shortly before an unusually long holiday break, which Mrs Z was going to make even longer by going away for an additional few days herself, for the most 'realistic' of reasons. Some form of acting out on breaks was not unusual for her, and we had discussed this new break and I had interpreted her response to it some weeks before the session I shall present. After these interpretations there followed two or three weeks of 'ordinary' sessions, and then gradually she became fed up and critical of herself, her analysis, and me, and I felt I did not fully understand why.

In the particular session I shall describe she came about ten minutes late and was silent for a long time. Eventually, on the basis of the quality of the silence, I said she gave the impression of feeling very negative and angry.

Again there was a long silence. At the end she launched into a description of a lot of inconveniences and minor grievances, mainly at work. She said it was a peculiar twist that analysis stirs things up in such a way that all these minor complaints turn into an attack here.

I said she wanted me to regard them as minor complaints, but . . .

'No', she said, 'only to know the difference between major and minor.' (There was utter contempt in her voice.) There was a short silence, then she said, 'I don't know whether it's you or me, but in the past ten days it seems to me you just totally and utterly keep missing the point.' (Her tone was exceedingly scathing.) 'Yesterday you apparently didn't notice it was so painful for me to admit that I find analysis and everything you do so terribly uninteresting. I can't stand it.'

I waited a bit, then started to speak, but she broke in almost shouting, 'Don't talk! You're just going to repeat what I said, or you're going to alter it. You don't take things in, you don't listen to what I say, or you listen and you just want to hear it the way you want it to be and you distort it.' (There could hardly be a better description of what she did to my interpretations, but interpreting projection directly is not usually helpful, especially when a patient is in a flight of paranoia.)

I was finding it hard to think, and I knew that my own self-doubt and feeling that I was a bad analyst were getting powerfully stirred up by her accusations. But I managed one small thought, which was that she must be feeling inadequate too, and that my leaving had a lot to do with it. Then came a second thought, that she hates herself for being cruel even though she gets excited by it. It felt to me as if I was like a damaged animal making her feel guilty, and she wanted to stamp me out.

I said she couldn't bear for me to know how painfully attacking she is, how much she wants to hurt me, how cruel she feels; but she also can't stand it if I don't know, don't react. It means she is unimportant.

'Can't you realize' – by now she was almost screaming – 'that I am totally and utterly uninterested in you! I don't care! I only care about myself. Take your pain to your analyst. Well, it's not my fault if you haven't got one.'

What I said, after quite a long pause, was that I thought she felt I treated her cruelly, with complete scorn and indifference, as if she was boring and utterly uninteresting, and that was why I was leaving her. I said she felt that the only way she could really get this through to me was by making me suffer in the same way.

There was another long silence. Then she said, 'None of this alters my being tired and having too many things to do.' (She sounded like a slightly mollified but still petulant child.) 'I suppose,' she went on, 'I am in a childish rage with you. I never could attack my parents, so I have to make up for it now.'

At the time I thought this reference to the past, although probably true, was a way of evading what was happening in the session. Now, on the contrary, I think she was living out in the session a painful situation of her past, which we both knew about, but in this living-out the roles were reversed: she was the abandoning parents, I was the helpless child.

What I actually said at the time was that nothing felt right to her. If she felt she hurt me, it made her feel so cruel that she couldn't bear herself, and she got furious with me for being the cause of her attack. But if I wasn't hurt she felt ignored, as if she had no power or importance at all.

She then repeated the last part of this interpretation almost as if she had not heard me and that it was her own idea; that is, she said if she didn't hurt me it meant she was a nothing. She then talked very indignantly about being left on her own. I said she thought I was cruel for leaving her on her own so arbitrarily and that she therefore had a right to attack me in kind. But she also felt I was leaving her because she was so attacking. She muttered that at least someone ought to notice that leaving was happening, as if implying that I was ignoring it. I said I thought she felt I was ignoring the time of the session as well as the holiday, and in fact it was time to stop now.

I would hardly present this as an ideal session, but I think it is an example of the way a patient may have an unconscious phantasy of projecting an experience into the analyst and may act in a way that makes the analyst feel it. I felt utterly trodden on, mistreated, immobilized. This is I think how she felt (unconsciously) about my leaving her, and how she had felt at the time of her traumatic abandonment by her parents in her childhood.

What particular thing was it, I asked myself later, that had made her so unable to express herself symbolically in this session, so intent on *doing* it instead of thinking it. In part I think it was the poignancy of the childhood situation which had become deeply embedded in her – it was part of her past that was forever present in her internal world, and at many levels of consciousness. But the fact that I was leaving her and that she sensed something in me – I think it was my self-doubt – that echoed her view of herself and of her parents also played a part.

Her reversal of roles, a characteristic disguise in this sort of situation, allowed her to remain unaware of the link between her past and the present, and confused me for some time as well. After a time I realized that my self-doubt was an important link both to her parents, whom she thought of as self-critical and self-doubting as well as abandoning, and also to herself, for she tacitly assumed that she was abandoned because she was unlovable. Of course rationally she knew, as an adult, that her parents had left her because of unavoidable circumstances, but to her unconscious mind that was no justification. And my holiday was equally arbitrary, an assertion of uncaring parental authority.

In this session I made some use, though with difficulty, of my knowledge of my patient's past and its links with her feelings and behaviour in the session. Through projective identification and role reversal, and without conscious awareness of what she was doing, Mrs Z got me to know what this past had felt like and how it had stayed deeply alive all through her life.

General discussion

Klein in my view uses her idea of the past in three ways. First, she thinks of it as consisting of the patient's conscious memories of his past. Second, the past involves what I call her ideal-typical model of the conscious and unconscious developments of infancy conceptualized, at least by the late period of Klein's theory, in her ideas of the paranoid-schizoid and depressive positions. And third, particular aspects of the past, particular 'situations', are lived out in the daily experiences of the transference and, as Klein says in her paper 'The origins of transference' (1952a), she thinks of the totality of these many situations as the 'total situation'.

I think these three definitions of the past have continued tacitly in the work of current Kleinian analysts, though without being categorized in quite the way I have suggested. In much current work, however, there is even more stress than Klein gave on the living-out of the patient's past in the transference. This emphasis is particularly evident in the work of Betty Joseph and several other Kleinian authors, for example Riesenberg-Malcolm (1986) and Feldman (unpublished, undated paper). It involves an apparent focus on the present, often referred to as 'the here-and-now' (though not by Joseph herself). It is assumed that the 'past' has become part of the patient's internal world which will reach its most alive expression in analysis in the emotional interchanges in the immediate present of the relationship between patient and analyst. Joseph describes the essence of her view about the past as follows:

> I myself can only go as far as to suggest that the useful integration of the past can only be achieved if we start from the present, from what is being enacted, however silently, with the analyst, making connections only if and when they form in one's own mind and seem to be immediately relevant, not starting from the past and explaining the present and the pathology from what one believes one knows of the past.
>
> (Joseph 1996)

Joseph thus starts with the transference, the relationship between patient and analyst in the session, and sees it as the living past. She puts more emphasis than Klein on those aspects of the past that are lived out in the transference, and less than Klein on links with the patient's own conscious view of his past or on his expressions of behaviour consistent with the theory of the paranoid-schizoid and depressive positions. Similarly in her paper 'Transference: the total situation' (1985) Joseph describes the 'total situation' as the many aspects and situations occurring in the transference, whereas Klein's usage of the term focuses on the complex and varied situations in the patient's experience. Of course this difference is more apparent than real because both Klein and Joseph think that the complex situations of the patient's experience are lived out in the transference.

In my own approach I think I start almost simultaneously with the transference situation and with what the patient says about his remembered past. But in thinking more generally about patients' experience of the past, I have also found myself increasingly but inconclusively occupied with general questions of time and causality.

Klein herself does not address general philosophical questions about time, nor do most contemporary Kleinian analysts. I think that most analysts assume – and I have been told both by philosophers and by anthropologists that the assumption is naive – that events that come first cause, or partly cause, related events that come later. I think that this belief coexists persistently and uncomfortably with the knowledge that one cannot have direct and independent knowledge of the 'facts' of one's patient's past or the actual effect that these experiences have had and may still have on the patient's present ways of being.

Dana Birksted-Breen, unlike most British analysts, has attempted to address the question of time in general conceptual terms (2003). She discusses the relevance of concepts of 'time', 'past' and 'present' to psychoanalytic theory and practice. She speaks in a general context of comparing the usages of British analysts with the usages of French analysts. She makes a distinction between 'developmental time', the idea of general progression from past to present to future (including death) and '*après-coup*', that is, Freud's idea of *Nachträglichkeit*, translated by Strachey as 'deferred action' (Freud 1918: 44), in which the past is resignified retrospectively by thoughts and feelings in the present. Her general conclusion is that British analysts have been bringing in the idea *of après-coup* without realizing it, while French analysts have been unintentionally bringing in the idea of developmental time because psychic acceptance of developmental time is necessary for the continual restructuring by *après-coup* to take place. Psychic acceptance of developmental time, as Money-Kyrle (1968) emphasizes, is often a difficult task. This connects with Klein's emphasis on the influence of unconscious phantasy on conscious perceptions and thoughts, including concepts of time as well as memories of the past.

Klein's approach to understanding the role of the past involves a putting together of the patient's conscious memories of the past with his living out of the past in the present analytic situation. Her theory of the paranoid-schizoid and depressive positions serves as a set of general guiding concepts that helps, in particular, to understand the expression of the past in the transference. Thus Mrs Z's abandonment by her parents which I have described above was what Klein describes as a 'situation'; Mrs Z had described it to me on many occasions. In the particular session I have described, however, she communicated what she felt about this situation much more evocatively by projective identification and role reversal instead of dispassionate verbal description.

As I have described above, I try to allow a simultaneous place in my mind for both the remembered events and the lived-out experience. At the same time I think it is important to remember that there is no way of directly testing one's assumption that a patient's apparent living-out in a session of a past experience is a true representation of the 'facts' of that experience, or even of the patient's experience of it at the time. Such experiences in sessions are deeply important both to patient and analyst, but that still does not tell us the 'facts' of the past or the full history of their relationship to the present.

Note

1   This material, in a slightly different form, has also been published in 'Clinical experiences of projective identification', in Anderson, R. (ed.) (1992) *Clinical Lectures on Klein and Bion*. London: Routledge, pp. 59–73.

5

Projective identification
Back to the future

I believe that Melanie Klein would be surprised by the interest her idea of projective identification has evoked, for she herself does not seem to have been particularly enthusiastic about it, at least not in her published work. I have been told, however, that Klein made much use of the concept in her teaching and supervision in the late 1950s (Gammill 1989) and she left a considerable number of unpublished notes about projective identification in her Archive.

In this chapter I will first describe Klein's own ideas about the concept, followed by a discussion of the way the idea has been developed and used by later Kleinian analysts in Britain.

Klein's views on projective identification

Klein was not the first person to use the term 'projective identification' in a publication. It had been used by Edoardo Weiss in 1925 along with the idea of 'introjective identification', especially in the context of describing choice of sexual partner (Weiss 1925). Klein refers to Weiss's work in her book *The Psychoanalysis of Children*, although without noting his use of the terms projective and introjective identification (Klein 1932a: 250n; see also Massidda 1999; Steiner 1999). Marjorie Brierley also described the idea of projective identification in a paper called 'Further notes on the implication of psycho-analysis: metapsychology and personology' just before Klein published her paper 'Notes on some schizoid mechanisms' (Brierley: 1945). In this paper Brierley says that 'projective identification of

106

ego-ideal with outer object, human or abstract, would appear to be a feature of the economy of all fanatics . . . the pedestrian everyday charity that begins at home, as distinct from fanatical devotion of ultra-personal interests, may depend upon projective identification with a fairly well-libidinzed operative self' (p. 96). Brierley mentions projective identification again in a second paper in 1947. It looks as if considerable thinking and discussion of introjection, projection and identification may have been going on among British analysts in the 1940s and that mention of projective identification was not so much a special focus as part of this general discussion.

In the original version of her paper 'Notes on some schizoid mechanisms', first published in the *International Journal of Psycho-analysis* in 1946, Klein describes the process of projective identification as follows:

> Together with these harmful excrements, expelled in hatred, split off parts of the ego are also projected on to the mother or, as I would rather call it, into the mother. These excrements and bad parts of the self are meant not only to injure the object but also to control it and take possession of it. Insofar as the mother comes to contain the bad parts of the self, she is not felt to be a separate individual but is felt to be the bad self.
>
> Much of the hatred against parts of the self is now directed towards the mother. This leads to a particular kind of identification which establishes the prototype of an aggressive object relation. Also, since the projection derives from the infant's impulse to harm or control the mother he feels her to be a persecutor . . .
>
> It is, however, not only the bad parts of the self which are expelled and projected, but also good parts of the self. Excrements then have the significance of gifts . . .
>
> (Klein 1946: 102)

In essence these three paragraphs are a definition of projective identification, but the concept is not mentioned by name. The actual term 'projective identification' is mentioned only in a passing comment two pages later where Klein says, 'I have referred to the weakening and impoverishment of the ego resulting from excessive splitting and projective identification' (1946: 104).[1] It was not until the 1952 version of 'Notes on some schizoid mechanisms' that Klein added the crucial sentence 'I suggest for these processes the term "projective identification"' ' to the defining paragraphs quoted above. There are other differences in the 1952 version: Klein added two paragraphs, one specifically on projective identification (1946: 11–12) and 13 new footnotes, mainly referring to her colleagues' work involving splitting, fragmentation and paranoia.[2]

There are occasional but important references to the concept of projective identification in Klein's later papers, as for example in 'Some theoretical conclusions regarding the emotional life of the infant' (1952c: 69), in *Envy and Gratitude* (1957: 181, 221) and in 'On the sense of loneliness' (1963: 304, 312), but the single paper in which Klein speaks of projective identification at considerable length is 'On identification' (1955b). This paper, however, is an analysis of a character in a novel who projects his *whole self* into various other people in order to acquire their identity. Although the term 'projective identification' is still used to describe this sort of psychic process, it is nowadays more usually used to describe the projection of *aspects* of the individual's self into other objects.

Klein's notes on projective identification in the Archive (B98, D17)

Because Klein published so little material on projective identification I have explored her unpublished material in the Archive. Here I found a file (B98) of 106 pages called 'Patients' material: theoretical thoughts' dating from 1946–7 and specifically devoted to clinical examples and theoretical thoughts about splitting and projective identification. I also found several pages of notes within the file D17 specifically on the subject of projective identification, one of which is dated 1958, and it seems possible that the other notes in this part of the file date from the same year. I have included these 1958 notes as an appendix to the present chapter (see p.110). It seems possible that by 1958 the term projective identification had acquired an identity of its own and was no longer thought of mainly in the context of general discussions of introjection, projection and identification. It also seems possible that in 1958 Klein was thinking of writing a paper on projective identification, although I did not find such a paper in the Archive.

Throughout these notes, and indeed throughout her work in general, it is clear that Klein thinks of projective identification as an unconscious phantasy. For her it was an intrapersonal not an interpersonal concept and she did not discuss the possibility that an individual's phantasies about projective identification might affect his behaviour in a way that would have an effect on his actual relationship with another person.

In her 1958 notes of D17 Klein states several views on projective identification.

First, she distinguishes between projection and projective identification as two steps in the same process. In the first step, which she calls 'projection', something of oneself that is very unpleasant or something that one feels one does not deserve to have is attributed to somebody else. In the second step, which is 'projective identification', this something, good or bad, is split off from the self and put into the object. The two steps, she says, 'need not be simultaneously experienced, though they very often are' (D17, frames 802, 840). I have not found this distinction useful – in fact I find it difficult to see how the second step is really different from the first – and so far as I can see none of her colleagues has adopted Klein's distinction.

Second, Klein thinks it is essential for the analyst to project himself into the patient in order to understand him, and that it is also essential that the analyst should introject the patient:

> Only is [if] the analyst can project himself into the analysand will he be able to understand him deeply enough . . . A conclusion from what I am saying would be that an optimum in identification with the patient, both by introjection and projection, is essential for a deeper understanding with the patient, together with a capacity to regain one's own self and ego sufficiently not to be misled by the identification.
>
> (D17, frame 804)

Third, she stresses that good as well as bad parts of the self may be projected into the object (D17, frame 801). There may be several motives for projecting bad aspects of oneself or for making 'bad' penetrations into the object: to get rid of something bad in oneself; greedily to control or rob the object; or to satisfy one's aggressive curiosity (D17, frame 805). The motive she cites for projecting good aspects of oneself is that one feels one does not deserve to have such aspects.

Fourth, Klein says nothing about countertransference in these notes, but we know from notes in other parts of the Archive such as the 'Discussion with young colleagues' which I have discussed in Chapter 3, that Klein did not agree with the idea that the analyst's countertransference could be a useful source of information about the patient (C72, frames 695–724). This is largely because of the way she defines countertransference: like Freud, she sees it as a sign of pathology in the analyst. She does imply in the notes of D17 in the Archive, however, that the analyst is bound to have a distinct emotional reaction to the patient, and she says explicitly that the analyst may be somewhat anxious both about projecting himself into the patient and about the patient's projecting himself into the analyst (D17, frames 805–6). She says:

> [But] if the analyst possesses the strength of ego and the other qualities to which I referred earlier, the anxiety of the patient projecting himself into him will not disturb him, and he can then analyse the projection of the patient.
>
> (D17, frame 806)

She seems to assume that the analyst's emotional reaction needs to be overcome because it will interfere with his capacity to think analytically.

Fifth, Klein clearly says that identification by both projection and introjection is essential in analysis and indeed in all object relationships (D17, frame 805):

> I think that depth of contact in relation to people is only possible with these processes [projective and introjective identification], together with the capacity to correct these processes by more objective judgement.
>
> (D17, frame 805)

Finally, Klein briefly describes a clinical session in which she shows how she analyses a particular instance of projective identification (D17, frames 802–3). Because she gives so little clinical illustration of her ideas about projective identification, I will quote her example here.

> In this connection, I wish again to stress the necessity to go step by step according to the emotions, anxieties etc. activated in the patient, and not to run ahead because the analyst knows already what is behind that. I have an example of this point. The analysand speaks in an early session of his analysis of some experience in . . . during the War. They had been warned

that there were man-eating tigers about, but they had not met any. Previous to that, his suspicions of me, very much stimulated by remarks made [by others] about me, had come up and had led to his distrust of his mother. His mother was supposed to have said, as an aunt reported to him, that, being in very bad circumstances, if she were starving, she would eat her son. Though Mr [X] actually knew quite well that that was not what she meant, he had never forgotten this remark, and it had come up in his suspicions of me, together with his suspicions of my possessiveness, dangerousness etc. I first analysed these suspicions and linked them with his suspicions of his mother, who had actually not been able to give him enough food at a certain period in his life, and linked these with the man-eating tiger he had mentioned, his fear that she would eat him and that she was starving him for bad and dangerous reasons. [He] went on about his stay in . . . and said that they had never actually met a man-eating tiger, but had met a bear, and then added laughingly that the bear did not eat them they ate the bear. My interpretations were then fully supported, that it was his wish to eat his mother's breast and that led to his suspicion that his mother was devouring him. At that moment [he] felt that the plants on my desk actually belonged to him, corrected this in the next moment, but found that this was a confirmation of what I said, because he had appropriated something that belonged to me.

(D17, frames 802–3)

It is worth noting here that Klein does not use her distinction between projection and projective identification in this brief account. It seems clear that she assumed that projection and projective identification were occurring simultaneously in this instance.

To summarise: the most important points in Klein's archival notes on projective identification are that she thinks *both good and bad aspects of the self are projected into the object*, and that *identification by both projection and introjection is essential in analysis and in all relationships*.

It is of interest that these two points have only begun to be stressed by contemporary Kleinian analysts in the last few years. This is shown in certain papers, especially that of Priscilla Roth (2001) and particularly that of Ignês Sodré (2004), which I discuss below, but the necessity and ubiquity of projective identification are also expressed in general discussions of clinical material. It is because of this concordance between Klein's thoughts in the Archive and recent Kleinian usage that I have used the phrase 'back to the future' in the title of this chapter.

111

Trends of change from Klein's usage to that of contemporary Kleinian analysts

One of the main trends concerning projective identification has been the remarkable number of papers about it both in Britain and in other countries. The British Contemporary Freudian analyst Joseph Sandler organized a conference on projective identification in Jerusalem in 1985 (Sandler 1987a) and contributed a paper on the concept himself (Sandler 1987b). Another conference was held on the topic in London in 1995. The spread of the idea has been described by Hinshelwood (1991), Canestri (2002), Hinz (2002), Jarast (in press), Quinodoz (2002; in press), O'Shaughnessy (in press b).

Three central ideas about projective identification have been adopted by most contemporary Kleinian analysts. The first is the idea that it is an unconscious phantasy but that it can also be actualized by evocative behaviour – 'actualization' being a term I have adopted from the work of Joseph Sandler (1976a, 1976b). The second is that no distinction is made between projection and projective identification; I believe this has occurred because of the emphasis on clinical expressions of projective identification, for in clinical work it is difficult to distinguish expressions of projection from expressions of projective identification. The third idea is that countertransference is to a considerable extent a response to the patient's projective identification.

Main conceptual developments by contemporary Kleinian analysts

The main conceptual developments in understanding projective identification have been made by Rosenfeld (1947, 1964, 1971b), Segal (1957) Bion (1955, 1959) and Sodré (2004), with additional and especially clinical contributions from Britton (1998b), Segal (1964a), Sohn (1985), Joseph (1987), Hinshelwood (1991), Feldman (1992, 1994, 1997), Spillius (1992), Riesenberg-Malcolm (1986), Bell (2001), Mason (in press) and O'Shaughnessy (in press a, in press b).

Herbert Rosenfeld

Rosenfeld has given one of the earliest and most telling clinical descriptions of projective identification in his paper 'Analysis of a schizophrenic state with depersonalization' (Rosenfeld 1947). In 1964 he emphasized his finding that in narcissistic patients both projective and introjective identification can both be used omnipotently *to deny the separate identity of the object*:

> Identification is an important factor in narcissistic object relations. It may take place by introjection or by projection. When the object is omnipotently incorporated, the self becomes so identified with the incorporated object that all separate identity or any boundary between self and object is denied. In projective identification parts of the self omnipotently enter an object, for example the mother, to take over certain qualities which would be experienced as desirable, and therefore claim to be the object or part-object. Identification by introjection and by projection usually occur simultaneously.
>
> (1964: 170–1)

In 1971 Rosenfeld developed a differentiation of several *motives for projective identification*: communication, which is based on the normal non-verbal communication between infant and mother; to rid the self of unwanted aspects, which leads to a denial of psychic reality; to control the mind and body of the other, the other in the analytic situation being the analyst; to get rid of awareness of separateness and envy; and, as a special form, particularly in the case of psychotic patients, parasitism, which involves the patient having an unconscious phantasy of virtually living inside the object (Rosenfeld 1971b). Further work by Rosenfeld on projective identification is described in his book *Impasse and Interpretation* (1987).

Hanna Segal

In her important paper of 1957, 'Notes on symbol formation', Hanna Segal describes the role of projective identification in concrete thinking: 'Parts of the ego and internal objects are projected into an object and identified with it. The differentiation between the self and the object is obscured. Then, since a part of the ego is confused with the

113

object, the symbol – which is a creation and a function of the ego – becomes, in turn, confused with the object which is symbolized' (1957: 393).

Wilfred Bion

Bion has developed the idea initiated by Paula Heimann (1950), Heinrich Racker (1953, 1957, 1958) and Roger Money-Kyrle (1956) about *countertransference as a source of information about the patient*. This issue about countertransference is partly a matter of definition. Thus when Bion uses the actual term 'countertransference' he often means it in the sense used by Freud (1910) and Klein as an expression, largely unconscious, of the analyst's pathology (see e.g. Bion 1962a: 24, 1963: 18.) At the same time it is clear from his papers, especially 'Attacks on linking' in 1959, that he uses his own emotional response as a source of information about the patient. In the wider definition of counter-transference used by Heimann and Racker this sort of response would be called countertransference. Bion describes this sort of response in 1952 in his paper 'Group dynamics: a review', and here he somewhat uncharacteristically actually uses the word 'countertransference' to describe the analyst's response to the patient's projective identification:

> Now the experience of counter-transference appears to me to have quite a distinct quality which should enable the analyst to differentiate the occasion when he is the object of a projective identification from the occasion when he is not. The analyst feels he is being manipulated so as to be playing a part, no matter how difficult to recognize, in somebody's [sic] else's phantasy – or he would do if it were not for what in recollection I can only call a temporary loss of insight, a sense of experiencing strong feelings and at the same time a belief that their existence is adequately justified by the objective situation without recourse to recondite explanation of their causation.
>
> (1952: 446)

I take this to mean that the emotions the analyst experiences are aroused by the patient's behaviour that is based on the patient's phantasies of projective identification, although the analyst is likely to feel that the emotions are largely of his own making.

In 'Language and the schizophrenic' (1955), Bion describes a similar process with a psychotic patient, saying that his interpretations
depended on the use of Klein's theory of projective identification first
to illuminate his countertransference, then to frame his interpretation.
He describes how in a session he at first felt a growing fear that the
patient would attack him. He interpreted that the patient was pushing
into his (Bion's) insides the patient's fear that he would murder Bion.
After this interpretation the tension lessened, but the patient clenched
his fists. Bion then interpreted that the patient had taken the fear back
into himself and was now afraid of actually making a murderous
attack. He goes on to say:

> This mode of procedure is open to grave theoretical objections and
> I think they should be faced ... I think there are signs that as
> experience accumulates it may be possible to detect and present
> facts which exist, but at present elude clinical acumen; they become
> observable, at second hand, through the pressure they exert to pro-
> duce what I am aware of as counter-transference. I would not have
> it thought that I advocate this use of counter-transference as a final
> solution; rather it is an expedient to which we must resort until
> something better presents itself.
>
> (1955: 224–5)

All Kleinian analysts now agree that countertransference in the
form of the analyst's feelings in response to a patient's projective
identification may be a useful source of information about the patient,
provided, of course, that the analyst is well-trained and reasonably
sensitive. The work of Bion, Segal and Joseph has been influential in
producing this change, but it has also involved a general change in the
definition of countertransference. All contemporary Kleinian analysts
have adopted the wider definition of countertransference advocated
by Paula Heimann and others rather than the narrower definition of
Freud and Klein.

Bion's second main contribution to the understanding of projective identification has been the distinction he makes between *normal*
and *pathological* projective identification. In his view projective identification is an early and very important form of non-verbal communication. He says: 'I shall suppose that there is a normal degree of
projective identification, without defining the limits within which
normality lies, and that associated with introjective identification

this is the foundation on which normal development rests' (1959: 103). He then describes several fascinating but obscure episodes of communication between patients and himself in which something pathological had apparently happened that damaged the patient's capacity for verbal communication. He goes on to say that an infant is dependent on the receptiveness of the object, typically his mother, to accept projections and to act in such a way that the messages of the projections are understood and responded to. If the object fails to receive the projections the infant will very probably increase his projective efforts, an escalation which is likely to be repeated later in the individual's analysis. Bion describes the process as follows:

> In the analysis a complex situation may be observed. The patient feels he is being allowed an opportunity of which he had hitherto been cheated; the poignancy of his deprivation is thereby rendered the more acute and so are the feelings of resentment at the deprivation. Gratitude for the opportunity co-exists with hostility to the analyst as the person who will not understand and refuses the patient the use of the only method of communication by which he feels he can make himself understood. Thus the link between patient and analyst, or infant and breast, is the mechanism of projective identification.
>
> (1959: 104–5)

But the object's imperviousness to projection is not the only form of attack on the link between infant and object. The infant (or later the patient) may be so envious of the object that he too attacks the link by assuming that the object's capacity to receive is a greedy attempt to take in the patient's projections in order to destroy them. Between the subject's envy and the object's unreceptiveness the links are damaged, communication is disrupted, curiosity is dulled and a destructive superego likely to be installed.

In later papers Bion goes on to develop further the idea of the subject's projective identification and the object's response, particularly in his model of the process of containment (1962a, 1963, 1965, 1970).

Ignês Sodré

Sodré makes two points about processes of identification. The first is to do with our beliefs about the 'good' and the 'bad' in projection and introjection. She says: 'Even though "projective identification" is used to describe normal as well as pathological processes, I think that we tend to think of projective processes as more pathological than introjective ones' (2004: 57).

Because of our assumption that projective identification is pathological and introjective identification is normal, we have tended to assume that when an identification is pathological it must be projective, and when it is normal it must be introjective. In contrast, Sodré argues that introjective processes and introjective identification can be just as pathological as projective identification. The pathological element in identification is not, she says, whether it is projective or introjective; it is whether the identification is concrete or symbolic.

Sodré goes on to remind us of Rosenfeld's assertion, quoted above, that identificatory processes tend to involve both projective and introjective identification, and she quotes from Rosenfeld's 1964 paper on narcissism to reinforce her reminder (Rosenfeld 1964: 170).

Thus we have tended to assume not only that projective identification is pathological and introjective identification is normal, but also – her second point – that episodes of identification involve either projective *or* introjective identification, whereas it is likely to be more useful to be prepared to see that particular instances of identification involve both.

I think that Sodré's paper has been both an expression of a growing tendency to recognize, as Klein had, the 'good' as well as the 'bad' aspects of projective identification, and has also been a further encouragement of such recognition. A similar point of view is expressed by Priscilla Roth in her paper on the paranoid–schizoid position (2001).

Ronald Britton

Britton (1998a) introduced the terms *acquisitive* and *attributive* projective identification to distinguish those types of identification in which the projective phantasy concerns an idea of entering the object to acquire some attribute that the object is thought to possess from processes of identification in which the projective phantasy consists of an idea of getting rid of some aspect of oneself into the object. Many phantasies of course include both elements of attribution and of acquisition, just as most phantasies of psychic interaction involve both phantasies of projection and of introjection. (Bollas's idea of 'extractive introjection' describes a similar sort of process as Britton's 'acquisitive projective identification' – Bollas 1987.)

Joseph Sandler

Sandler (1976a, 1976b), a Contemporary Freudian analyst, has made particularly explicit the difference between projective identification as an unconscious phantasy and projective identification when it is 'actualized' by evocative behaviour.

An example of my own usage of projective identification

I have of course absorbed both Klein's and contemporary Kleinian views on projective identification, especially the emphasis on counter-transference as a response to the patient's projective identification and Sodré's idea that concrete and symbolic forms of thinking are found in both introjective and projective identification. I have also found useful the unpublished views of Klein, especially on the ubiquity of projective and introjective identification in analysis and in all social relationships, her observation that 'good' as well as 'bad' aspects of the self are projected and her stress on the need to go 'step by step' in the analysis of projective identification. All these ideas and attitudes played a part in my work with a patient I shall call Mrs R.

At the time of the session I shall describe, Mrs R had a somewhat idealized form of conscious transference. It was the fourth session (of five weekly sessions) after a holiday break.

She began by describing a woman at work who had presented her work in a strong, straightforward way in contrast to someone else who tried to be amusing but in such a way that one could not take him seriously. She went on to describe a dream.

In the dream either she or her partner had been condemned to be imprisoned, incarcerated. The imprisonment took the form of being placed in a dinghy on the dismal Thames at night. It was dark and cold, and she thought, 'If I do that I'll die.' She said the dream was the opposite of being in a comfortable place. It was about being alone. I linked it to her having said yesterday that she and her partner were really alone although together, in spite of their good relationship. I added that she felt alone with me today, especially because I had come back from the holiday break and was trying to give her something.

She said she could not take in what I said, but felt my attitude was gentle and friendly. She suddenly remembered that she had forgotten to pay the bill I had given her.

She was silent and then with some hesitancy said it was quite compelling, this thought of my trying to put something inside her. When something like that happened long ago with her first boyfriend he had said, 'No wonder sex is difficult.' She then described a mother feeding a baby in a machine-like way although the baby seemed happy.

I linked the mechanical breastfeeding, her having at first ignored the content of my interpretation, her and her partner's slight alone-ness with each other and the deathly coldness in the dream – all in contrast to the happy baby, the warm feeling towards me, her gener-ally decent and loving feeling towards her partner. She said it had something to do with what she'd said at the beginning about the person who presented material in a straightforward way and the other one who did it like a puppet show. I said she had found it difficult at first to hear my clear, straightforward statement. In the words of her former boyfriend she had evidently experienced it as too threatening and sexual. Instead of hearing it she had idealized the warm friendly attitude with which she thought I had said it. I think that this made something of a puppet show of what I had said. And her feeling of a warm and friendly me was accompanied by forgetting her cheque. She said 'Hmm' and seemed to be thoughtful, and after a short silence I said it was time to stop.

In brief, she projected her capacity for an affectionate attitude into me and saw me as warm and friendly, toning down anything that she might not have liked, seeing the positive as much as possible, so that in this case her projective identification with me was mainly positive. She said she admired straightforward presentations but was reluctant to hear at first when I made a straightforward interpretation. I think that she was playing down any criticism or bad feeling between us, and displacing any bad aspects of me into other people or else

119

blaming herself – very ready to realize that she had forgotten her cheque, for example.

This was not only a matter of projective identification. She also introjected and identified with the images of a good and friendly me (and mother) and of a straightforward but rather threatening me (also mother, and others) so that at this time she saw herself and was experienced by me – and presumably by others as well – as usually warm and affectionate but sometimes as straightforward and somewhat critical.

In conclusion

As I have described, Klein defines projective identification but says relatively little about it in her published work. In the unpublished notes of the Archive she says much more, emphasizing particularly the ubiquity of projective and introjective identification, the projection of good as well as bad aspects of the self, and the importance of project-ive identification in all analytic and social relationships. She also makes a somewhat unclear distinction between projection and projective identification which no one else has adopted.

Contemporary Kleinians now recognize that countertransference in the widest sense of the term can be a useful source of information about the patient, including information about the patient's project-ive identifications. Many Kleinian analysts use Sandler's term 'actual-ization' to describe the expression of phantasies of projective identifi-cation in interpersonal behaviour (Sandler 1976a, 1976b). Tracking the expression of projective identification and the analyst's responses to it has proved to be very useful clinically.

Following Bion, a distinction is now made between normal and pathological projective identification (Bion 1959). Following Rosenfeld, Segal and Joseph, numerous motives for projective iden-tification are now envisaged: communication, sometimes unintentional, of psychic states; ridding the self of unwanted aspects; controlling the mind and body of the other; taking over the object's capacities; ridding the self of awareness of separateness and envy; and parasitism. Rosenfeld also stresses 'intrusive' projective identification which he relates to infantile experiences of being intrusively pro-jected into by parents. But there is also, especially recently, an emphasis on the role of the projection of good aspects of the self in developing constructive relationships with others (Roth 2001; Sodré 2004).

Following Britton, a distinction is now recognized between 'attributive' and 'acquisitive' projective identification. And following Sodré, there is general recognition that projective identification can include both 'good' and 'bad' aspects of the self and of internal objects, and, similarly, introjective identification can involve both 'good' and 'bad' motives and aspects of the object.

I have given a clinical example to show an aspect of my own interpretation of the interplay of projective identification, introjective identification and countertransference in an analytic session.

Notes

1 I am grateful to Riccardo Steiner for pointing out that Klein uses the term 'projective identification' in the 1946 version of her paper even though it is not part of her definition of the concept.

2 The 1952 version of 'Notes on some schizoid mechanisms' was first published in Klein, Heimann, Isaacs and Riviere, 1952, pp. 292–320. This 1952 version has been reprinted in Klein's *Writings*, vol. 3 (1975) pp. 1–24. The 1952 version is usually referred to in the psychoanalytic literature as 'Klein 1946'.

Appendix: notes in the Melanie Klein Archive specifically on projective identification (D17, frames 799–806; 837–8, 840)

Frame number 799

(in handwriting) to be used in a paper on projective identification.

Frame number 800

situation. Loving parts of the self, which are felt to be good and valuable, are split off and projected into objects, and therefore the self is felt to be poorer, whereas the object is felt to be richer. These good parts are in a sense regained by reintrojecting the loved object. These may not be felt to be quite identical with what has been given out and contribute to a sense of impoverishment and incompleteness. This feeling of having lost good parts of the self which can never be fully regained is in some measure due to a deficient early capacity for

121

integration. If integration in the working through of the depressive position has led to a relative wholeness of the self, projecting parts of the self into others is only temporary and does not lead to a feeling of having irretrievably lost something valuable.

Frame number 801 (in the Archive Frame 801 repeats most of Frame 800)

However, there is another aspect in this situation. Loving parts of the self, which are felt to be good and valuable, are split off and projected into objects, and therefore the self is felt to be poorer, whereas the object is felt to be richer. These good parts are in a sense regained by reintrojecting the loved object. These may not be felt to be quite identical with what has been given out and contribute to a sense of impoverishment and incompleteness. This feeling of having lost good parts of the self which can never be fully regained is in some measure due to a deficient early capacity for integration. If integration in the working through of the depressive position has led to a relative wholeness of the self, projecting parts of the self into others is only temporary and does not lead to a feeling of having irretrievably lost something valuable.

Frame number 802

Additional Views on Projective Identification

The question whether the process of projection is identical with projective identification needs consideration. I am inclined to think of two steps. On an upper layer, projection means attributing to another person something which one feels unpleasant in oneself – not 'I am mean', but 'you are mean', for instance, not 'I am wrong' but 'you are wrong'. It could also be 'I am good, no, you are good'. I believe that, in a deeper layer, such projection always mobilises the feeling 'I am putting into you what either I do not want to have – for instance, I am wrong – or something which I feel I do not deserve having – for instance, I put goodness into the other person', but that already is projective identification. The conclusion, therefore, would be that the two steps, projection as described above, and projective identification, need not be simultaneously experienced, though they very often are. As regards technique, it is my belief that one should carefully consider, as I have often pointed out, the layer which is activated, that is to say, if my impression is that an upper layer is just operating, then interpretation would go to the first of the two steps which I have described.

Note

The rest of Frame number 802 and most of Frame number 803 have been quoted earlier on pp.110–11.

In this connection, I wish again to stress the necessity to go step by step according to the emotions, anxieties etc. activated in the patient, and not to run ahead because the analyst knows already what is behind that. I have an example of this point. The analysand speaks in an early session of his analysis of some experience in . . . during the War. They had been warned that there were man-eating tigers about, but they had not met any. Previous to

Frame number 803

that, his suspicions of me, very much stimulated by remarks made about me, had come up and had led to his distrust of his mother. His mother was supposed to have said, as an aunt reported to him, that, being in very bad circumstances, if she were starving, she would eat her son. Though Mr . . . actually knew quite well that that was not what she meant, he had never forgotten this remark, and it had come up in his suspicions of me, together with his suspicions of my possessiveness, dangerousness etc. I first analysed these suspicions and linked them with his suspicions of his mother, who had actually not been able to give him enough food at a certain period in his life, and linked these with the man-eating tiger he had mentioned, his fear that she would eat him and that she was starving him for bad and dangerous reasons. [He] went on about his stay in . . . and said that they had never actually met a man-eating tiger, but had met a bear, and then added laughingly that the bear did not eat them they ate the bear. My interpretations were then fully supported, that it was his wish to eat his mother's breast and that led to his suspicion that his mother was devouring him. At that moment [he] felt that the plants on my desk actually belonged to him, corrected this in the next moment, but found that this was a confirmation of what I said, because he had appropriated something that belonged to me.

The question whether projection always leads to projective identification has many years ago been put to me about introjection. Does identification always imply introjection? This is not an exact parallel, as can be seen, but it is on similar lines. After years of experience, I have found an answer to this question. There is no identification possible without having taken the object in and,

Frame number 804

even if the identification is a very transient one, I believe that, for the time being, the object has been taken in in order for the subject to be identified with it. I shall go back to the difference between the identification resulting from projection and the identification resulting from introjection at a later point.

To continue my additional views on projective identification. I believe that any relation implies projective identification, but I wish to point out that this process is one of the fundamental steps in analysis. Only [if] the analyst can project himself into the analysand will he be able to understand him deeply enough. Now that is a point at which a failure of the analytic procedure is very near at hand, because, if that projection is too strong, too intense, too lasting, the analyst is bound to go wrong. He has then put too much of himself into the patient to understand him objectively. The degree etc. in which that projection takes place depends on the strength of the ego of the analyst, on the ways of splitting, and his capacity to project, as well as to take parts of himself back again, and then correct any error which may have resulted from that projection. That is to say, he can judge the patient's feelings, tendencies etc. objectively. I have no doubt that part of the analytic procedure is the introjection of the patient and here again the same pre-conditions of failure or success enter. A conclusion from what I am saying would be that an optimum in identification with the patient, both by introjection and projection, is essential for a deeper understanding with the patient, together with a capacity to regain one's own self and ego sufficiently not to be misled by the identification.

Frame number 805

A very important point in the success of this process is the motivation of projective and introjective identification. For success it is important that this identification is motivated by the wish to help and understand. If other elements, such as greed, the wish to control, the tendency to rob, are more prominent, the process fails; but this applies also, although with some differences, to all object relations. I think that depth of contact in relation to people is only possible with these processes, together with a capacity to correct these processes by more objective judgement. If it is only for a very short time, if I do not put myself into the place of the person in whom I am interested, the relation will remain shallow and will never lead to good contact. On the other hand, if that is excessive, for the reasons I have explained, the relation will also go wrong.

Speaking of motivation, we would think of the child who projects himself into the analyst, either to control, to rob, to satisfy an aggressive curiosity. If these motives are predominant, the relation to the mother will be impaired. If the wish to make reparation, to protect the mother, both by introjection and projection, to keep her safe, is predominant, the controlling etc. aspect is sufficiently counteracted. From the technical point of view, it is extremely important again to see which motivation is most operative. This does not mean ignoring other motivations but to give full weight to those which are predominant at the moment.

There is another aspect of projective identification entering

Frame number 806

into the analytic procedure, and that is the fear of the analyst of projecting himself into the patient, because of anxiety that he might do it too strongly and that his motivations are detrimental, but, as I have said, if he is not able to identify himself with the patient in the way which I have described, he will not be able to analyse correctly. The counterpart of this anxiety is the anxiety stirred up by the patient projecting himself into the analyst, a process which is quite unavoidable in the analysis. But again, if the analyst possesses the strength of ego and the other qualities to which I referred earlier, the anxiety of the patient projecting himself into him will not disturb him, and he can then analyse the projection of the patient.

I have already referred to the inevitability of identification in a deep-going analysis. If this does not occur, the analyst aloof, is incapable of close contact.

Frame number 837

Notes

I have come across in several supervisions of the analysis of young children a feature of which seems to me of interest. The split between the parent and the analyst is well known. We know that very often either love or hate is directed against the analyst and split off from the home situation and the parents. But more recently I have found that an element enters into this split which I want now to enlarge on. The whole analytic situation, the analyst, the toys, the means of attack when aggressive feelings come out, can be experienced by the child as fantasy, in contrast to the actual mother who is felt to be real. The wish to destroy the analyst, standing for the bad or hated mother or father, is then experienced as something unreal. The analyst, in the cases I am referring to, was not simply standing for the bad or hated parent, but there are also

125

feelings of love and the wish to preserve. These children wanted to come to the analysis, felt relieve[d], and were loath to finish the analytic hour, and yet during the session the destructive attitudes were expressed with full strength.

From the technical point of view I find it important that then not only the split between good and bad mother or good and bad father, is interpreted, but also the feeling of unreality bound up with the strong expression of destructive attacks. For instance, a young child who attempted to set the analyst on fire would in the same session show not only guilt about that, but it was quite obvious that even at the moment of attack he took the match, the room and the analyst to be fantasies. The real analyst, as it were, though hate might be experienced he would not have set on fire.

Frame number 838

One element in this fantasy situation is projective identification. So much of the destructive and hating impulses in parts of the personality have been projected into the analyst that he had lost as it were his identity for the child. I think this connection between the fantastic nature of another person is bound up with strong projective identification. The person in whom this projection has taken place has stopped being the actual person whom the child – or adult for that matter – at other times would see in a different light. Another aspect of this connection with projective identification is that in my view nobody is so much hated as the destructive part of one's own personality.

In thinking over my own cases, child and adult, I found that these observations apply quite frequently.

Dr Segal mentioned to me something quite independently regarding a similar observation in an adult, and I therefore suggested to her to put these observations, arrived at from different angles, together in a communication.

Frame number 840

Technique   **27th March 1958**

There are two steps in projective identification. The first is projection due to feeling something very unpleasant is rather attributed to somebody else, such as meanness, envy etc. The next step, which I think always follows after projection pure, is projective identification, which means that, having attributed it to another object, it is actually split off from the self and put into the object.

PART THREE

Interaction of Ideas and Clinical Work

6

Clinical reflections on the negative therapeutic reaction[1]

When Freud first discussed the negative therapeutic reaction in *The Ego and the Id* in 1923 he gave both a clinical description of it and a psychological explanation. In this chapter I want to suggest that the clinical description and the psychological explanation may not be as intrinsically connected as Freud thought.

Freud does not give actual case material, but his clinical description is as follows:

> There are certain people who behave in a quite peculiar fashion during the work of analysis. When one speaks hopefully to them or expresses satisfaction with the progress of the treatment, they show signs of discontent and their condition invariably becomes worse. One begins by regarding this as defiance and as an attempt to prove their superiority to the physician, but later one comes to take a deeper and juster view. One becomes convinced, not only that such people cannot endure any praise or appreciation, but that they react inversely to the progress of the treatment. Every partial solution that ought to result, and in other people does result, in an improvement or a temporary suspension of symptoms produces in them for the time being an exacerbation of their illness; they get worse during the treatment instead of getting better. They exhibit what is known as a 'negative therapeutic reaction'.
>
> (1923: 49)

Thus the clinical phenomenon, according to Freud, is that when the analyst thinks and says that progress has occurred, the patient gets worse; he 'backtracks' on his earlier progress. Freud had already touched on a similar phenomenon in one of his papers on character, 'Those wrecked by success' (1916).

Freud's explanation of the negative therapeutic reaction is that it occurs because of an unconscious sense of guilt, or need for punishment. Indeed, he drew attention to the clinical phenomenon mainly because he thought it provided evidence for the usefulness of the concept of the superego. This is how he puts it:

> In the end we come to see that we are dealing with what may be called a 'moral' factor, a sense of guilt, which is finding its satisfaction in the illness and refuses to give up the punishment of suffering. We shall be right in regarding this disheartening explanation as final. But as far as the patient is concerned this sense of guilt is dumb; it does not tell him he is guilty; he does not feel guilty, he feels ill. This sense of guilt expresses itself only as a resistance to recovery which it is extremely difficult to overcome.
>
> (1923: 49–50)

Freud discusses this theme further in 'The economic problem of masochism' (1924) and in 'Analysis terminable and interminable' (1937), and he relates it to moral masochism and the destructive or death instinct.

From Freud's original thesis two main lines of thought have developed, the first concentrating on Freud's explanation of the negative therapeutic reaction as caused by unconscious guilt, and the second focusing on envy and narcissism as an explanation. Freud had of course considered but abandoned the 'envy and narcissism' sort of explanation when he said that 'One begins by regarding this [patients' discontent and worsening condition] as defiance and as an attempt to prove their superiority to the physician, but later one comes to take a deeper and juster view.'

The main adherent of the 'unconscious guilt' explanation, at least in Britain, is Joan Riviere (1936). The main authors of the 'envy and narcissism' explanation are Abraham (1919), Horney (1936), Klein (1957) and Rosenfeld (1975).

Riviere relates the negative therapeutic reaction to the patient's fear that progress in analysis and in life will make him aware of the desolate state of his attacked and unrestored internal objects and that he will feel intolerable guilt and pain. Bion (1953) and Segal (1956) give clinical material which exemplifies Riviere's point. Riviere, like Freud, focuses on guilt and depression, but her explanation of the role of guilt in the negative therapeutic reaction is somewhat different, because while Freud regards the reaction as an expression of guilt, she regards it as a defence against the experience of guilt.

Recently there has been an increasing number of American papers about the negative therapeutic reaction which follow, more or less, the first line of development in that they deal with patients who are dominated by unconscious guilt and moral masochism. Only a few of these papers give specific clinical material, but it is my impression that these depressed and sado-masochistic patients show many types of resistance and negativism in addition to the negative therapeutic reaction (see Feigenbaum 1934; Gero 1936; Eidelberg 1948; Bernstein 1957; Brenner 1959; Olinick 1964, 1970; Loewald 1972; Valenstein 1973; Asch 1976; Spiegel 1978).

The fact that two separate lines of explanation have developed from Freud's original formulation already suggests that the clinical phenomenon and the psychological explanation may not be as closely associated as he thought. I want to suggest that the clinical phenomenon Freud described, the patient's 'backtracking' on earlier progress, is usually found to be associated with envy and narcissism, whereas unconscious guilt is likely to give rise to many sorts of generalized resistance and negative reaction, of which the negative therapeutic reaction is only one. Further, when patients dominated by unconscious guilt *do* show a negative therapeutic reaction, it is likely to be considerably disguised and defended against.

I will first discuss Freud's clinical description of the negative therapeutic reaction and then I will describe two clinical examples of it from my own practice. My first case fits Freud's clinical description but not his psychological explanation; the second fits his psychological explanation but is not so clear-cut an instance of the clinical phenomenon.

Freud's clinical definition of the negative therapeutic reaction

Freud's clinical definition is unfortunately imprecise, which has allowed the term to be interpreted in many ways. Several authors bemoan a current trend to use the term in a very general way, often to mean any sort of intractable resistance that the analyst finds great difficulty in coping with (Olinick 1964; Sandler *et al.* 1970; Loewald 1972; Baranger 1974). Every now and again an analyst suggests that we should stick to Freud's original definition (or to the particular author's interpretation of Freud's original definition), but these injunctions have not had much effect, for the trend towards loose usage continues. Several analysts have also pointed out that negative responses by the patient are a function of the interaction between patient and analyst, not just a function of the patient's psycho-pathology (e.g. Langs 1976); some analysts are very critical of the concept because they think it is used as an excuse for bad technique (Reich 1933; Salzman 1960). I do not want to discuss this aspect of the concept further except to say that I think the loose usage and misuse of the concept have been caused not only by imprecision in the original definition but also by the tendency to assume rather than to investigate the causal connection between the clinical phenomenon and its psychological explanation.

There are three elements in Freud's original clinical description.

First, the analyst speaks hopefully about the progress of treatment, or there is a partial solution which in other patients would lead to improvement. This part of the definition is crucial because it outlines the situation in which the negative therapeutic reaction occurs. Freud's description is somewhat unsatisfying, for what is to happen if the analyst does *not* speak hopefully about the progress of treatment, and who is to say that the patient should have improved or that another patient would have improved in similar circumstances? It is not entirely clear whether Freud thought that the *patient* as well as the analyst had recognized that improvement had taken place. I think that discussions of the negative therapeutic reaction would be greatly clarified if authors stated whether it was the analyst, the patient or both who thought that there had been improvement. In my own work I stress the importance not only of my own but also of the patient's judgement of progress. Of course including the patient's own definition of progress does not free the situation from problems of judgement, for patients can be as mistaken, secretive and defensive about their own progress as analysts can be. But I think this criterion is of some help in distinguishing the negative therapeutic reaction from other forms of resistance.

Second, the patient goes back on his progress in some form or other, usually including a worsening of symptoms. This element of 'backtracking' also distinguishes the negative therapeutic reaction from other forms of resistance.

In emphasizing the sequence of these two elements – the patient's own definition of progress followed by going back on it – I follow Klein, who described this sequence as characteristic of envy. 'Needless to say,' she writes, 'our patients criticize us for a variety of reasons, sometimes with justification. But a patient's need to devalue the analytic work which he has experienced as helpful is the expression of envy' (1957: 184). She regards envy as intrinsic to the negative therapeutic reaction (1957: 184–5, 220–5). This stress on envy, especially unconscious envy, is her distinctive contribution to the analysis of the negative therapeutic reaction.

Third, in the clinical phenomenon of the negative therapeutic reaction there is an element of attack on the analyst. Freud thinks this is not the real issue, for he says that the explanation about unconscious guilt is 'a deeper and juster view' implying that the attack on the analyst is a byproduct rather than an intrinsic part of the negative therapeutic reaction. Klein, on the contrary, stresses the attack on the analyst as a central component. I think the actual clinical examples given in the literature support her view, as do the two clinical examples I describe. In one of my cases the attack was open; in the other it was heavily defended against, but in both cases the attack was definitely there.

In brief, then, I am defining the negative therapeutic reaction as a sequence of behaviour in which a tacit or explicit recognition of progress by the patient is followed by a worsening of his condition and by an open or disguised attack on the analyst.

Clinical material

The first patient to be discussed here, Mr B, expressed a negative therapeutic reaction and, in my view, felt more envy and rivalry than unconscious and conscious guilt. The material of the first patient is very similar to that of patients described by Rosenfeld in his papers on the negative therapeutic reaction (1975) and 'delusional narcissism' (1971a), except that my patient was less ill than most of those described by Rosenfeld. Rosenfeld's formulation of this sort of negative therapeutic reaction is that an omnipotent, arrogant aspect of the self makes an envious attack on the analyst and on a trusting, infantile part of the self which has been allowing progress to occur in the form of letting itself be helped by the analyst; the usual state of affairs in this type of patient is that the trusting, infantile part of the self is dominated by the omnipotent, arrogant aspect of the self, thus achieving a form of narcissistic self-sufficiency.

Here is the material of my patient.

He was the eldest of three children of a Catholic family in a Latin country. He worked as a biologist and suffered, among other things, from difficulty in designing and following through original research. However, for some months before the bit of material I want to report, he had been effectively at work completing his first independent research project. From time to time he realized, though rather incidentally, that his analysis was helping him to become more effective and constructive in his work. Eventually he finished his research and several people complimented him on it. He began to feel worse and worse. The research was no good, he said, not truly creative or original; he did not belong anywhere; he felt utterly inert; he was fed up with me and analysis because I was not helping him to feel more alive in himself. In one session he had a sudden fantasy, which he described as grandiose, of developing his so-called 'small' research into a major undertaking, with a special grant from an American foundation, a large staff of assistants, housed in a special wing of a new university building etc. I said he was telling me this plan in a way perhaps designed to lure me into making some sort of punitive interpretation about omnipotence, as if he wanted me to belittle and ignore both the validity of his research and the work we had done together to make the doing of it possible. He proceeded to talk about something else as if he had not heard what I had said. He was being as lofty towards me, in other words, as he was in his research plan.

In the next session he reported the following dream. He was on his way home to his own country for a holiday. On the way he saw an accident but no one was badly hurt. Once home, he heard from a casual acquaintance that his close friend Mario had got married. Mario had not invited the patient to the wedding, and he felt dreadfully left out.

He woke feeling life was not worth living and nothing was enjoyable. He was utterly incapable of taking pleasure in anything. Most of his associations centred around his opinion that Mario was someone probably incapable of marriage or any kind of deep relationship.

I said I thought Mario represented that part of himself that had been incapable of any sort of relationship with me, but that in recent months this Mario aspect of himself had come into contact with me more and more, which he described in the dream as a marriage. It was even producing 'children' in the form of his research. I suggested that the non-Mario part of himself felt left out of the growing alliance between Mario and me and it had been trying to reassert its control over both of us.

He thought about this and then said he could not see why he should feel so left out by his getting better. After a short silence he said that Mario's mother was an immaculate, attractive woman, very nice to all Mario's friends, and in fact she had hinted to the patient that she wished Mario were more like the patient. He thought Mario's mother wanted Mario to be successful and to get married, but only to prove that she was a successful mother, not for Mario's sake. I said he seemed to be saying that my growing relationship with the Mario aspect of himself was not to be trusted because I only wanted him to grow up and develop so that I could congratulate myself on being a successful analyst.

In subsequent sessions he was gradually able to recognize himself in the qualities he attributed to me and to Mario's mother – especially his narcissistic self-centredness and his grudging attitude towards his own and my enjoyment of the analysis and of his success.

The second patient, Mrs D, was a woman dominated by conscious and unconscious guilt, but showing a hidden and defended form of negative therapeutic reaction. This patient suffered from the sort of unresolved depression and moral masochism that Freud and many later authors think is characteristic of patients who exhibit the negative therapeutic reaction. Although she was cooperative in the analysis, she was at this time locked in recurrent attacks of self-punishment, persecution, remorse and identification with damaged internal objects, especially her mother. Clearly defined negative therapeutic reactions were not characteristic of her material. It was much more usual for her to nip a negative therapeutic reaction in the bud, so to speak, by not having enough therapeutic improvement for there to be a negative reaction about. Even the instance of negative therapeutic reaction I describe here was at first difficult to identify.

Some time before the sessions I will describe I had had a minor illness. In the first session I shall describe, which occurred some time after I had returned to work, the patient described a dream. There had

135

been an ill woman; the patient realized that she could not help the woman very much herself; the right person to ask to help the woman was her boss, who was a highly qualified person but not overly conscientious. I interpreted this dream as a move towards recognition that in spite of his deficiencies father was the right person to look after and repair damage to mother, that the patient could not do it all herself. (It was her internal parents we were talking about; her real parents had died years before.) I also suggested that she felt I was the ill woman who needed looking after and whose care and cure she was trying to relinquish control of. Right near the end of the hour the patient told me she had received a minor promotion at work. She managed to say it in such an offhand way that I almost overlooked it.

In the next session, a Friday, she felt bleak and had a memory of feeling utterly desolate when she had been sent away to boarding school. At first I did not think of her desolation as a negative therapeutic reaction, for she had already played down her bit of success so much that I had not realized she was tacitly thinking of it as success. At first I linked her desolation with the weekend, though that did not seem to make sense of the extent of her feeling. Then I suggested she was feeling more grown up, in that she was trying to give up her insistence that she was the one who had power over me by looking after me, but that made her feel abandoned, as she had felt when she had been thought grown up enough to be sent away to school. I said she was warning me that she could not stand yesterday's minor successes, either the success at work or in analysis; she had to fail now as she had at school. But I still felt there was something about this session I did not understand. (What I did not see until several weeks later, when the theme came up again, was that she was also feeling overwhelmed and confused by an identification with her ill, fragile mother who had experienced every bit of growth by her child, my patient, as an abandonment of her, so that my patient, paradoxically, had had to fail in order to please her mother.)

On Monday she was in a very different mood, rather excited. She had had three dreams. In the first, she met one of my male patients, who found her sexually interesting. I interpreted this as her way of getting control of her feeling that I had abandoned her at the weekend to be with my partner. In the second dream one of her former university professors told her about a new university department that was opening nearby where she might do a special course. In the third dream a junior colleague was telling her that she was overexcited.

136

Eventually I suggested that she was my junior colleague warning me that if I was able to open a new department for her so that she could enjoy a bit of success, she would get overexcited, and the excitement would turn into triumph directed against me and her analysis. With some reservations she agreed with this. I said she evidently felt she could not enjoy any success without its turning into a triumph.

On Tuesday she felt desolate again and on Wednesday she was once again excited, as she had been on Monday. I did not see it at the time, but I think she was repeating the sequence of the 'low' session and the 'high' session in order to show me that there was a lot I had failed to understand. I think the 'low' response had two roots. The first was that unconsciously she felt guilty because she felt she had attacked her mother by improving, which meant leaving her; she punished herself by identifying with this fragile, attacked mother who could not let her grow up and 'go to school'. Second, the 'low' response was a way of avoiding making an envious, resentful attack against me for threatening to help her grow up. The excited, rather seductive mood of the 'high' sessions was more an expression of triumph over me for having missed the meaning of the 'low' sessions than an expression of triumph because of her improvement the week before.

Discussion

If one compares these two patients, it is clear that the first gave a much more direct expression of the negative therapeutic reaction than the second, although I think both reactions fit the definition I have given above.

The first patient was openly envious and resentful about his own progress and my contribution to it, even though he was not actually conscious of being envious. His progress hurt him, and he could only just bear to recognize it. Contrary to Freud's thesis, however, he did not suffer acutely from unconscious guilt or moral masochism. At this stage of his analysis he was mainly persecuted by his internal objects rather than concerned or guilty about them, for he was projecting into them the envy and self-centredness that he did not recognize in himself.

The second patient, on the other hand, was dominated by both conscious and unconscious guilt and unresolved depression. According to Freud's formulation she should have been a clear case of the negative therapeutic reaction, but in fact her reaction was much less open than that of the first patient. It consisted of defences against envy and destructiveness rather than open expressions of them, and although she got 'worse' in the low sessions it was not easy at first to relate her depressed feeling to the preceding recognition of progress. She was more depressive than the first patient and it was her capacity for concern for her objects that prevented her from making an openly envious attack. She had loved her fragile mother and could not accept her own wishes to attack her. Similarly she had strong positive feelings about me and had difficulty in recognizing her wish to attack me. She spared me and her mother by attacking herself. But she was not only trying to spare her objects when she did herself down; she was also trying to avoid accepting responsibility for her own enviousness and aggressiveness. In trying to avoid pain and responsibility by attacking herself she of course caused even more damage than if she had made a direct attack in the first place: she kept her mother fragile, and she also made it hard for me to find out what was going on. It was difficult for me to recognize that unconsciously she believed that the way to look after both her mother and me was by her own failure.

My general conclusion from these two cases, from my practice as a whole, and from the literature, is that open expressions of negative therapeutic reaction are likely to be a prominent and recurrent feature in patients of narcissistic and envious character structure, but that in patients who suffer from unresolved depression, especially persecutory depression (Klein 1957), the negative therapeutic reaction is likely to be heavily disguised, as in the case of my second patient. General resistance, negativism and avoidance of success are more typical of such patients than is the obvious backtracking of the negative therapeutic reaction of the sort I have described in my first patient, in whom I think envy and rivalry were more important than unconscious guilt. Freud's clinical phenomenon and his psychological explanation, in other words, are not as closely linked as he thought.

What, then, is one to conclude about the negative therapeutic reaction? Is it a useful concept? I think it is, for it alerts the analyst to the presence of an acute conflict about progress, whatever the character structure of the patient. It may be, of course, that a patient reacts negatively not to progress in analysis and in life but to mistakes by the analyst and deprivation in his life, a possibility that should be explored as openly as possible by analyst and patient together. Assuming that the progress is genuine and the interpretations reasonably accurate, an openly expressed negative therapeutic reaction means the patient is protesting about the disturbance of his status quo and the indignity of being helped by an analyst, which is, after all, hardly surprising. In mild and transitory forms it is surely very common.

But what of patients dominated by unconscious guilt? Should one describe their chronic resistance, failure to thrive and avoidance of success as negative therapeutic reaction? Sandler *et al.* (1970) think it most unwise to widen the concept of negative therapeutic reaction to include chronic resistance of this sort. In a way I agree, for there is an obvious empirical difference between the open negative therapeutic reaction and chronic resistance. Nevertheless one cannot escape a feeling that Freud was right in saying that unconscious guilt stops patients from getting better. In the long run, chronic resistance and the negative therapeutic reaction are not so very different from each other. Patients who suffer from unconscious guilt get stuck in their illness and misery; very occasionally they improve a bit and allow themselves to recognize the improvement, and then they have to resort to a more open negative therapeutic reaction to restore the status quo. Usually, however, they express a sort of hidden negative therapeutic reaction all the time, which is unconsciously designed to prevent open improvement, with the result that an open negative therapeutic reaction is unnecessary.

And so, in conclusion, where Freud suggested one clinical phenomenon, I would suggest two: an open and a hidden negative therapeutic reaction. And where Freud suggested one explanation I would suggest two: envy and narcissism associated with the open negative therapeutic reaction, and unconscious guilt associated with the hidden negative therapeutic reaction.

Note

1   A slightly different version of this chapter has been published as a paper in the *Bulletin of the European Psychoanalytic Federation* in 1980, 15: 31–9.

7

Varieties of envious experience[1]

Envy is disturbing – a disturbing feeling and a disturbing concept in psychoanalysis. Freud's idea of penis envy has aroused anger in many women, especially feminists. Klein's idea of constitutional envy evoked a storm of protest by many analysts. In this chapter I discuss envy as defined and used by Klein herself and by later Kleinian analysts, but I also describe clinically two ways of experiencing and expressing envy that I think show qualitative as well as quantitative differences. I then describe a model of the conscious and unconscious feelings accompanying processes of giving and receiving, not only because I believe that these processes are central to understanding envy but also because I have found them to be clinically useful.

Freud was the first analyst to use the concept of envy both in the idea of penis envy and in the idea that the members of a group can forego their envious rivalry with one another in a common idealization of the group leader (Freud 1921). Abraham (1919) uses the idea of envy to explain a destructive attack that certain patients make on psychoanalytic work. Eisler (1922) notes that envy derives from the oral instinct. In 1932 in 'Jealousy as a mechanism of defence' Joan Riviere regards pathological jealousy as a mechanism of defence against unconscious oral envy of the parents in coitus. Melanie Klein, however, was the first analyst to make the concept of envy central to her psychoanalytic theory.

Klein had used the idea of envy in much of her earlier work (Klein 1929a, 1929b, 1932b, 1945, 1952c, 1955b) but towards the end of her life she wrote about it much more systematically in *Envy and Gratitude*: 'I consider', she writes, 'that envy is an oral-sadistic and anal-sadistic expression of destructive impulses, operative from the beginning of life, and that it has a constitutional basis' (1957: 176). A little later she describes it as '. . . the angry feeling that another person possesses and enjoys something desirable – the envious impulse being to take it away or spoil it' (p. 181). In her view it is a manifestation of death instinct, which she thinks of as an instinctual, internal destructive force felt as fear of annihilation.

Klein distinguishes with care between envy, greed and jealousy. *Greed* she defines as '. . . an impetuous and insatiable craving, exceeding what the subject needs and what the object is willing and able to give . . . its aim is destructive introjection; whereas envy [aims] . . . also to put badness . . . into the mother . . . in order to spoil and destroy her' (1957: 181). *Jealousy* she describes as a three-person situation in which the 'love that the subject feels is his due has been taken away, or is in danger of being taken away, from him by his rival' (1957: 181).

These three states of mind are frequently found in close association. Greedy acquisition can be a defence against being aware of the envy of those who have or who are what one wishes one had or was oneself. Analysts are familiar with the sort of patient who makes insatiable demands on the analyst but rubbishes whatever he is given – a mixture of greed and envy. The jealous lover is often driven less by love than by envious hatred of his lover's capacity to arouse the love of another. And in everyday English the words 'jealousy' and more rarely 'envy' are often used where 'admiration' would be appropriate, as for example in statements such as 'I am jealous (or envious) of your lovely garden.' Even Shakespeare (*Othello* c. 1603) has Iago describe the crucial element of jealousy in terms that are an excellent description of the core of envy:

Oh! Beware, my Lord, of jealousy;
It is the green-ey'ed monster which doth mock
The meat it feeds on.

                    (III, 2, lines 165–7)

Thus in literary and everyday usage the terms envy and jealousy overlap, vary in meaning, and have a large penumbra of associations. These varying and overlapping usages are enshrined in the *Oxford English Dictionary*. Klein's definition of envy is well within the dominant traditional usage, though it emphasizes the malignant aspects. There are difficulties, however, in treating much-used words like envy and jealousy as technical terms, as Klein does, for people are sure to add in the various associated and overlapping meanings.

According to Hanna Segal (personal communication), Klein developed her ideas about envy in the course of analysing three particularly difficult patients. Jaques (1969) adds that some of Klein's evidence for envy and for its early nature derived from her work with 'Richard', a 10-year-old patient who, after acknowledging a particularly helpful bit of the analytic work, often used to attack and belittle it; these attacks appeared particularly often in the context of Richard's feeling that Klein and his mother possessed the feeding 'breast' which was giving mental nourishment not only to him but also to others (Klein 1960). More generally Klein thought that envy was a major motive for the sort of negative therapeutic reaction that sometimes sets in after helpful work has been acknowledged by the patient (see also Rosenfeld 1975 and Chapter 6 of the present book). She was impressed too by the intense pain and depression that many patients experienced when attempting to integrate their conscious positive feeling towards the analyst with their increasing awareness of making envious attacks on what they had experienced as their analyst's goodness. She gives several moving examples of such struggles in *Envy and Gratitude*.

Klein lays especial emphasis on the fact that envy leads to psychic attacks on the experience of the goodness of the object, which, if unchecked, leads to great difficulty in taking in and in learning. Because envy leads to attacks on the individual's sense of the goodness of the object, it is likely to result in confusion between the object's goodness and badness, which impairs processes of differentiation and the development of rational thought (see also Rosenfeld 1947, 1950). Klein thinks that envious attacks on the goodness of the object, which are much more difficult to acknowledge than attacks on badness, are likely to lead to a premature development of guilt before the individual is able to stand the pain of it, leading to confusion between depressive guilt (Klein 1935) and paranoid-schizoid persecution (Klein 1946), and sometimes to confusional states. In satisfactory development, by contrast, Klein says that a deep-rooted relation with a good object is built up and internalized, and then the child can withstand temporary states of envy, hatred and grievance which arise even in children who are loved and well mothered.

Klein does not assert, as is sometimes thought, that envy is entirely constitutional. As she puts it: 'In speaking of an innate conflict between love and hate, I am implying that the capacity for both love and for destructive impulses is, to some extent, constitutional, though varying individually in strength and *interacting from the beginning with external conditions*' (1957: 180, emphasis added). Or again: 'Furthermore, whether or not the child is adequately fed and mothered, whether the mother fully enjoys the care of the child or is anxious and has psychological difficulties over feeding – all these factors influence the infant's capacity to accept the milk with enjoyment and to internalise the good breast' (1957: 179).

The experience and expression of envy, and indeed of love and hate in general, occur and develop in relationships with objects, so that one can never meet the constitutional component unmodified by experience. Nor can one tell, from the perspective of the consulting room, how much of a patient's envy is constitutional, how much has developed because of his experiences with objects, or how much is the result of the process of interaction between the two. What one *can* tell from the way a patient behaves in the consulting room is what his envy is like in his internal world now, how severe it is, how it expresses itself in relation to the analyst and what defences the patient uses.

Klein's work on envy provoked a storm of disagreement in the British Psychoanalytical Society, chiefly on the grounds that it was preposterous to regard such pernicious attacks on goodness as inherent in human nature; that the death instinct, of which envy was an expression, was not a viable concept; that Klein ignored the environment; that what she described as envy in infants could better be described as 'eagerness'; that she was attributing to infants thoughts of which they were not capable; that her theory of envy was a theory of despair, scientifically unproved; and that Kleinians' preconceived theoretical expectations of envy were leading them to find confirmation of intractable, vicious and destructive envy in all their patients' clinical material.

These criticisms were voiced in a symposium on envy and jealousy which was held by the British Psychoanalytical Society in 1969; the main critical paper, by Walter Joffe, was published in 1969; other unpublished criticisms were made by Winnicott, Khan, Gillespie, King, Bonnard, Heimann and Limentani. Much of the discussion focused on whether or not envy was constitutional, and there was little examination of the clinical material Klein described or her particular use of the concept of envy in elucidating it. Another assumption seemed to suffuse this discussion, namely that if envy proved to be intractable in analysis it was probably inherited. I think this assumption is questionable. Indeed, it *was* questioned at the Envy and Jealousy Symposium, in which Rosenfeld maintained that there was no reason to assume that inherited dispositions were immutable and impervious to analysis. Further, we know that early infant/caregiver exchanges can have profound emotional effects which are difficult to change, and there is no reason to assume that envy that proves to be intractable in analysis should not have been affected by early infant/caregiver exchanges, whatever its constitutional basis. The discussions at the Envy and Jealousy Symposium were also complicated by the fact that many speakers were tacitly emphasizing other aspects of the traditional usages of the term envy in addition to the ones focused on by Klein. All the participants were influenced by the presence of complex theoretical issues which have still not been fully clarified or agreed: the relationship to one another of the concepts of instinct, mental state, affect, character trait and object relationship.

Joffe and other British colleagues have not been the only critics of Klein's use of the concept of envy. In 1958 Elizabeth Zetzel said that 'the hypothesis developed in *Envy and Gratitude* suggests that Melanie Klein is moving further away from, rather than toward the mainstream of contemporary psychoanalysis' (1958: 412). Zetzel was critical not only of Klein's work on envy but also of her whole approach (Zetzel 1956). In 1961 Guntrip expressed dismay at Klein's treatment of envy as '. . . unmotivated and ultimate, and as a basic manifestation of death instinct' (1961: 344). More recently (1992) Earl Hopper has said that 'The critique [in the Envy and Jealousy Symposium of 1969] was telling, if not devastating, and remains so.' Feldman and De Paola are also critical of Klein's idea about envy because she speaks of it 'alternately as a feeling or as an impulse . . . not maintain[ing] a consistent approach to the problem of its [psychic] category' (1994: 221).

I believe that most of the antagonism to Klein's idea of envy is based on her assertion that it has a constitutional basis, which many critics have taken to mean that she thinks envy is an instinctual impulse rather than a feeling. One, at least, of Klein's inner circle questioned her closely about this aspect and its implications. In a letter of 18 April 1956 Joan Riviere wrote to Klein:

In your letter you mention your Envy paper as again showing that you connect object–relations with instincts: here what I am going to say is not criticism or doubt, I am hoping you will make it clearer in the book how 'innate envy' can arise. The idea is not clear in itself. It implies an object-relation before birth – a difficult proposition to many people. If that is what you mean, it is <u>new</u> in theory, and you need to discuss it fully and give your evidence for it. The difficulty is expressed in Bowlby's letter to you about it, which is circularized, and it should not be ignored. You may be perfectly right, as you so often have been; but in scientific work the conclusion should be worked out on the basis of evidence, or else it should be put forward <u>as</u> a speculation, which Freud did about the L & D instincts, though giving all the evidence he could.

(Riviere 1956)

It is typical of Klein's unfussy and rather unsystematic approach to theory that she saw no problem in the idea of something starting off as an instinctual impulse and interacting with experience to become a feeling, and, indeed, when she expanded her 1955 paper on envy into her book *Envy and Gratitude* (Klein 1957) she did make much clearer how she used her idea of envy in clinical work – not that that stopped the criticisms of its instinctual basis, however.

In spite of criticisms of the concept of envy, most Kleinian analysts have continued to treat the concept as a cornerstone of their theory and their clinical approach even though few papers have been specifically written about it (but see Segal 1964a; Joseph 1986; Etchegoyen *et al.* 1987; Brenman 1980; Lussana 1992). The fact that so many of the criticisms of Klein's concept of envy came from non-Kleinians perhaps increased the feeling among Kleinian analysts that stress on envy was a distinctive sign of their identity, but they also adopted the concept because of its immense clinical usefulness. One of the hard-won clinical understandings arising from Klein's insight about envy is that in some patients envy can be extremely destructive both to the individual and to his objects, including the analyst. In severe cases it is as if envy holds the patient in thrall; the patient feels that his convictions and his defensive system are infinitely preferable to his tentative positive relationship with the analyst as a good object, and he attacks this relationship remorselessly, especially when he feels the analyst has been helpful (see especially Rosenfeld 1971a; Joseph 1982).

Klein assumes that a propensity for envy is present from birth, a view that is consistent with her idea that some form of self/object differentiation and some rudimentary form of object relationship is present from the beginning. This assumption has also been much criticized, especially by Winnicott and other psychoanalysts who assume that the neonate does not distinguish between self and non-self (Feldman and De Paola 1994 give a sensitive hypothetical reconstruction of the development of envious feelings starting from this hypothesis of undifferentiation at birth). We cannot of course know what preverbal infants think – nor, for that matter, what anyone thinks except by inference – but Klein's assumption is consistent with certain observations of babies, some systematic and 'scientific' (Stern 1985: 10), some much more casual. A very young baby, for example, characteristically did not take hold of the nipple readily; his father, watching him, said, 'He only takes hold of it if he thinks he has come across it by accident. I don't think he likes to feel he really needs it.' The father was assuming, taking it for granted really – and probably also reading his own feelings into the baby – that his baby would not like having to get too much involved with this 'other', this 'not-me' thing that fed him. It was clear too that the father did not think his baby's behaviour was 'bad', only that he was perhaps precociously independent and did not like acknowledging his need for help. Both parents were sympathetic to their baby and his expressions of envy or proto-envy, an important attitude for analysts as well as parents.

Klein and her colleagues assume that when an individual approaches the depressive position (Klein 1935, 1940) he experiences his object in a much more fully developed way. The object is known to be needed by the individual, but is also known to have an independent existence, to be both good and bad, loved and hated, to have relationships with others. The stage is set for much more explicit awareness of envy and jealousy. And in the case of patients' fluctuations between the depressive and the paranoid-schizoid positions in the analytic situation, it is when they approach the depressive position mode of thinking, with its tendency towards integration and awareness of the object's separateness, that envy is likely to be experienced most acutely, sometimes consciously, and retreat to the defences of the paranoid-schizoid position may ensue.

All contemporary Kleinians consider envy to be an important and clinically useful concept, although there is some variation in definition and usage. Some Kleinian analysts define envy and death instinct in even more generalized and forceful terms than Klein herself used. John Steiner, for example, thinks of death instinct and envy as forces whose aim is to reduce differentiation and diminish structure, especially structure that involves differences between subject and object.

Any difference may be attacked by envy, but goodness is its special target. He places much stress on the 'malignant destructiveness of envy, which is anti-life, anti-creativity, and anti growth and development' (Steiner 1992b and personal communications). To those who hold this view, degrees of envy are recognized, but the idea that there might be qualitatively different sorts of envy or even different subjective experiences of envy is not really a meaningful one; envy, if consciously experienced at all, is thought to be experienced by the individual as a bad, destructive attack on an object recognized to be good. This usage is probably more restricted than Klein's own, but it has become a hallmark of the current approach of many Kleinian colleagues.

Some other Kleinian analysts, however, perhaps most notably Britton (1998a: 58 and personal communications), think of envy as less intrinsic and fixed. In his terms envy is 'molecular' rather than 'atomic'. In his notion of development, individuals struggle not so much with different balances of life and death instinct as with different balances of allergy and attraction to 'otherness'. He finds the developmental and clinical significance of envy essential and convincing, but he does not find its description in infancy as an irreducible, malignant element to be satisfactory. He thinks that Bion's -K (Bion 1962a) rather than envy in itself might be a factor underlying what Britton calls *'psychic atopia'*, meaning an antipathy to knowing anything that is different, a counterpart in the psychic constitution to the somatic immune system. And whatever the unknown constitutional basis of envy and of psychic atopia may be, it is my assumption (and I think Britton's) that envy and gratitude evolve in myriads of infant-caregiver, child-caregiver and later person–person exchanges, conscious and unconscious, whose exact nature we cannot know from the perspective of the consulting room. All that we can investigate in the consulting room is the role that envy plays in the internal world of the patient and in his exchanges with the analyst.

'Ordinary' and 'impenitent' envy

I used to think that envy was only destructive to the individual and to those around him when it was unconscious and split off, and that in analysis it would become conscious, arouse guilt and gradually become integrated with more positive dispositions. I soon found, however, that this first expectation was too simple. In some patients envy appears to be experienced consciously, but without arousing the individual's guilt or remorse.

In all the clinical examples given by Klein in *Envy and Gratitude*, in one of Segal's (1964a) and most of Joseph's (1986), the envious reactions are of the first type described above: envy was mainly unconscious and usually well contained. It rarely expressed itself directly, though its unconscious operation led to inhibition, sometimes severe inhibition, of the patient's creativity in work and in personal relationships. Conscious envy emerged late in the analysis in the case of these patients, at moments when the patient was feeling the analytic work to be deeply helpful, and the patient experienced acute mental pain and a sort of circumscribed depression as he integrated the awareness of his envy into his picture of himself. When this sort of envy is relatively mild I think of it as *'ordinary* envy'. To the sort of patient I have in mind, this ordinary envy is *ego-dystonic*, or, perhaps more accurately, *consciousness-dystonic*; his envy is usually unconscious and intense guilt is aroused if the individual becomes fully aware of it. In such cases, analyst and patient are using the same definition of envy. Like Britton, and like the father described above watching his baby's approach to the breast, I assume that everyone tends to be somewhat allergic to otherness, especially to goodness in others. Ordinary envy may become malignant, but some degree of it is universal.

But in some of my patients, and in a few reported cases including some of Joffe's (1969) and one of Segal's (1964a), and in many of the 'social' examples described by Schoeck (1969) and Berke (l986), envy is very obvious to the outside observer and is conscious at least to some degree to the person expressing it. I use the term *'impenitent'* for this sort of envy; in everyday usage such envy is often called *'grievance'*. I assumed at first that impenitent envy, being virtually or actually conscious, would be less severe than the cases of ordinary, ego-dystonic envy described by Klein and others. In fact, however, I have found that this is rarely so. In my experience there is a considerable range in severity and destructiveness in both ways of experiencing envy. Further, there may well be other ways of experiencing envy. Several colleagues have suggested that severely manic and schizophrenic patients use other modes than the two I have described. Nevertheless it is the ordinary and impenitent modes that I have chiefly encountered in my practice and that I want to discuss here.

According to the *Oxford English Dictionary* envy may be felt when the individual compares himself with someone superior in happiness, reputation or the possession of anything desirable. In my view envy is especially likely to be felt when the individual has to *depend* on someone who is experienced as this sort of superior person, and all envious patients defend themselves to some extent against being aware of such dependence. The person whose envy is ego-dystonic directs defences against becoming aware that envy may be the basis of his behaviour, especially his various forms of attack on good objects. In the analysis of this sort of patient and this sort of envy, analyst and patient have the same or potentially the same definition of envy: it is a destructive attack on a good object. If the ordinarily envious individual becomes aware of his envy, he feels guilty and unhappy. The impenitently envious person, however, is consciously aware of his envy, but he does not suffer from conscious guilt and a sense of responsibility for his envy; he thinks it is the envied person's fault that he, the envier, feels envy. The analyst may feel that his impenitently envious patient is making a destructive attack on a good object, but the patient thinks he is making a legitimate attack on an envied object who deserves to be hated. Splitting the object into 'good' and 'bad' is a common defence by a person who experiences impenitent envy: the perceived goodness of the object is held to be the proper possession of the envier; the perceived badness of the object is held in contempt or is angrily attacked.

This sort of impenitent envy without guilt is also described by Kernberg as typical of narcissistic personality disorder, especially when this disorder takes the form of pathological narcissism or antisocial personality disorder (Kernberg 1984: 193, 197, 303, 1989: 559). Impenitent envy is particularly clearly described by Dennis Carpy in an unpublished and undated paper called 'Fantasy vs. reality in childhood trauma: who's to blame?'

Aggrieved people frequently have a belief that they have been unfairly treated and are entitled to redress. In analysis this emerges as a belief, at times as an insistence, that the analyst *must* agree with the patient, that only then will the patient feel really understood, only than can he be cured. The patient offers the analyst what Michael Feldman describes as a 'deal': 'You agree about the rightfulness of my grievance and I will let you help me' (Feldman, undated and unpublished paper on grievance, and personal communication; Britton, personal communication; Kohon 2000).

A frequent aspect of the defensive arrangements of an impenitently envious person is that he feels *unconsciously* that he is profoundly unlovable and inferior, qualities which he projects into others towards whom he feels superior. Thus the person with impenitent envy and a persistent sense of grievance tends to find himself in a world in which some people are unfairly superior to him while others are justifiably inferior. Such patients remind one of Milton's Satan (*Paradise Lost*, 1667) with his abandoning of hope, good and remorse, and his welcoming of evil and power:

> So farewell hope, and with hope farewell fear,
> Farewell remorse: all good to me is lost;
> Evil be thou my Good.
>   (Book 4: lines 108–10)

Like Carpy, however, I have found that in cases of impenitent envy and grievance, defences are used not only to maintain and enhance the sense of grievance but also to evade acknowledging the acute pain and sense of loss, sometimes fear of psychic collapse, that would come from realizing that one wants a good object but really feels that one does not have it or has not had it. Such recognition of loss would mean having to face the acute feelings of conscious envy not only of the good object one should have had, but also of the self one should have been but will never be, and to acknowledge realistically the actual qualities of the objects one has had, such as they are and were. Feeling perpetual grievance and blame, however miserable, is less painful than facing such losses. Better to hate than to mourn. Viewed from this angle, impenitent envy is a form of narcissistic defence. 'Envy and narcissism', as Segal said at the Symposium on Envy and Jealousy in 1969, 'can be seen as two sides of the same coin.'

Defences against envy are multiple, and frequently reinforce one another, especially in the case of impenitent envy, to form what has been called a 'defensive' or 'pathological' organization (Rosenfeld 1971a; O'Shaughnessy 1981b; Steiner 1987, 1993a). Looked at singly, the main defences against envy, as described by Klein and elaborated by her colleagues are: (1) denigration of the good qualities of the object, which will then provoke less admiration and dependency (Klein 1957; Segal 1964a; Joseph 1986); (2) projection of envy so that the individual sees himself as a non-envious person surrounded by envious destructive people (Klein 1957; Joseph 1986); (3) idealization of the envied object so that comparisons with oneself become

150

irrelevant (Klein 1957; Joseph 1986), or it may take the form of denigration of the envied object and idealization of some other object, or some aspects of the envied object may be denigrated and others idealized; (4) identification with the idealized object or idealized aspects of the object through projection and introjection so that the individual feels that he is the possessor of the admired attributes of the envied object (Klein 1952c: 68–9; Rosenfeld 1964: 71; Sohn 1985); (5) stifling feelings of love and correspondingly an intensifying of hate, sometimes expressing itself as indifference or emotional withdrawal (Klein 1957; Rosenfeld 1969); (6) a form of masochistic defence in which the individual feels himself to be omnipotently hopeless so that the envied object, who cannot cure the individual's despair, is proved to be worthless (Joseph 1982, 1986).

Examples of ordinary and impenitent envy

I want now to describe sessions with two patients which illustrate the expression of ordinary and impenitent envy. In the sessions, both patients somewhat resented the fact that recent analytic sessions had been helpful, and both expressed some degree of negative therapeutic reaction. Mrs A's envy is ego- or consciousness-dystonic and, although she was considerably upset when she became aware of it in the sessions I report, her envy is not pervasive or deeply destructive. Mrs B feels impenitent envy and, although she would not be described as deeply disturbed or fragmented, I think she is considerably more troubled by envy than Mrs A. Her defences are more complex but also less effective than those of Mrs A. She constantly feels how unfair it is that other people have qualities and advantages that make her feel envious.

Ordinary envy: Mrs A

Mrs A mistakenly came to her session 15 minutes early. While waiting to start the session I was puzzled, for Mrs A was generally punctual. Was she in an unusual state of eagerness? In a panic? Was it connected with the yesterday's apparently 'good' session? Once the session began she explained that she hadn't realized at first that she had come early, and she had felt angry with me for keeping her waiting. Then she realized what had happened and felt very embarrassed, as if she was caught in the act of spying on me. She had found it reassuring while she was waiting to hear me talking to the woman who cleans my house. It meant that I was involved in all the sounds of domesticity. 'Because you too make pretty much the same sort of sound,' I said, 'so it means you and I are alike.'

She agreed and went on to tell me that she had found yesterday's session particularly helpful, that she had understood many things that she hadn't thought of before. I said she was very grateful for this but it also seemed possible that it had made her feel that she couldn't provide for herself the sort of understanding that I had, so she regained her balance by arranging to hear me in my domestic role in which I was reassuringly similar to her.

She thought briefly and then agreed, saying that it wasn't very nice. Then she talked about one of her colleagues with whom she was having a lot of difficulty because he said that one of his bosses was 'past it' and hardly worth bothering about. 'Oh dear,' she said.

'You seem to have started listening to what you were saying and translating it,' I said.

'Yes, and it seems to be that I'm saying you're "past it". Even worse.' She paused, and then went on to tell me that a close friend of her brother had rung last night and how important it was because they had been somewhat estranged. Then she told me a long, harrowing and extremely interesting story about the heroism of this brother's friend during the recent revolutions in Eastern Europe.

For some time I was completely caught up in listening to the story, then I began to think about why I had got so involved in it, and wondered whether it was possible that her telling of the story had something to do with the situation we had been talking about earlier. Eventually I said I thought she was worried I might think she was past it, and she was regaining her balance, this time by telling me a very interesting and dramatic story which she thought I would find utterly absorbing. It was a way of arranging things so that she felt she was the one who had the valuable stuff and I was the one who was being enriched by it – she was the giver, I the receiver, reversing the roles she felt we'd been in yesterday.

'I've suddenly remembered a dream,' she said. 'It was pretty dreadful. I was with my sister. All my crowns fell off my teeth. I was trying to push them back on but even the stumps were falling out. I was a wreck. Then I saw an old friend walking past with her back very straight. She looked very regal, wearing a kaftan. Father used to tell me off for not walking with my back straight.'

I said that she'd remembered the dream almost at the end of the session so that if I talked about it I would be pronouncing on it in the sort of regal manner that she felt was characteristic of her sister. I thought she felt that in the dream the repair work we had being doing had fallen to pieces, that there wasn't even a foundation for it. It wasn't clear whether she felt my supposed repair work was attacking her teeth, or she was attacking the work we had been doing together, but it did seem that I was queening it over her and she was a wreck.

Reflecting on the session after she had left, it seemed to me that as the session proceeded she had gradually moved closer to a more explicit recognition of making an envious attack.

Mrs A's further sessions

At the next session Mrs A went back to the dream at once. She agreed, with some discomfort, that her self-attack was really an attack on the work we had been doing. The straight-backed old friend, it emerged, was her view of me in which I was made out to be haughty and regal rather than helpful. Further, she thought she had wanted to be like this sort of person herself, hardly a compliment to the analytic enterprise. Then she talked in detail and with pain and seriousness about the difficulty she had in getting hold of things in herself that she really didn't like.

As time went on in successive sessions, she realized that her envious attacks on me and on her own progress were not as deeply spoiling as she feared. She became more objective about my vices and virtues and more forgiving towards herself for her periodic impulses of envious attack. Very gradually, too, she became less inclined to blame herself endlessly for what she felt to be her mother's defects.

Impenitent envy: Mrs B

Before the sessions I shall report, Mrs B had had several sessions in which she felt I had understood something particularly painful that she had undergone.

153

Session 1

She seemed to be in a bad mood. She said her students hadn't turned up so she'd cancelled her seminar. Then she'd had a piano lesson and felt it had gone well; it made her furious that she was dependent on something external like that.

Furious also, I said, that she'd felt better during yesterday's session, another external something she perhaps felt dependent on.

She said I could add her mother's visit. It went well and that made her disgruntled too. Silence. Then she said she'd had a dream but didn't propose to tell me. The atmosphere was heavy with resentment. I waited for quite a long time and then said I thought she didn't want me to have the pleasure of working with her to understand the dream.

'I suppose not,' she said. A long silence, then she said, 'Having said I won't tell you, here it is. I'm with my grandmother. She was dancing with me in a lively fashion. I was half enjoying it but half afraid she would have a heart attack and die.' She said she couldn't make much sense of it. Then she spent quite a long time explaining that her grandmother had a weak constitution, a constitutional defect. After a pause she talked about a woman colleague whose marriage looked very trendy and successful but she thought it was all a great strain on the couple and their children. She, the woman, and her husband were the same – everything looked fine on the surface but things weren't really right.

'As in the dream,' I said, 'in which your grandmother looked full of life, but seems to have been unaware of the fact that she might have a heart attack and die at any moment.' I went on to say that I thought she had similar mixed feelings about me. I looked all right on the surface, she'd been told I was a respected training analyst etc., but what sort of strain was going on under that supposedly trendy exterior? What sort of strain was the dance between us putting on us? Would I be overwhelmed and would she be blamed?

Silence. 'You mean because of my telling you about feeling troubled yesterday. Yes, perhaps.'

I waited some time, then said that, like her grandmother in the dream, I thought my patient felt I was unaware of the danger I was in. She thought I was idealizing my energy and my dancing partnership with her, just as her colleague at work idealized her trendy marriage. So there was a constitutional weakness in me that she knew about and I didn't.

There was a longish pause. Then she said that there was something ridiculous about her grandmother in the dream. 'You're right. I've just realized there is something I've been feeling about you that is ridiculous. It's about your garden. It makes me think you're silly. Why did you choose a house that is overlooked? At first I thought it must be some American custom – you're so urbanized you don't care about being overlooked. Anyway, so long as you only had a mess out there it didn't matter, there was nothing to see. But now you've put in grass and plants. Surely you must realize there is no point in doing that when you're overlooked. It's silly.'

Normally I would have explored her choice of my garden a bit further, but it was getting near the end of the session. I said the garden was her analysis. So long as it was barren and a mess, she could overlook it and it didn't matter. But now I was aspiring to grow things in her analysis with her, and it made her furious. It made her feel overlooked, resentful, shut out, and she dealt with it by thinking she was the one overlooking me, superior. I was unaware of this and silly.

'Yes,' she said, 'and *you* overlook that there is something in me that is going to spoil everything – my inheritance, my bad constitution.' (This was said with a mixture of grievance and contempt, as if she did not have to carry any responsibility for spoiling everything because it was her bad constitution that was to blame, and I was too stupid to have seen this.)

I said she put it cogently, triumphantly. She felt I deserved to be put down. And, as in the dream, she felt I was a slightly absurd, vulnerable granny, oblivious of the dance of death she was doing with me, and oblivious too, perhaps, of her fear that she would get blamed for the terrible outcome it might have.

(In addition to the three meanings of 'overlook' in this interchange, namely, (1) to see into or over; (2) to ignore; and (3) to look down upon, there is another meaning according to the *Oxford English Dictionary* which is 'to look with the evil eye', a concept very close to envy. I doubt very much, however, whether my patient knew this; certainly I did not know it at the time.)

Mrs B's further sessions

Mrs B felt marvellous and sounded absolutely triumphant in the next session. Three good students had appeared and she had assigned them all to her own seminar. She didn't see why her colleagues should expect to share in her decision. After all, their work wasn't any better than hers just because they had Ph.D.s.

I said she felt she was not only the equal of her colleagues with Ph.D.s, but also the equal of the me, who had a Ph.D. She had become me, or, rather, the impressive Ph.D. aspects of me.

Gradually in the course of the session it became clear that her image of me was increasingly split. The incompetent granny me was being denigrated more and more, and was arousing in my patient not a sense of responsibility but the persecutory guilt that Klein describes. The Ph.D. me was exalted, idealized; she had taken it over and had become identified with it to the extent that she was almost talking as if she had a Ph.D. herself. Certainly she was as good as me.

Eventually, though not in this session, her spell of narcissistic self-sufficiency collapsed into futility and hopelessness, which she felt I could do nothing to help her with. It became clearer that she found it very difficult indeed to bear the intense pain of the loss of all the good experience that she wished she had had, good experience that had in part been denied her by others, but that she herself had also spoiled.

Looking back now on these sessions of Mrs B's, I think there was something that had been particularly provoking to her in the sessions before the ones I have reported. In these earlier sessions she had felt very troubled and felt I had understood this not only in the sense of interpreting her pain in a way that made sense to her but also in the sense of registering her pain empathically. But she was very threatened by this sort of empathic understanding, which I think was too close to the love she longed for but could not let herself know she wanted. She dealt with such emotions by denigration: empathy was a sign of weakness, even lack of insight. To her, goodness was weak, inferior, unsafe, even persecuting. Strength was cruel, superior, safe. Something that is good cannot be strong and vice versa. Kernberg (1984: 299) describes the same sort of belief but in much more pathological types of character than Mrs B. Mrs B has a sense of grievance against her parents for being weak, and in the sessions she had a sense of grievance against me for being a 'weak granny' who might easily be overwhelmed and she, Mrs B, would be blamed. Perhaps my capacity to see that she felt I was a weak granny provoked an even greater sense of grievance. Certainly she did not see my capacity to see this as a strength that could help her. Only my (irrelevant) Ph.D. was impressive and desirable.

Envy in both Mrs A and Mrs B can be described as relatively mild compared, say, to some of the cases described by Segal (1964a and personal communication), Steiner (personal communication), Kernberg (1984, 1989) and Schoeck (1969). Of the two patients I have described, I found Mrs B's envy somewhat more severe and difficult to work with than Mrs A's. Both patients were provoked by 'good' sessions which made them feel dependent, but Mrs B was more humiliated than Mrs A. Both picked on something to idealize and identify with, but Mrs A's identification (with the old friend in the kaftan) was transitory, Mrs B's (taking over my Ph.D.) more insistent. Mrs A's denigration of me was slight, Mrs B's was more intense. But in this respect there was a difference of kind as well as degree. To Mrs A, I remained a basically good figure whom she discovered, to her chagrin, she was attacking for what she thought were base reasons; Mrs B felt that when I was attacked by her 'constitutional defect' I was damaged and became a bad persecuting figure, and she would be blamed for something she really should not have had to be responsible for. The splitting between the good me and the bad me was more profound in Mrs B than in Mrs A. But the main difference was that, whereas Mrs A's defences worked tentatively and singly, Mrs B's worked together to make a strong system that maintained her view of herself as someone with a legitimate grievance and justifiable envy.

Because it is comparatively mild as well as consciousness–dystonic, the 'ordinary' envy of my first patient, Mrs A, is easier for both her and me to deal with than the sort of grievance and impenitent envy with which Mrs B makes herself so miserable. I find that the doctrines of the Catholic Church recognize something like this difference – hardly surprising as the Church has had nearly 2000 years of trying to understand the nature of goodness and sin. Envy, corresponding roughly to the sort of envy of Mrs A, is one of the seven deadly sins: envy, pride, avarice, lust, anger, gluttony, sloth. But there is another type of envy, called 'envy of another's spiritual good', which is much more serious and is one of 'the six sins against the Holy Ghost': envy of another's spiritual good, presumption, despair, resisting the known truth, obstinacy in sin, final impenitence. These six more serious sins 'do not arise from mere frailty or ignorance, but are generally accompanied with so much malice and such wilful obstinacy to the Spirit of God and the known truth that they who are guilty of them are seldom converted' (Hart 1916: 370–1).

It is of some interest that both patients described their childhoods in similar terms. Both felt they had over-busy and chronically pre-occupied parents who were basically unhappy, and both patients thought they had missed out on the love and attention they wished they had had. If anything, Mrs A felt even more left out than Mrs B because she felt that her mother greatly preferred some of the other children to her. But Mrs A had a profound feeling of concern and responsibility about both parents, particularly her mother; she worried about her and wished more than anything that analysis would show that her mother had really loved her after all. Mrs B respected those members of her family who she felt were strong and successful and felt ashamed of those who she thought were weak. As I have described above, she closely associated weakness with goodness and ineffectualness, and all three were unsafe and contemptible. I believe that she despised weakness in others because she believed unconsciously that she herself was weak, inferior and unlovable. Perhaps her greatest difficulty was in mourning not only the loss of the ideal parents she would like to have had but also the loss of the ideal self that she would like to have been.

I do not of course know what the parents of Mrs A and Mrs B were actually like, and the very different outcome in my two patients' expectations of life makes one aware of the enormous complexity of the interplay of psychic and material reality, and aware, too, of how cautious one needs to be in assuming that in analysis one can discover historical as distinct from remembered truth. I do not think it would be right to assume that Mrs B's parents were 'worse' than Mrs A's; I simply do not know. Nor would it be correct even to say that Mrs B *thought* they were worse. What *is* clear is that in analysis, Mrs A was better able than Mrs B to mourn the loss of the good parents (and the good analyst) that she would like to have had.

One could describe the way Mrs A expressed envy in the session I report as envy in the depressive position, whereas the way Mrs B expressed envy, at least on this occasion, could be characterized as envy largely in the paranoid–schizoid mode, a defensive retreat to persecutory anxiety and schizoid defences. I do not mean that Mrs A's sort of envy is the only type that is found in the depressive position: it can often be more severe, as shown in the cases described by Klein and others, and it may be different at different periods in an analysis. Nor do I think it would be right to assert that impenitent envy is the only form of envy that one encounters in patients who are enmeshed in the pathology of the paranoid–schizoid position.

Rather than characterize the comparison between ordinary and impenitent envy solely in terms of the paranoid–schizoid and depressive positions, however, I want to describe in greater detail a model that I have gradually constructed of the factors which I think mitigate envy or exacerbate it. My model centres on the *perceived relation between giver and receiver*, partly because it is this relation that one sees especially clearly in analysis, as in infancy, but also because it is the relation in which envy is particularly likely to be aroused.

Models of envy in relation to giving and receiving

One crucial factor seems to me to be the conscious and unconscious feelings of the giver about giving, and the way these feelings are perceived or misperceived, consciously and unconsciously, by the receiver. Already it must be apparent that my model is potentially highly complex. Presumably there is some 'factual' reality about the nature of the giving and receiving, but this reality is enormously complicated by the conscious and unconscious feelings and perceptions of both giver and receiver, and it is these psychic realities that are especially important in the experience of envy.

Let us suppose that the giver takes pleasure in giving and, further, that he is not, for example, giving in order to establish superiority over the receiver. Let us suppose too that the receiver is able to perceive this accurately and to realize also that the giver knows that he, the receiver, might resent being given to, like the father described above observing his baby's approach to the breast. In this type of giving and this type of perception by the receiver, it is likely to be easier for the receiver to acknowledge envy and to feel positive feelings as well; in particular, the receiver may feel able to give something back to the giver in the form of feeling pleasure as well as some resentment about being given to. If the giver can recognize and accept this return gift, this gratitude, a benign circle may be set up in which both parties give something of value to each other. The receiver's capacity to be given to is a return gift to the original giver. Goodness in the other becomes bearable, even enjoyable. The receiver introjects and identifies with an object who enjoys giving and receiving, and an internal basis for admiration can develop, and hence emulation of the generous giver becomes possible.

Let us suppose, by contrast, that the giver takes little pleasure in giving or is actually hostile or inconsistent towards the receiver, or that he feels consciously or unconsciously that the receiver is making unreasonable demands or draining his resources unfairly; or suppose that the giver gives eagerly and with pleasure but only in order to demonstrate his superiority over the receiver. Or, further, let us suppose that he gives reluctantly and unwillingly because he is trying to conceal the fact that he feels what he gives is bad. And, still further, let us suppose that the giver's lack of genuine pleasure and generosity is accurately perceived by the receiver. In any of these examples, envy is likely to be exacerbated. Pleasure in receiving cannot easily develop, and the receiver will not readily feel grateful. The receiver is likely to feel resentful and to give as little as possible back to the giver. The giver, deprived of gratitude, gives less, or more aggressively, and the deprivation/envy circle continues. So, somewhat paradoxically, envy is likely to be greatest when the giving object is felt to give little or badly. The receiver takes in and identifies with a giver object who does not enjoy giving and receiving, and the vicious circle is perpetuated internally. Genuine emulation becomes very difficult, and is likely to involve splitting, projection and a takeover of the giver's power, like Mrs B's identification with my Ph.D.

The contrast I have drawn so far is of course much too simple. It takes some account of the giver's motives and mode of giving, but it assumes that the receiver perceives and interprets these modes correctly. In reality, however, the receiver may make many types and degrees of misperception and misinterpretation.

The giver may give with pleasure and in good faith, for example, but the receiver may misinterpret the gift as an attempt by the giver to establish superiority. A giver may have a reasonable expectation of gratitude for a gift generously given, but the receiver may be so resentful that the giver has the capacity to give whereas he, the receiver cannot supply the good thing for himself that he reacts with hatred, contempt, conventional politeness or simply ignores the fact that the gift has been given – all of these being forms of spoiling. Or – another example – the giver may give diffidently because of a conviction, conscious or unconscious, that what he has to give is really bad, and the receiver may misperceive this as stinginess, superiority or indifference. The immediately preceding examples of misperception have concerned cases where the giver's emotions are basically good but the receiver misinterprets them. But there are also cases of 'bad' giving which the receiver misconstrues as good. It took some years of

160

analysis, for example, before Mrs A could realize that I had made a bad interpretation or that I should have made a particular interpretation but had failed to do so; it took still longer before she could tell me immediately that I was wrong instead of waiting until the next session.

I have not tried to exhaust the possible variations, and it is obvious that there can be very complex interactions of giving, receiving, further response by the original giver and yet further response by the receiver. One has only to think of an hour or two in the life of a mother and baby or a session or two in the course of an analysis to realize how complex these interchanges can be.

Several colleagues with whom I have discussed this chapter have assumed I was saying that the model of giving and receiving I have described could be used to describe the role of the 'environment' in shaping the development of envy in childhood. This is true only in the most general sense, in that whatever potential for envy an infant may have had, the giving/receiving exchanges with caregivers will have had an effect on it. But from the perspective of the consulting room I do not think any patient and analyst can determine what *really* happened in the infancy of a particular patient, nor even, in many cases, what the patient *thinks* happened, for the crucial interchanges cannot be remembered. Even the interchanges of later childhood will have been affected by earlier and largely unconscious templates of giving and receiving and by the retrospective projection of the state of giving and receiving in the adult patient's inner world in the present. Thus I think one must be very cautious in attempting to make causal explanations of envy in terms of the effects of past experience. I think, for example, that I have a fairly clear picture of the role of 'ordinary' ego-dystonic envy in Mrs A's current life and the role of grievance in Mrs B's life, but if I were asked to explain the ultimate cause of the differences between them I do not think I could answer.

I have devised and used my model of giving and receiving to describe how envy works in the inner world of these two patients in the present and in their analyses. The model might be useful in developmental observations of children, and I find it useful to keep it in mind when reflecting on my patients' early experiences, but the imaginary and tentative nature of these reflections must always be kept in mind.

Note

1 An earlier version of this paper has been published in the *International Journal of Psychoanalysis* (1993), 74: 1199–212.

Freud and Klein on the concept of phantasy[1]

One of Freud's earliest discoveries was that in the unconscious, memories and phantasies are not distinguished – hence his abandonment of his earliest theory of neurosis, the 'seduction' or 'affect trauma' theory. From that time onwards phantasies have been of central interest. In this chapter I discuss the ideas of Freud and Klein regarding this interesting and complex concept. Throughout the discussion of their ideas about phantasy I refer briefly to the Controversial Discussions of the British Society in the 1940s in which the concept of phantasy played a central role. I then describe certain more recent but minor changes in the Kleinian use of the concept. The chapter ends with brief conjectures about the use of the concept in other current schools of psychoanalysis.

Considering its importance, it is perhaps surprising that Freud did not devote even a paper to the concept of phantasy, let alone a book. His ideas on it are scattered about in the first 20 years of his psychoanalytic writings. His most explicit theoretical statements about it are to be found in his paper 'Formulations on the two principles of mental functioning' in 1911 and in Lecture 23 of the *Introductory Lectures in Psychoanalysis* (1916). In her work with children Klein gradually developed a rather different view from that of Freud. Klein's view was explicitly stated by Susan Isaacs in a paper called 'The nature and function of phantasy' which was the central theoretical issue of the Controversial Discussions in the British Psychoanalytical Society in 1943 (King and Steiner 1991). The various views on phantasy voiced at the Discussions are clearly described and discussed by Anne Hayman (1989).

163

One of the difficulties in describing the differences between Freud's and Klein's views on phantasy is that Freud uses the term rather differently in different places. In 'Formulations on the two principles of mental functioning' (1911), which is the place where he comes closest to making a formal definition, he speaks of phantasy as a wish-fulfilling activity that can arise when an instinctual wish is frustrated. Phantasies derive ultimately from unconscious impulses, the basic instincts of sex and aggression. I shall call this Freud's 'central usage' (it is well expounded by Sandler and Nagera 1963).

In understanding Freud's central usage it is important to remember that his idea of phantasy, like his work on dreams, is closely bound up with the development of his topographical model of the mind (see Chapter 7 of *The Interpretation of Dreams*, 1900; his papers 'Repression', 1915b and 'The unconscious', 1915c; Sandler *et al.* 1997). In the topographical model of the mind, conceptualized as the System Unconscious, the System Preconscious and the System Conscious, there is a double focus, first on the attributes of consciousness and unconsciousness, and second on primary and secondary process. The 'secondary process' Freud defined as the rational thinking of ordinary logic; the 'primary process' he thought of as a much more peculiar system of logic, characteristic of the System Unconscious, in which opposites are equated, there is no sense of time, no negation, no conflict.

Although Freud thought that some unconscious phantasies might be 'unconscious all along', he also thought that most phantasies originated as conscious or preconscious daydreams and might subsequently be repressed. As he puts it in 'Hysterical phantasies and their relation to bisexuality' (1908), the unconscious phantasies of hysterics 'have either been unconscious all along and have been formed in the unconscious; or — as is more often the case — they were once conscious phantasies, day-dreams, and have been purposely forgotten and have become unconscious through "repression" ' (p. 160). In Freud's view the basic motive force for making phantasies is an unconscious wish that is blocked from fulfilment, and the phantasy is a disguised expression and partial fulfilment of this unconscious wish. If phantasies are formed in the System Conscious or if they are allowed into it, that is, if they are daydreams, they are known not to be true. If they are formed in the System Preconscious or if they are repressed into it, they will be descriptively unconscious but formed according to the everyday logic of the secondary process. If phantasies are further repressed into the System Unconscious, they become subject to the peculiar logic of the primary process; they 'proliferate in the dark', as Freud put it, and from their position in the System Unconscious they may become indistinguishable from memories and may also find their way into dreams, symptoms, symptomatic acts, further preconscious and conscious phantasies and other drive derivatives.

Freud's 'central usage', with its emphasis on phantasies being formed according to the logical thinking of the secondary process, is the usage that was adopted by Anna Freud and the other Viennese analysts during the Controversial Discussions, and by several British analysts, notably Marjorie Brierley and to some extent by Ella Freeman Sharpe and Sylvia Payne (King and Steiner 1991). This is the usage that has been adopted by ego psychologists (Beres 1962; Arlow 1969a, 1969b, 1995; Inderbitzen and Levy 1990), by the Contemporary Freudian group of analysts in Britain (especially Sandler 1986; Sandler and Sandler 1986, 1994, 1995) and also by many Independent group analysts.

In Freud's view, although there *are* phantasies in the System Unconscious, the basic unit of the System Unconscious is not phantasy but the unconscious instinctual wish. The making of dreams and the making of phantasies are parallel processes; one might speak of 'phantasy work' as comparable to the 'dream work'; both involve transformation of primary unconscious content into a disguised form. For Klein, on the contrary, unconscious phantasies *are* the primary unconscious content, and dreams are a transformation of it. For Freud, the prime mover, so to speak, is the unconscious wish; dreams and phantasies are both disguised derivatives of it. For Klein the prime mover is unconscious phantasy.

I think that Freud and Klein emphasized contrasting aspects of the everyday usage of the word 'phantasy'. The word conveys contrasting implications in English and I believe also in German. It has a connotation of the imagination and creativity that underlie all thought and feeling, but it also has a connotation of make-believe, a daydream, something that is untrue by the standards of material reality (see Rycroft 1968; Laplanche and Pontalis 1973; Steiner 1988; Britton 1995, 1998a). Freud's central usage emphasizes the fictitious, wish-fulfilling aspect of the everyday usage whereas Klein's tends to focus on the imaginative aspect (see especially Britton 1998a).

But this relatively clear-cut contrast between Freud and Klein is complicated by the fact that Freud's 'central usage' is not by any means his only usage. Further, he moves easily from one implied definition to another without being finicky about his formulations. In some of his early work he seems at times almost to equate unconscious phantasy with unconscious wish (1900: 574); at others he speaks of phantasies largely as conscious or preconscious daydreams (1900: 491–8). In his clinical work he deduces phantasies of quite surprising content, phantasies of which the patient was presumably unaware. He assumes, for example, that the Wolf Man when he was 18 months old had a phantasy of being inside his mother's womb so as to intercept his father's penis (1918: 101–3). It is not clear whether Freud thought the Wolf Man was consciously aware of this phantasy at the time and repressed it later, or whether it never became conscious at all. Freud deduces similarly striking phantasies in the case of Dora (1905), though again he does not discuss their precise topographical status. Some of Dora's phantasies were presumably conscious, such as her phantasy of revenge on her father. Some may have been descriptively unconscious, such as her phantasy of fellatio, of the female genital (the 'nymphs' in the 'thick wood', that is, the labia minora in the pubic hair), her phantasy of defloration, of bearing Herr K's child, and her homosexual love for Frau K.

It seems likely that Freud always tacitly assumed that at least some phantasies may originate directly in the System Unconscious without being originally preconscious or conscious derivatives of unconscious wishes. Indeed, in 1916 he speaks of 'primal phantasies' which he thinks are inherited: these are the phantasies of the primal scene, of castration, of seduction by an adult. He does not mean, he makes clear, that parental intercourse is never seen, that threats of castration do not occur, or that seduction does not happen in reality. But he thinks that these phantasies will occur even if external reality does not support them because they were once, to quote him, 'real occurrences in the primeval times of the human family, and . . . children in their phantasies are simply filling in the gaps in individual truth with prehistoric truth' (1916: 371). Most of Freud's followers have not adopted this view, presumably because of thinking it too Lamarckian. But with some alteration I think it is not far away from Klein's notion of inherent knowledge of bodily organs, birth and intercourse (Klein 1927b: 175–6) or from Bion's idea of 'preconceptions' waiting to mate with experience to form conceptions (Bion 1962a, 1962b). And in French psychoanalysis these primal phantasies are considered to be of fundamental significance both in theory and in clinical work (Roussillon 1998).

In summary, Freud is not punctilious in his definition of phantasy. He uses the term in several senses and, as Laplanche and Pontalis point out, he is more concerned with the transformation of one sort of phantasy into another than with any static definition (1973: 314–19). What I have called his 'central usage', however, is the one that has been adopted by most of his immediate followers.

What, then, is Klein's view of unconscious phantasy and why did it arouse so much controversy?

Essentially Klein focuses on the 'unconscious all along' aspect of phantasy. She regards phantasy as a basic mental activity present in rudimentary form from birth onwards and essential for mental growth, though it can also be used defensively. Klein developed this view of phantasy through her work with children, especially through discovering that children accompanied all their activities by a constant stream of phantasy even when they were not being frustrated by external reality. As for example Fritz and the letters of the alphabet, one of many examples:

> For in his phantasies the lines in his exercise book were roads, the book itself was the whole world and the letters rode into it on motor bicycles, i.e. on the pen. Again, the pen was a boat and the exercise book a lake . . . In general he regarded the small letters as the children of the capital letters. The capital S he looked upon as the emperor of the long German s's; it had two hooks at the end of it to distinguish it from the empress, the terminal s, which had only one hook.
>
> (Klein 1923: 100)

Klein developed her idea of phantasy gradually from 1919 onwards, stressing the damaging effect of inhibition of phantasy on the development of the child, the ubiquity of phantasies about the mother's body and its contents, the variety of phantasies about the primal scene and the Oedipus complex, the intensity of both aggressive and loving phantasies, the combination of several phantasies to form what she called the depressive position (Klein 1935: 1940) – the paranoid-schizoid position was to come later, in 1946 – the development of phantasies of internal objects, and, of course, the expression of all these phantasies in the play of children and the thinking and behaviour of adults. Essentially I think that Klein viewed unconscious phantasy as synonymous with unconscious thought and feeling, and that she perhaps used the term 'phantasy' rather than 'thought' because the thoughts of her child patients were more imaginative and less rational than ordinary adult thought is supposed to be. Further, Klein thought that it was possible to deduce the phantasies of infants from her analyses of small children, assuming that she was discovering the infant in the child much as Freud had discovered the child in the adult (Britton 1995).

So important was the concept of phantasy in Klein's thinking that the British Society made it the central scientific topic of the Controversial Discussions of the 1940s (King and Steiner 1991), the aim of the discussions being to see whether Klein's ideas were to be regarded as heresy or development. It was Susan Isaacs, however, who gave the definitive paper, 'The nature and function of phantasy' first given in the Discussions, then published in revised form in 1948 and 1952. In this paper Isaacs stressed the link between Klein's concept of phantasy and Freud's concept of drive. She defined phantasy as 'the primary content of unconscious mental processes', 'the mental corollary, the psychic representative, of instinct'. Phantasies are the equivalent of what Freud meant by the 'instinctual representative' or the 'psychic representative of an instinctual drive'.

Isaacs, like Klein, particularly emphasizes the idea that everyone has a continual stream of unconscious phantasy and, further, that abnormality or normality rest not on the presence or absence of unconscious phantasy but on how it is expressed, modified and related to external reality. She distinguishes between conscious and unconscious phantasy and suggests the 'ph' spelling to distinguish the latter. (Nowadays most British analysts use the 'ph' spelling for all phantasies, I believe because it is sometimes difficult to be sure whether phantasies are conscious or unconscious.)

Isaacs's and Klein's definition of phantasy is thus much wider than Freud's central usage. In the Kleinian view, unconscious phantasy is the mainspring, the original and essential content of the unconscious mind. It includes very early forms of infantile thought, but it also includes other forms that emerge later on in development through change in the original phantasies. And, as described by Freud, some unconscious phantasies may start off as conscious daydreams or theories which are later repressed. But, unlike many of Freud's successors, Klein does not think that repression of once conscious daydreams is the *only* or even the main source of unconscious phantasies. Freud's central usage, the wish-fulfilling definition of phantasy, is a specific and more limited form, a particular type of phantasy within Klein's more inclusive definition. In the Controversial Discussions Klein and Isaacs did not stress this relation between their all-inclusive definition and the wish-fulfilling definition of phantasy as a particular type within it. Certainly the argument in the Discussions was made more difficult by the fact that each faction was using the same word for a different concept: much of the time the two factions talked past each other. Sometimes the Viennese seemed to assume that Klein's definition of phantasy was the same as their own, so that they could not understand how Klein could possibly say that phantasies occurred in very early infantile life, since this would have meant that very small infants were capable of secondary process thinking. At other times Glover and Anna Freud specifically criticized Klein for broadening the concept of phantasy so much that it included everything and hence had become meaningless (King and Steiner 1991: 399, 423–4). Ronald Britton has suggested that Isaacs probably did not fully clarify the difference in definitions because she did not want to emphasize Klein's difference from Freud, for Klein and her colleagues were worried that Glover might succeed in banishing them from the Society on the grounds that they differed from Freud and were therefore not 'legitimate' (Britton 1998b).

Freud is not very specific in making conjectures about the nature of early infantile thought. Klein called such thought phantasy and assumed that it was closely linked to bodily experience. She assumes that phantasizing starts very early, in some primitive form 'from the beginning' as she was fond of saying. She did not bother much about Freud's distinction between the System Unconscious and the System Preconscious, between primary and secondary process thinking. Klein and Isaacs assumed that phantasies could be formed according to primary process thinking – indeed that primary and secondary process thinking were very much intertwined.

Isaacs assumes that the earliest phantasies are experienced mainly as visceral sensations and urges, the other senses of touch, smell, sound, taste and sight being added later and gradually. Such unconscious phantasies can perhaps be regarded as similar to the 'thing presentations' that Freud describes in 'The unconscious' (1915c). Isaacs makes much use of the principle of genetic continuity to link these very early phantasies with the more structured verbal phantasies of the older child and the adult. She assumes that what is experienced is a sensation and an impulse, together with a feeling of something happening that is involved with the sensation and may have an effect on it; looked at from the perspective of an outside observer, the 'something' is some aspect of external reality. From the perspective of the infant, things are assumed to be inside him. Hinshelwood (1991: 34–5) describes it as follows:

> An unconscious phantasy is a belief in the activity of concretely felt 'internal' objects. This is a difficult concept to grasp. A somatic sensation tugs along with it a mental experience that is interpreted as a relationship with an object that wishes to cause that sensation, and is loved or hated by the subject according to whether the object is well-meaning or has evil intentions (i.e. a pleasant or unpleasant sensation). Thus an unpleasant sensation is mentally represented as a relationship with a 'bad' object that intends to hurt and damage the subject . . . Conversely, when he is fed, the infant's experience is of an object, which *we* can identify as mother, or her milk, but which *the infant* identifies as an object in his tummy benevolently motivated to cause pleasant sensations there.

Slowly, through introjection and projection, a complex phantasy world of self and internal objects is built up, some of it conscious, but reaching to the unconscious depths. This notion of internal objects and the internal world was and has continued to be central in Kleinian thought. This internal world is imaginary by the standards of material reality, but possesses what Freud calls 'psychic' reality, that is, to the individual concerned it feels real at some level, conscious or unconscious, and it is also real in the sense that it affects his behaviour. It is noteworthy too that in the unconscious aspects of the internal world Klein and Isaacs think of phantasies as combining both ideas and feeling, another difference from Freud, who spoke of the System Unconscious as the realm of ideas and memory traces and was never entirely resolved about the status of unconscious feelings.

Early phantasies are omnipotent: 'I want it, I've got it.' 'I don't want it, it's gone!' They are stated by Isaacs to have many attributes Freud thought to be characteristic of the primary process – no coordination of impulses, no sense of time, no contradiction, no negation. But Klein also thought of unconscious impulses and phantasies as being in conflict with each other in the unconscious; unconscious conflict between love and hate, between a good self and a bad self, between a good parent and a bad parent were conceptions she found appropriate and useful, though in Freud's topographical conceptualization wishes (and wishful phantasies) in the system unconscious are in conflict not directly with each other but indirectly through their contact with the regulating ego.

Klein's discoveries about the phantasies of small children led her to be very much aware of their intense bodily concreteness, their concern with birth, death, the primal scene, babies, faeces, urine, murderous hatred and equally violent love. Her descriptions of phantasies are as graphic and surprising as those of Freud. For example:

> One day while Ruth was once again devoting her attention exclusively to her sister, she drew a picture of a tumbler with some small round balls inside and a kind of lid on top. I asked her what the lid was for, but she would not answer me. On her sister repeating the question, she said it was 'to prevent the balls from rolling out'. Before this, she had gone through her sister's bag and then shut it tightly 'so that nothing should fall out of it'. She had done the same with the purse inside the bag so as to keep the coins safely shut up . . . I now made a venture and told Ruth that the balls in the tumbler, the coins in the purse and the contents of the bag all meant children in her Mummy's inside, and that she wanted to keep them safely shut up so as not to have any more brothers and sisters. The effect of my interpretation was astonishing. For the first time Ruth turned her attention to me and began to play in a different, less constrained way.
>
> (Klein 1932a: 26–7)

Or again:

> As I was putting a wet sponge beside one of them [a doll] as she had done, she burst out crying again and screamed, 'No, she mustn't have the *big* sponge, that's not for children, that's for grown ups!' I may remark that in her two previous sessions she had brought up a lot of material concerning her envy of her mother. I now interpreted this material in connection with her protest against the big sponge which represented her father's penis. I showed her in every detail how she envied and hated her mother because the latter had incorporated her father's penis during coitus, and how she wanted

to steal his penis and the children out of her mother's inside and kill her mother. I explained to her that this was why she was frightened and believed that she had killed her mother or would be deserted by her . . . Gradually she sat up and watched the course of the play with growing interest and even began to take an active part in it herself . . . [When] the nurse came . . . she was surprised to find her happy and cheerful and to see her say goodbye to me in a friendly and even affectionate way.

(Klein 1932a: 28)

Nowadays, like our classical colleagues, many Kleinian analysts have become more cautious about interpreting phantasies so boldly and so concretely. (I have discussed this elsewhere, Spillius 1988 vol. 2: 8–9, and in Chapter 2 of this book.) In spite of this change, I think that emphasis on the unconscious and on adult forms of living out infant-ile experiences and phantasies has remained characteristic of Kleinian analysis. Like Klein herself, her present-day followers take it for granted that in thinking, in dreaming, in creativity, in all experiencing there is a constant and often uncomfortable mixture of logic and illogic. Further, unconscious phantasy is the mainspring of both cre-ativity and destructiveness. It gives meaning to the external world and richness to the internal world.

Klein and Isaacs assume that the expression of unconscious phantasy in words comes very much later than their original sensory formulation. Indeed, in current Kleinian thought it is assumed that some unconscious phantasies about infantile experience are never formally articulated in words, though words may be the means unconsciously used to communicate them by evoking them in an external person. To give an example: in the course of a preliminary consultation an articulate young woman suddenly said, 'Hollow inside,' and then continued with what she had been saying. At a suitable pause I asked, 'Did you say "Hollow inside?" ' She asked what I meant, adding that she had no memory of having said anything about 'hollow inside'. I felt rather disoriented. Once her sessions began she talked intelligently and apparently meaningfully about her history and her current life, but I felt detached and unable to find any real meaning or emotional connection with what she was saying. Eventually it occurred to me that now *I* was experiencing the 'hollow inside' that she had so accurately and so disconcertingly put into words. Gradually this split-off experience became the focus of our sessions.

Klein and Isaacs assume that phantasies affect the perception of external reality, but, equally, that external reality affects phantasies, that there is a continual interplay between them. This assumption, namely, that actual external events are interpreted and understood, experienced in other words, in terms of pre-existing phantasies and that phantasies may be modified to take experience of events into account, is a basic premise in Kleinian thought. It comes, for example, into the Kleinian idea that the infant gradually develops the more realistic thinking of the depressive position (Klein 1935, 1940; Segal 1964b) alongside and partially replacing the omnipotent thinking of the paranoid–schizoid position (Klein 1946), although each infant and each adult will have his own characteristic realization of the two forms of thought in the particular content of his phantasies.

The first part of Klein's idea about the interaction of phantasies and external events, namely, her idea that external events are interpreted and understood in terms of pre-existing phantasies, caused considerable argument during the Controversial Discussions and subsequently as well, for many analysts disputed Klein's assertion that an infant or child could have, say, attacking and destructive phantasies without having been destructively attacked. In the Kleinian view such phantasies of attack may conceivably be a realization of a hereditary disposition, though they may also arise from earlier experiences of bodily sensations of discomfort, as described above in the quotation from Hinshelwood. External reality thus often operates not only as a stimulus or cause of phantasies but as a confirmation or disproof of them. One does not have to see a breast being cut to pieces to have a phantasy of it, but for one's mother's breast to ooze blood and pus is likely to be felt as an alarming confirmation of a phantasy of attack, or a disturbing disproof of a phantasy of a loving and well-cared for breast able to stand up to attack. The argument about which is primary, pre-existing phantasies or external events is an expression of a more general, and in my opinion unproductive, psychoanalytic argument about the relative priority of heredity and environment – unproductive because the relevant psychoanalytic evidence for deciding the issue in particular cases, especially direct evidence about the past, is usually not available.

Klein and Isaacs assume that phantasies are not used solely to express unconscious impulses and wishes. Mechanisms of defence too are expressed through phantasy. Projection, introjection, splitting, idealization, denial and repression are abstract terms that describe general psychic processes, but a given individual's use of them is expressed through particular phantasies.

Phantasies expressing particular impulses and defences do not operate in isolation. Gradually some of them may build up into a complex system which involves the individual's own unique way of being, of relating to the world, of maintaining his balance. The concept of phantasy is thus central to the idea of the organization of the personality as a whole. This is the main sense of the term 'unconscious fantasy' favoured by Arlow (1969a, 1969b, 1995), by Shane and Shane as 'global fantasies' (1990) and by Inderbitzen and Levy (1990). Kleinian usage includes such central or 'global' phantasies but does not confine the general term to such particular sorts of phantasy.

The fate of the concept of phantasy after the Controversial Discussions

It is hardly surprising that in the Controversial Discussions of the 1940s Anna Freud, Glover and their associates were not convinced by Isaacs's arguments nor she by theirs. As I have said, they meant such different things by the same term, phantasy, that they were talking past each other. Since 1943 the differences of definition and usage have continued, though most of the heat has gone out of this particular debate.

Later Kleinian developments

Kleinians' changes in their definition and use of the concept of phantasy have been minimal. Considering that Kleinians regard unconscious phantasy as such an important concept, it is perhaps surprising that little has been written about it since Isaacs's original paper (but see Segal 1964b, 1997; Joseph 1981; Hinshelwood 1991; Britton 1995). I think so little has been written because the concept is now taken for granted. Many of the developments in Kleinian thought have used the concept of phantasy without changing Klein's view of it. Much of the work on the development of thinking, for example, uses the idea of changes in the content and functions of phantasy in the movement from the paranoid schizoid to the depressive position, as I have briefly described above. Bion takes the concept of phantasy for granted in describing his model of the container and the contained and its role in the development of thinking (1962a). Similarly, much of the work on psychic equilibrium and on pathological organizations uses the concept of phantasy, especially in the course of describing the relevant clinical material (Riviere 1936; Rosenfeld 1971a; Segal 1972; O'Shaughnessy 1981b; Joseph 1982; Steiner 1993a). Phantasy comes into everything.

Although Klein's successors have thus made little fundamental change to her concept of phantasy, they have in my view made three minor changes: more emphasis on the role of phantasy in the development of logical thought; a change in the language used to describe unconscious phantasies to the patient; and more emphasis on the enactment of phantasies by the patient in the analytic situation.

First, phantasies are now viewed by Kleinians as crucially important in the development of logical thought since they may be used as hypotheses to be confirmed or disproved by experiences of external reality, an idea implicit in Klein's thought but explicitly added to the Kleinian conception of phantasy by Hanna Segal (1964b, 1991). The testing of phantasies against reality does not mean that earlier more omnipotent phantasies are necessarily abandoned; they remain but are added to by more sophisticated versions in keeping with experiences of external reality. And often the more sophisticated versions are used to deny the continuing psychic reality of the cruder and perhaps earlier phantasies (Segal 1991; Britton 1995).

Second, as I have briefly mentioned above, many Kleinians have become more cautious about using part-object anatomical language in describing the content of unconscious phantasies to patients (Spillius 1988, 1994a; Chapter 2 of the present volume).

Third, in describing clinical material there has been a tendency to devote attention not only to the symbolic content of phantasies but also (and increasingly) to the way they are lived out in the session. This has been a notable trend in the very influential work of Betty Joseph (1989).

To give an example of the enactment of an unconscious phantasy, I now summarize some clinical material described in more detail in Spillius (1992).

Mr C was the child of wealthy but preoccupied parents who seem to have had little idea that their child might have emotional needs. My patient imagined that he had lived in a little secluded world of his own, sitting in his corner playing with his toys, quite happy and self-sufficient. Later he spent a lot of time playing with the village boys until he was sent away to boarding school. I got no impression of his consciously protesting against parental neglect. On the contrary he stressed the cultural duty of respecting and honouring parents. He was almost always very polite to me and, although he missed many sessions because of his work, when he did come he was punctilious about arriving on time. He thought it very odd that I might expect him to be in any way disturbed by holidays or weekends, or even to notice them. Only the ends of sessions sometimes bothered him: why should he have to stop just when he had got interested in something? He was often silent and preoccupied in sessions, and sometimes found it hard to begin talking.

He arrived on a Friday saying he had been sitting outside in his car making phone calls and couldn't leave his thoughts about them. He went on to say that most of the sessions were useless, nothing happened, but then sometimes something really did happen and it was very important to him, but it was always when he felt that he was 'really here'. It was like a dream world almost, like the thing I had called his 'world of freedom'.

He was silent. I asked, 'Where is that dream world now?'

He answered literally. He said he never remembered dreams well. He always knew he had them but could never remember them. Last night he was having one and his little daughter woke him – it was a dream about his dogs. They were puppies. He bent down to pat one and it nipped him, in fact tried to bite him quite hard. He patted the puppy on the head again and said to someone, 'Would you believe it, that little puppy really daring to bite me like that!' There was a lot more but he couldn't remember it.

He went back to talking about how he couldn't stop thinking about his phone calls and his busy weekend. He told me what he was going to do during the weekend. I found my mind starting to wander to my own weekend. (This was a clue to what was happening. I was feeling an impulse to fit in with a projection from my patient. He was the busy preoccupied father, I was the child who was managing his lack of interest in me by thinking about my own weekend, my toys in my corner. I was the puppy.)

I said he was leaving me and felt he couldn't be here, he was too busy with his own concerns. I said I thought he expected me to get involved in my own thoughts quite happily and just leave him to get on with whatever he was thinking and planning.

He was silent for quite a long time. Then he said that what I had said reminded him of a friend of his who was an inventor. This inventor said that he was very much left on his own in childhood, and he was so desperately lonely that he took to inventing things so as to drive away his loneliness. But he (my patient) was never lonely. He liked being alone. He didn't feel badly that his parents were so busy and didn't notice him.

I said that similarly he didn't feel badly when I left him, as I was doing today, as it was Friday. On the contrary, he felt that it was he who was leaving me, and he expected me to be happy in my little world and not to mind that he didn't notice me.

He was silent, but I felt that now he was present, in the session. I waited for quite a long time, then said I thought he felt he took advantage of his parents' neglect, that he felt he liked being in his little private world just as he expected me to like being in mine. But somehow he was also encouraging me to protest, to be a brave little puppy and give him a bite. He had given me a little pat on the head and thought it would be brave of me to protest.

Silence. 'You mean', he said, 'that it would have been braver of me to protest?'

I said yes, though I thought he didn't usually let himself know that.

He sighed. It was nearly the end of the session. And then he gave me a little bite.

'Oh,' he said, 'I didn't tell you. I won't be here on Monday. I'm going hang-gliding. That Italian professor wants me to leave it. I don't want to help him. It's the competition, I don't want to miss it. I suppose I should. He's so crazy he needs me to help.'

Later, on reflection, I was struck by how disjointed these short sentences were. At the time I didn't know about the Italian professor, the help he needed, the competition, the craziness. I hadn't known whether my patient was just uncomfortable about being so impolite as to miss another session, or if he was really confused, feeling a bit crazy.

What I actually said was that I thought he felt I was so crazy that I needed him to come to his session on Monday to look after me. He laughed. 'But you *know* it's the time of year for my hang-gliding,' he said.

I said it was time to stop now.

I think that Mr C had a pervasive feeling of loneliness and sadness although he did not consciously connect it with the neglect of his parents or even with neglect by people in his current life. I think the idea of the neglect existed in his mind as an unconscious phantasy, and part of the phantasy was a feeling that he was essentially unlovable and that it was because of this unlovableness that he had been so much neglected by his parents. But all this was covered up and denied by another phantasy, a belief that he did not mind the neglect, that he was self-sufficient and even happy in his self-sufficiency. As an adult he was likeable and occupationally successful, which partially helped to conceal his loneliness and sadness. In analysis, as I have described in the session, he tended to project the neglected child into me and he became the busy preoccupied parent. In his own family he was very attentive to his children, and in this way he succeeded to some extent in putting right the neglect he had suffered as a child.

A final word about the Kleinian view of unconscious phantasy

It is clear that in the Kleinian view, unconscious phantasy is really synonymous with the content of the unconscious mind. That, of course, was one of the objections that Glover, Anna Freud and others made to Klein's usage: all mental functions were encapsulated into this one concept. And of course it is clear that all analysts, regardless of school of thought and regardless of their definition of the concept of phantasy, use the idea of unconscious thoughts and feelings. In Kleinian analysis such thoughts and feelings are called unconscious phantasy, in classical analysis they are called drive derivatives and the term phantasy is used mainly for one particular form of drive derivative. But the conception of unconscious thoughts and feelings occurs in all schools of analysis. Perhaps the importance of the Kleinian notion of unconscious phantasy, overall, is that it has tended to keep the attention of Kleinian analysts even more focused on unconscious anxieties and defences than is the case in other schools of psychoanalytic thought.

Later Independent views on phantasy

The concept of phantasy has not been central in the thinking of psychoanalysts of the Independent group, but Harold Stewart thinks that Independent analysts have made an important contribution to it by stressing the particular importance of actual external experiences in contributing to patients' phantasies (Stewart 1992b and personal communication). This is in keeping with the general Independent stress on the importance of actual external experience in shaping the internal world.

Later Contemporary Freudian views

Contemporary Freudians, as described above, use Freud's central definition of phantasy. Joseph Sandler has been especially interested in the definition and use of the concept of phantasy (Sandler and Nagera 1963; Sandler 1986). He and his wife Anne Marie Sandler constructed a model of the mind involving what they called the 'past unconscious' and the 'present unconscious' (Sandler and Sandler 1983, 1984, 1986, 1987 and particularly 1994, 1995) which corresponds roughly to Freud's System Unconscious and System Preconscious of the topographical model, in which the concept of unconscious phantasy is most at home.

Phantasy in Continental and especially French psychoanalysis

The idea of unconscious phantasy is particularly important in French psychoanalysis, especially the primal phantasies of the primal scene, seduction, castration and the Oedipus complex. This emphasis on unconscious phantasy has not occurred because of British or Kleinian influence but because of interest in Freud, especially perhaps the earlier Freud of the topographical model.

Phantasy in American psychoanalysis

It is my impression, though there are many exceptions to it (especially Jacob Arlow) that less attention is paid to manifestations of unconscious phantasy or of the unconscious in general in American psychoanalysis than in British and Continental analysis. The American Psychoanalytical Association held a panel on unconscious phantasy in 1989 (papers by Shapiro, Trosman, Abend, Morton and Estelle Shane, Dowling and Inderbitzen and Levy). This was the first panel on the topic for many years and in it Shapiro (1990) specifically remarked that the concept of phantasy had been neglected. I think that such neglect is perhaps encouraged by the structural model of id/ego/superego, which focuses attention on conflict between these three conceptualized agencies of the mind and on the defences and adaptations of the ego. The two distinctions of conscious/unconscious and primary/secondary process, which cut across each other and which are so important in Freud's characterizing of different types of phantasy, also cut across the id/ego/superego classification, which does not provide a natural 'home' for unconscious phantasy. Of course the concept of unconscious phantasy is clinically useful, essential even, and talented clinicians have found ways of focusing attention on it even though the structural model tends to discourage focus on the dynamic unconscious.

Although yet again there are many exceptions (e.g. Shane and Shane 1990) it seems to me that decreasing focus on unconscious phantasy is even more apparent among self-psychologists, intersubjectivists and relational analysts than among other sorts of American psychoanalyst. Presumably this decreased emphasis on the unconscious of the analysand occurs because it is felt that the interpersonal perspective on both the analytic relationship and the analysand's personal history offers a more cogent understanding of personality, normal as well as pathological, than do the concepts of unconscious phantasy and, more generally, of conflict between conscious and unconscious. I do not see any logical reason why the interpersonal focus should necessarily diminish the importance of the unconscious, but empirically it does seem to be so.

Summary

In brief, I think Freud's idea is that the prime mover of psychic life is the unconscious wish, not phantasy. The 'work' of making phantasies and the 'work' of making dreams are parallel processes in which forbidden unconscious wishes achieve disguised expression and partial fulfilment. For Freud himself, especially in his central usage, and even more for his immediate followers, phantasies are conceived as imagined fulfilments of frustrated wishes. Whether they originate in the system conscious or the system preconscious, they are an activity of the ego and are formed according to the principles of the secondary process. That is not the whole story, however, because phantasies may get repressed into the System Unconscious where they become associated with the instinctual wishes, become subject to the laws of the primary process, and may find their way into dreams and many other derivatives. And for Freud, and for French psychoanalysts particularly, there are the primal phantasies, 'unconscious all along', of the primal scene, castration and seduction, also capable of being directly incorporated into dreams and expressed through other derivatives.

For Klein, phantasy is an even more central concept than for Freud and it has continued to be used by her successors with only minor changes. In Klein's thinking unconscious phantasies play the part that Freud assigned to the unconscious wish. They underlie dreams rather than being parallel to them − a much more inclusive definition of phantasy than Freud's. The earliest and most deeply unconscious phantasies are bodily, and only gradually, with maturation and developing experience through introjection and projection, do some of them come to take a verbal form. Freud's central usage, the wish-fulfilling definition of phantasy, is a particular type of phantasy within Klein's more inclusive definition. And, as in Freud's formulation, conscious phantasies may be repressed, but in Klein's formulation this is not the only or even the main source of unconscious phantasies. In Klein's usage, unconscious phantasies underlie not only dreams but all thought and activity, both creative and destructive, including the expression of internal object relations in the analytic situation.

Finally, it is my tentative suggestion that conceptual and clinical focus on the concept of phantasy, especially unconscious phantasy, as in Britain and France, tends to involve a heightened awareness of the unconscious − hardly surprising, since unconscious phantasy is such a fundamental aspect of the unconscious. I have suggested that, although there are many individual variations, the structural model and the self-psychology, relational and intersubjectivist models tend to discourage focus on the dynamic unconscious, that is, on Freud's System Unconscious.

Acknowledgement

I am grateful to several colleagues for help in writing the paper on which this chapter is based, especially Dr H. Segal, Dr R. Steiner and Dr R. Britton.

Note

1   An earlier version of this chapter was published in the *International Journal of Psychoanalysis*, (2001), 82: 361–73.

Developments in Kleinian technique

In this chapter I describe some of what I regard as the central themes in the development and current practice of technique among British Kleinian psychoanalysts.

It is important, as always, to remember that Melanie Klein's work began with the analysis of children. Looking back now to her earliest work, she seems to have had a touchingly naive faith in Freud's method. When she began analysing children (in addition to her own child, 'Fritz') she tried to get them to lie down on the couch and to free-associate, and it was some time before she realized that this method was not really appropriate (Frank 2000). Eventually she went to get an armful of her own children's toys for one of her younger patients to use and so embarked on the famous 'play technique' (Klein 1955a). But in spite of the play technique Klein stuck as closely as possible to Freud's method: sessions five times a week, rigorous maintenance of the setting, emphasis on transference as the central focus of analyst-patient interaction, and emphasis on interpretation as the main agent of therapeutic change. These features are not, of course, specifically Kleinian; they are characteristic, though to varying degrees, of most psychoanalysts.

There is something very vivid about Klein's way of working, a sense of immediacy and immense bodily concreteness about the children's phantasies that she deduced. Looking back now, some of this early work seems striking but hardly surprising, though at the time it must have been quite shocking. For example, here is Peter, aged 3 years and 9 months, in his first and second session (Klein 1932a: 17).

> At the very beginning of his first session Peter took the toy carriages and cars and put them first one behind the other and then

side by side, and alternated this arrangement several times. In between he took two horse-drawn carriages and bumped one into another, so that the horses' feet knocked together, and said: 'I've got a new little brother called Fritz.' I asked him what the carriages were doing. He answered: 'That's not nice,' and stopped bumping them together at once, but started again quite soon. Then he knocked two toy horses together in the same way. Upon which I said: 'Look here, the horses are two people bumping together.' At first he said: 'No, that's not nice,' but then, 'Yes, that's two people bumping together,' and added: 'The horses have bumped together too, and now they're going to sleep.' Then he covered them up with bricks and said: 'Now they're quite dead; I've buried them.' In his second session he at once arranged the cars and carts in the same two ways as before – in a long file and side by side; and at the same time he once again knocked two carriages together, and then two engines – just as in the first session. He next put two swings side by side and, showing me the inner and longish part that hung down and swung, said: 'Look how it dangles and bumps.' I then proceeded to interpret. Pointing to the 'dangling' swings, the engines, the carriages and the horses, I said that in each case they were two people – Daddy and Mummy – bumping their 'thing-ummies' (his word for genitals) together. He objected, saying: 'No, that isn't nice,' but went on knocking the carts together, and said: '*That's* how they bumped their thingummies together.' Immediately afterwards he spoke about his little brother again . . .

There is another feature that was typical of Klein's early work and that has continued to be a leitmotif in Kleinian analysis: the negative transference (See especially Klein 1955a; Frank 2000). Where Anna Freud and her Viennese colleagues at first thought the analyst should cultivate the positive transference with children (A. Freud 1927), Klein thought the analyst would get the analytic situation more effectively established by interpreting the child's negative as well as positive feelings, both about the analyst and the analytic situation and, more generally, about what was going on in his inner world. Klein did not do this in order to convince the child – and later the adult – of his own badness, but because she thought negative feelings were the greatest source of anxiety and needed to be fully known in order to be lived with, possibly modified, or used as constructively as possible.

Klein thought that unconscious phantasy was always based on bodily functions and she phrased her interpretations to children in vivid bodily language. This indeed was one of criticisms levelled at her during the Controversial Discussions of the British Society (King and Steiner 1991), namely, that she was assuming that infants and small children were having phantasies and thoughts of which they would not have been capable. Anna Freud is especially pungent about the absurdity of so-called 'deep' interpretations. 'It has always puzzled me,' she says, 'how it was possible in Kleinian technique to interpret deeply repressed cannibalistic phantasies in the beginning of analysis without meeting absolute disbelief in the patient or without strengthening his resistance' (King and Steiner 1991: 425). But in spite of criticisms, Klein always retained her emphasis on unconscious phantasy and the usefulness of interpreting it, although in her work with adults, as described for example in *Envy and Gratitude* in 1957, she phrased it in a language less specifically 'bodily', though never losing in directness. This change in linguistic phrasing continued among her successors after her death. Where Klein would have talked about 'breast' and 'penis,' we are now more likely to talk about functions: taking in, swallowing, listening, thinking, evacuating. It all sounds more reasonable, less shocking. But there is a danger in this approach too, a danger that Klein's concepts of unconscious phantasy and the inner world will get so much watered down that some of the clinical richness and imaginativeness of her approach may get lost.

In addition to changes of the content of interpretations, there are three respects in which Klein and her various colleagues have developed and changed Freud's technical approach. First there is Strachey's idea of the mutative interpretation (1934). Second is Klein's idea of transference as a 'total situation' (1952a). Third is the idea of the role of projective identification and countertransference in the analytic relationship leading to what I will describe as 'transference/countertransference as enactment'.

Strachey and the 'mutative interpretation'

As is well known, it was Strachey's idea that the patient projects his archaic superego onto the analyst and that the analyst, by behaving differently from the patient's expectation, may be able to show the patient, in a series of small steps, that he is not acting like the patient's archaic superego, and the patient may be able to take in these new aspects of what Strachey calls the 'auxiliary superego' (1934). The point that Strachey makes, and certainly the point that Klein emphasizes, is that it is transference interpretations that are most likely to be mutative. But what exactly did Klein mean by 'transference interpretation'?

Klein's idea of transference as the 'total situation'

Freud defines transference as the revival and expression in analysis of experiences with early primary objects. He describes this revival as being felt 'not as belonging to the past but as applying to the person of the physician at the present moment' (1905a: 116). Klein extends this idea, saying that what is transferred into the analytic relationship is not so much the actual relationship that existed with a particular person of the past, but rather the place of that person in the patient's inner world, which is an amalgam of actual experience and unconscious phantasy, constantly processed by projection, perception, reintrojection, and re-projection, so that the mother of the inner world, for example, may be rather different from the actual mother of the past. This is the way Klein puts it in her paper 'The origins of transference':

> I hold that transference originates in the same processes which in the earliest stages determine object-relations. Therefore we have to go back again and again in analysis to the fluctuations between objects, loved and hated, external and internal, which dominate early infancy . . . It is my experience that in unravelling the details of the transference it is essential to think in terms of *total situations* transferred from the past into the present, as well as of emotions, defences, and object-relations.
>
> For many years – and this is up to a point still true today – transference was understood in terms of direct references to the analyst in the patient's material. My conception of transference as rooted in the earliest stages of development and in deep layers of the unconscious is much wider and entails a technique by which from the whole material presented the *unconscious elements* of the transference are deduced. For instance, reports of patients about their everyday life, relations, and activities not only give an insight

into the functioning of the ego, but also reveal – if we explore their unconscious content – the defences against the anxieties stirred up in the transference situation. For the patient is bound to deal with conflicts and anxieties re-experienced towards the analyst by the same methods he used in the past.

(1952a: 53, 55)

Klein also began to think that transference was even more central than Freud had thought, although it is also clear that in her own clinical work she made many extra-transference interpretations. She makes clear, especially in unpublished lectures in the Klein Archive, that she does not think any transference interpretation is complete if it only refers to the 'here-and-now' of the session; she thinks the analyst should link the present up to the phantasies and if possible to the realities of the remembered past (see Chapter 4 and also the Klein Archive, C59). This approach led her to a less explanatory sort of analysis and to richer and more varied clinical work. So, where Freud had at first made didactic explanations to his patients and then began to stress the role of transference and to use it as evidence for his deductions and reconstructions, Klein carried this trend further, focusing even more than Freud on the analyst-patient relationship, which left the way open for many contemporary analysts to take this trend even further.

The role of projective identification and countertransference in the analytic relationship

Klein developed the idea of projective identification in 1946 in the course of describing the paranoid-schizoid position, a way of thinking and feeling she thought was characteristic of early infancy but which she also thought might be continued by many individuals into childhood and adulthood (Klein 1946). As I have described in earlier chapters,[1] in the paranoid-schizoid position good and bad experiences are omnipotently kept split apart as much as possible, the good being idealized and the bad demonized. In phantasy, good and bad feelings are projected into external objects so that they too are seen as split. The individual thus lives in a world in which he and some of his objects are felt to be very good, sometimes unrealistically good, whereas others are felt to be very bad, and whole objects, that is, objects recognized to be both good and bad, are not yet perceived as such. Klein thinks that in this constellation of anxieties and typical object relationships, omnipotent projection, introjection, splitting, idealization and denial are the major processes and defences. She describes projective identification as a process in which the individual splits off aspects of himself, projects them in phantasy into an external object, and then reacts to the object as if it were the self or the part of the self that has been projected into it. This can happen with both good and bad aspects of the self, though until fairly recently (e.g. Roth 2001; Sodré 2004) it has been the bad aspects that have mainly been described in the Kleinian literature.

Klein's colleagues and students gradually began to use her idea of projective identification and found that it greatly enriched their understanding of object relations in general and of the analytic relationship in particular. So much is this the case that projective identification, as I have described above, has become perhaps Klein's most well-known concept, having been adopted or at least written about by many other schools of thought.

It is important to stress that Klein thought of projective identification as the patient's *phantasy*. In cases of projection by a patient into the analyst, Klein thought that the analyst should not be emotionally affected by the projection. If the analyst *were* affected, Klein thought it was because the analyst was not working properly. But Bion, in particular, began to show how a patient's projection might affect the analyst emotionally and how, if the analyst understood what was happening correctly, he could use his own emotional responses as a source of information about the patient. In 'Language and the schizophrenic' (1955), as I described in Chapter 5, Bion gives a striking illustration of a session with a psychotic patient in which, although the patient at first seemed calm, Bion felt a growing fear that the patient would attack him. Bion interpreted that the patient was pushing into Bion's insides the patient's fear that he would attack Bion. The tension in the room then lessened, but the patient clenched his fists. Bion then interpreted that the patient had taken his fear of murdering Bion back into himself, and was now afraid that he might actually make a murderous attack on Bion.

In my opinion this changed conception of countertransference and its potential usefulness is the main difference between Klein's theory and technique and that of contemporary Kleinians. Such use by the analyst of his own emotional responses makes for vivid analysis but is of course susceptible to error and misuse. The dangers are that the analyst will be overwhelmed by the patient's projection and will become unable to think, that he will refuse to take in the projected emotion, or that he will get caught up in some form of mutual acting out with the patient such as mutual idealization or a sado-masochistic encounter. The basic difficulty for the analyst, as Money-Kyrle describes it, 'is in differentiating the patient's contribution from his own' (1956). Klein herself thought that too much departure from the idea of projective identification as the patient's phantasy and from countertransference as the analyst's pathology would lead the analyst to blame patients for the analyst's deficiencies and mistakes (Segal, personal communication). For the same reason Klein also did not like Paula Heimann's idea of widening the notion of countertransference to include all the analyst's emotional responses to the patient and using them as a source of information about the patient (Heimann 1950). And, indeed, although I think the use of the ideas of projective identification and countertransference have greatly enriched our understanding of the analytic relationship, we also need to be aware of the dangers of placing too much emphasis on our own feelings instead of closely observing the patient.

But projective identification and countertransference have won the day. Taken together, they have greatly influenced our view of the analyst–patient relationship and have led us to look increasingly at understanding the actions of the patient, his unconscious pressures – sometimes gross, sometimes very subtle – to get the analyst to feel certain feelings, think certain thoughts, act in certain ways. All this has become as important as, sometimes more important than, the actual verbal content of sessions. This emphasis has been particularly central in the work of Betty Joseph (1989), who describes in a series of technical papers how patients constantly 'nudge' their analyst to behave in accordance with the patient's unconscious phantasies and expectations. This is Joseph's way of describing what Joseph Sandler calls 'actualization' (Sandler 1976a, 1976b). At first Joseph spoke of this process as the patient 'acting out' in the session, then as his 'acting in'; more recently this process has been described as transference/countertransference 'enactment'.

Like Klein, Joseph speaks of the 'total situation,' but makes a subtle change in emphasis. Where Klein thought of the total situation as all the complex experiences and phantasies of the past and present that are likely to be expressed in the analysis, Joseph focuses more on the totality of their expression in the current analyst-patient relationship, saying, for example:

> What he [the patient] brings in can best be gauged by our focusing our attention on what is going on within the relationship, how he is using the analyst, alongside and beyond what he is saying. Much of our understanding of the transference comes through our understanding of how our patients act on us to feel things for many varied reasons; how they try to draw us into their defensive systems; how they unconsciously act out with us in the transference, trying to get us to act out with them; how they convey aspects of their inner world built up from infancy − elaborated in childhood and adulthood, experiences often beyond the use of words, which we can often only capture through the feelings aroused in us, through our countertransference, used in the broad sense of the word.
>
> (1985: 157)

Joseph tends to focus on the immediate analyst-patient relationship first before linking it with the patient's view of his past (Joseph 1985), but this is a topic on which there is considerable variation from analyst to analyst (Spillius 1988 vol. 2: 15–16; see also Chapter 4).

In spite of increasing emphasis on understanding the analyst-patient relationship, it is important to stress that such understanding is viewed as a means to another end, the end being that of the patient coming to understand himself better. Understanding the analyst-patient relationship is not regarded as an end in itself.

Stereotypes, variation, my own view

Kleinian technique is sometimes seen as rigid, with too much stress on transference interpretation, too little appreciation of the therapeutic effect of extra-transference interpretation, too much focus on what Rickman (1951) described as the 'here-and-now' of the session, and too much emphasis on destructiveness and too little on the 'environment' (see especially Winnicott 1956a, 1956b; Greenson 1974; Gill 1982; Blum 1983; Couch 1995; Stewart 1992b). Of course being a Kleinian analyst I do not agree with the general sort of stereotyping that this characterization suggests, though individual instances must occur of one sort or another.

My own view is that more attention tends to be paid nowadays by both Kleinians and many other analytic schools (see Cooper 1987) to transference as enactment than was the case 20 or 30 years ago, but there is much variation in the way Kleinian analysts have combined the three ideas of the mutative interpretation, transference as a total situation, and transference/countertransference as enactment. There is variation both from analyst to analyst and from work with one patient to work with another (Britton 1998c). Klein herself made many extra-transference interpretations, as her work with Richard shows (Klein 1960) and she had a remarkable clinical gift for sensing and describing unconscious phantasies. As I have said, she was more cautious than many of her colleagues about making full clinical use of the concepts of projective identification and countertransference. Bion, as I have described, led the way in developing the idea of enactment and use of countertransference in understanding the analytic relationship and hence the patient. Betty Joseph has continued and developed his approach; she focuses primarily on the immediate analyst-patient situation (Joseph 1985, 1989). Segal's way of working is perhaps closest to Klein's though she uses the idea of transference as enactment more than Klein did (Segal 1989). Rosenfeld did not focus as strictly on the analyst-patient relationship as did many of his colleagues; he believed that the important thing was to take up whatever was urgent in the material, wherever it was located (see especially Rosenfeld 1987). He thought that insistent transference interpretations were unwise with traumatized patients and that one should pay close attention to the patient's perceptions of the analyst, especially of the analyst's failings (1986, 1987). He was critical of what he called the 'me too' school of interpretation in which everything the patient says is translated into a statement about the analyst. Thus there is considerable variation among Kleinian analysts and this has continued in the younger generation (see especially Steiner 1984, 1993b: Ch. 11 Brenman Pick 1985; Britton 1989; O'Shaughnessy 1992b; Riesenberg-Malcolm 1994; Feldman 1997; Roth 2001; Sodré 2004).

In my own work I find that thoughts about both the patient's immediate and long-standing relationship with me are always in my mind, though not always in the foreground of it. This attitude is similar to the French distinction between analysis *in* the transference and analysis *of* the transference (Laplanche 1999: 216). I think too that whatever one's view of transference may be – and I think it important to know that whether one likes it or not one is bound to have a theoretical view – it should be sufficiently formulated and accepted by oneself to be allowed to be in the back of one's mind. If the analyst becomes too preoccupied with it either consciously or unconsciously he is likely to foist it on his patient. Freud (1912), Bion (1967b) and Sandler (1976b) all warn against having too set an idea of what one *should* see. I would rephrase this somewhat: I think it is when one is preoccupied or troubled about what one should see that one's receptiveness is most likely to be disturbed. Further, psychoanalytic work involves both uncertainty and clinical responsibility, a difficult combination which can foster both anxiety to conform and determination to be original, neither of which is a good basis for impartial curiosity. I find it important when working to have a free-floating expectancy about the complexities of the patient's inner world and the way he may use the opportunities presented by the session to express them. I frequently find myself musing about the patient's remembered history even when I am interpreting something in the immediate relationship; and conversely I often find that I am keeping in mind the current atmosphere and relationship in the session when I am verbally addressing something in the past. It is my belief that the analyst should work from a double perspective. His readiness to focus on the interaction of transference and countertrans-ference involves a form of what anthropologists, who I believe invented the term, call 'participant observation', that is, an emotional involvement and interaction with the patient which is, however, combined with the study of that involvement from an outside per-spective. One hopes, as James McLaughlin felicitously puts it, to achieve binocular vision not double vision (McLaughlin 1993).

My own way of working and some of its variations

To illustrate, I will describe sessions with two patients, the first being Linda, aged 3 years 6 months.

This session took place when Kleinian analysts were beginning to shift away from interpretations involving anatomical part-object lan-guage and more towards focus on mental functions and the immedi-ate transference/countertransference situation. I was very much aware of Linda's current situation outside the analysis, and it was my sudden realization that she seemed to be living this out in the session that led to the particular interpretation of the primal scene that I made.

After saying some words normally when she was about 18 months, Linda had stopped speaking. At that time her parents had moved into a one-room flat while waiting to be rehoused. Another child was born when Linda was 2 and a quarter years, and since that time she had refused to say a word. She was also said by her mother to be stubborn and disobedient. When I first met her I saw a small, sturdy, determined little girl who seemed to be silently saying, 'I'm not having any nonsense from *you*!' She was courageous as well as defiant: she came with me to the consulting room on the very first day without asking her mother to come with her, even though she looked quite frightened. As the sessions went on she soon began playing with the toys I had provided and much of her play involved making things. When I said I thought she was making a baby the way her mother and father had, she looked at me rather contemptuously as if to say, 'Why would you need to say something so obvious?' It was clear that her understanding was intact in spite of her not talking.

After the first long break in her analysis Linda came along readily to the playroom and the minute I had shut the door she grabbed hold of the bottom edges of my coverall and gave a sharp jerk, which sent several buttons flying around the room. She looked intently at my abdomen.

After a pause for thought, I said she thought that when I'd left her for so long I'd been with my husband making a baby, and she was looking to find it.

She turned away and with great vigour got out several plastic cups and filled them with water. Then she put some bits of paper and Plasticine in one, put another on top of it to make a lid, and gave it good shake. I said she was trying to show me that she could make a baby too, and furthermore she could do it all by herself. She gave me a withering look, but she took the top cup off and peered inside. Then she threw the whole thing on the floor in my direction.

I said she was furious – it was only water and paper and Plasticine. It was just pooh and pee, no baby. While I was saying this she quickly pushed a small table beside a bookcase, climbed on top of the bookcase and marched up and down.

I said she wanted me to think she didn't care if she couldn't make a baby. She was getting very excited and wanted to show me that she was bigger and more important than I was even if she couldn't make a baby. She hummed the tune of 'I'm the king of the castle and you're the dirty rascal'. Unwisely I turned my head away for a moment and in that moment she leaped on my back and the two of us crashed noisily down together onto the floor. After I had made sure that neither of us was hurt, I said *she* was being the daddy and leaping on my back the way she thought her daddy did to her mummy when they were together in bed and made babies – and I added that she wanted to bash up both me and the baby she thought I might have been making. She looked a bit sobered. Then she nodded. Shortly afterwards she began to speak, first at home and then in her sessions.

But her talking to me was not quite open or clear. That would have given me too much credit. Instead she sang all the verses of 'Ten green bottles hanging on the wall', with a specially penetrating look at me when she got to the bit about 'If *one* green bottle should accidentally *fall* . . .', and on she went happily till all the bottles had fallen. We had a tacit agreement, which I eventually tried to put into words, that although I had helped to make things better, I was not to rub it in. And I thought too that Linda agreed with her parents that analysis was all very well but it was soon time to stop.

When Linda acted out her idea of the primal scene I thought it was not a simple transference onto me of feelings about her mother or her father. It *was* that, but more too. It was an enactment of the aggressive, damaging sort of intercourse she felt that her parents were having and that she wanted me to have; she was attacking both me as mother and the baby inside me. I do not of course know whether her parents' intercourse was as violent as Linda thought; whatever its nature, I assume that her perception of it was influenced by her own impulses. Although I did not interpret it fully at the time, I think Linda was expressing something else in addition to her sadistic view of inter-course. She had given me quite a shock, and I think that in so doing she was giving me a graphic demonstration of how violent and per-secuting she felt her parents' intercourse was and how frightened and resentful she felt at constantly having to witness it – she was always provoked, always excluded, but never excluded enough to feel even partially free of it. I suppose one could say that her elective mutism was her way of saying that she felt that what she was going through was unspeakable. Unconsciously she was trying to evoke in me her own feelings of shock and outrage – an example of the communica-tive potential of projective identification, of transference viewed as enactment.

The second patient is an adult, Mrs X.

In this session we both became absorbed in analysing an unusually expressive dream, perhaps too much absorbed, I thought later, so that I missed some of the importance of the dream as an enactment in the session.

It was the penultimate session of Mrs X's long analysis and, although I do not want to give all the details of the session, it touched on many issues of her infancy, the difficult years of her adolescence and adulthood, and her current situation, including the analysis itself and its end. In the course of the session Mrs X reported a dream. She was in New Zealand. She was travelling through the interior. She knew that she was a foreigner there and she was allowed to travel through the country but wasn't allowed to settle there. As she drove along she wondered what would happen if the car broke down. She was in a wood and there were people there who seemed to be blue. They looked almost as if they were the trunks of trees but they were actually people. They were the native people. She knew that there was some idea that she ought not to disturb them, that they were very primitive but they had their own lives and their own way of doing things, their strange customs, which shouldn't be disturbed. Then she saw one of them lying down in the road and she thought to herself, 'I must be careful. I mustn't kill that one.' That was the end of the dream.

Although I did not say so directly to my patient, I found this dream very moving. In a compressed and visual form it conveyed her conception of the experience of analysis, including its imminent ending, but beyond that the dream seemed to link this situation with earlier, sensual, preverbal experiences, probably originating in infancy, perhaps concerned with observing and being observed. I thought that she did not literally remember these experiences, but unconsciously felt them to be alive in the present as feelings in her inner world – the kind of experience that Klein describes as 'memories in feeling' (1957).

I asked why did she think it was New Zealand and she said she'd no idea. I said I thought 'New Zealand' meant 'new-seeing-land,' and she laughed (she had occasionally described analysis as a new way of seeing things). 'It was a strange dream,' she went on to say, 'and I think it's about the world inside my mind, inside mine and perhaps yours too, the strange world I have been in here. Just the way it actually is, I'm allowed to visit but I can't stay permanently.'

I agreed and went on to say that this strange land with its primitive people was an attempt to describe her feelings not only about her

195

analysis and about me, but about the way, as she'd said, she felt about the 'interior', the inside of my mind. These were the thoughts and people inside me that gave me my particular character and individuality and that made it possible for me to give her something that was different from what she could give herself. It was as if I had a sort of intercourse with these strange beings, an intercourse whose outcome was valuable to her, but which at the same time made her feel angry, even murderous. (I was thinking at this moment in the session, perhaps too explicitly, about the strange wood as an internal version of the primal scene with herself as observer which Britton 1989 describes as 'triangular space'.)

'You mean because there was that one I had to be careful not to kill. I suppose what you're saying is that I wouldn't have had to think about *not* killing him if I hadn't wanted to. It's jealousy again.'

'And yet you make it clear', I said, 'how much you've valued being in that strange world even if it does make you so jealous. And you've said too that it's a picture of the inside of your own mind as well as mine.'

She reminded me that she had very mixed feelings about the objects in my room (these are various bits and pieces from my anthropological past). I said her description of this primitive land where people had their own dignity and their own customs had some connection with her knowledge that I was an anthropologist and that she knew I had lived and worked in so-called 'primitive' societies. I thought the atmosphere of the dream conveyed much of what she felt about her analysis: she felt not only that she was visiting my room and my mind, but also that I was a temporary visitor/anthropologist to her mind, observing the world of her past and her present as it lived inside her now. The blue of the bodies, it emerged, came from the feeling of the consulting room with its blue rug. And perhaps the people were like trees because of the Tree of Life pattern of the blue rug. She said she thought the unconscious mind was extraordinary.

As the session drew to a close she talked of leaving, loss and fear of a possible breakdown – a reference to her difficult past and perhaps future, and to the detail in the dream about what would happen if her car broke down. She also expressed gratitude for my having given her 'gifts', especially the gift of greater tolerance of her mother's unhappiness and its effect on herself. And she expressed a wish that there would be some sort of gift she could give me. Perhaps the gift was the dream itself, I said, and I went on to describe the complex atmosphere of the session: the pervasive feeling of sadness and hope; the wish and fear that I would be unrealistically encouraging; her pride and misgiving about having to manage all this on her own.

Later I thought about another less idealizing aspect of the dream which would have added depth to the understanding of it. The predominant theme in the content of the dream was that she was visiting me and my world rather than my visiting hers. Perhaps this expressed a feeling that she was now the anthropologist/analyst – a way of coping with the ending by taking over my role and my identity. But the session was also suffused with feelings of loss about ending which were having a powerful effect on both of us. If I were doing it again I would stress even more the presence of both feelings, the loss but also the taking over of my role, and I would recognize more explicitly the pressure we both felt to idealize the work and for mutual harmony in the face of the deficiencies in the analysis and the inevitable uncertainties about ending. This would have given a more complete view of the total situation.

In conclusion

I have described my view of the particular features of Kleinian technique, namely, the combination of the ideas of mutative interpretation, transference as a total situation, and interpretation of the role of projective identification and countertransference in the analyst-patient relationship. I have also indicated ways in which the technique of contemporary Kleinian analysts differs from that of Klein herself. Contemporary Kleinians are more likely than Klein to use their responses to the patient as a source of information about the patient, while recognizing that caution is required in such usage; analysts as well as patients are likely to enact aspects of their inner world in the analytic situation, so that the analyst needs to the best of his ability to observe himself as well as his patient. In general, contemporary Kleinians are probably more likely than Klein to focus on the 'here-and-now' of the session rather than on the 'past,' although there is considerable variation in this respect. Contemporary Kleinians are less likely than Klein to phrase interpretations in terms of anatomical bodily language, although Klein herself was more cautious in using such language with adults than with children.

I have also stressed that it is inevitable that every analyst should use ideas about technique according to his own character and experience and according to differences in his patients, and I have described sessions with two of my own patients as examples of such variation.

Note

1   The role of projective identification and countertransference and the nature of the paranoid–schizoid and depressive positions have been discussed in Chapters 3 and 5.

10

Recognition of separateness and otherness

Freud says little about the child's development in earliest infancy, his interest in childhood being particularly focused on the development of sexuality (Freud 1905, 1909). Klein, by contrast, makes a point of saying that there is a rudimentary ego at birth and that object relations begin virtually at birth (Klein 1946: 2, 1952b: 57, 1955a: 138, 1958: 236, 246, 1959: 251).

Klein's view of the early ego and early object relations contrasts markedly with the work of a large number of psychologists, psychoanalysts and infant researchers who have been concerned to observe, experiment on and develop theories about the development of the infant's awareness of his own 'separateness' from others and of his attachment to them. In the USA most researchers have focused on the development of awareness of separateness (Mahler *et al.* 1975; Stern 1977, 1983, 1985, 1988; Blatt and Blass 1990; Blass and Blatt 1992, 1996; Pine 1992). In Britain, as Blatt and Blass point out (1990: 109), there has been more focus on the importance of the attachment aspect of infant and child development as shown in the work of Fairbairn (1952, 1963), Bowlby (1944, 1951) and Winnicott (1958, 1969).

My own view is that attachment and separateness are so intrinsically involved with each other that efforts to separate them are bound to be artificial. In any case I think it is unlikely that we are ever going to know what infants think, which is what psychoanalysts and psychologists would most like to discover. We know a great deal about what infants *do*, but what they think is another matter; all we can do is make hypotheses based on what we observe. Of course all interpretations about what adults and older, verbal children do, say and think are also bound to be based on inference and conjecture, but inferring what infants *think* from what they *do* is particularly problematic.

In the 1980s I was interested to note that in his book *The Interpersonal World of the Infant* Daniel Stern shows that newly-born infants behave as if they are aware of objects, meaning that his findings and his interpretations of them agree, at least in part, with Klein's beliefs about very young infants being aware of objects. I was struck too by the fact that none of my Kleinian colleagues had remarked on the fact that Stern's findings agreed with the views of Klein, and I concluded that they had not been very much aware of the research of Stern and other infant researchers, or of Stern's critique of Mahler's beliefs and findings. Mahler and her colleagues (1975) had attempted to show that infants were 'autistic' for their first 1 or 2 months, then submerged in a 'symbiotic' form of attachment with their mothers from 2 to 5 months, after which they were thought to go through a long and gradual process of 'separation–individuation' from 5 to 36 months. Stern's critique of Mahler's approach and findings has been gradually accepted, at least to a considerable extent, by most psychologists and psychoanalysts in the USA (see e.g. Pine 1992).

The fact that Kleinians ignored the work of both Mahler and Stern suggests that other factors were at work in their lack of interest in infant research. I think that by the 1980s contemporary Kleinians were no longer very much interested in Klein's or anyone else's theories of early infancy. By this time they were regarding Klein's ideas of the paranoid–schizoid and depressive positions not as descriptions of psychic states in infancy but rather as ways of understanding the various behaviours of children and adults in analysis.

Although Klein assumes that very young infants have a rudimentary ego and that object relations begin virtually at birth, she thinks that the perception of self and others in early infancy, in the early paranoid–schizoid position, is not very realistic. She believes that the infant thinks of his object as 'good' when it satisfies him and 'bad' when it does not, and that the infant's own impulses of love and hate powerfully affect his perceptions (1946). She thinks that in early infancy there are rapid shifts in perception and feeling depending not only on the behaviour of the mother but also on the shifting attitudes and perceptions of the infant. It is her view that binary splitting of good and bad experiences and objects is characteristic of the paranoid–schizoid position and that this binary splitting is a necessary basis for the later integration of perceptions and feelings of good and bad in the depressive position (1957: 184). And she believes too that the attitudes and object relations of the two positions are not 'stages' which the individual lives through and then abandons – hence her use of the term 'position' instead of 'stage' or 'phase' (1952c: 93).

I have thought for some time that there has been a gradual though largely tacit recognition among Kleinian analysts that one of the essential aspects of the depressive position is the individual's increasingly realistic perception of the 'otherness' and 'separateness' of his objects, together with recognition of his own identity as separate from but related to his objects (see also Spillius 1988 vol. 1: 4). Klein herself does not describe such recognition of the 'otherness' and the 'separateness' of objects and self as an essential aspect of the depressive position, but I think she comes close to it when she says, for example, 'Where the persecution-anxiety for the ego is in the ascendant, a full and stable identification with another object, in the sense of looking at it and understanding it as it really is, and a full capacity for love, are not possible' (1935: 271). (It is notable in this example, however, that Klein's description is negative, that is, she describes one of the important essences of the depressive position by noting a factor that interferes with it.) I believe that continuing experiences of fluctuation between the anxieties, defences and object relations of the paranoid-schizoid and depressive positions involve further developments of awareness of the separateness of oneself together with awareness of the 'otherness of the other', to use André Green's phrase (2000: 157).

In this chapter I will describe instances of separation and reunion which illustrate aspects of awareness of separation, attachment and otherness in a baby, a 3-year-old child and an adult returning to analysis after a brief separation. I will then describe in more detail the analysis of three episodes of separation/reunion in the analysis of a woman which show her development of greater understanding of their psychic ramifications in her internal world. I saw the baby and her mother once a week, the child and one adult five times a week, and the other adult four times a week.

Katie: separation/reunion in an 8-week-old baby

Katie was the first child of a young and rather insecure mother. I was observing Katie and her mother for a seminar on infant observation supervised by Esther Bick (see Bick 1964). By the age of 8 weeks it seemed clear that Katie had a very clear responsiveness to her mother as the central figure in her life, rather different from her attitude towards her father, her grandmother, the health visitor and me.

The night before the observation I shall describe the mother had for the first time put Katie to sleep in her own room, at her husband's insistence. The husband was older than the mother, gentle and supportive to his wife. On the night in question both Katie and her parents had slept well.

Soon after I arrived the next morning for the weekly observation Katie woke and cried very hard for at least five minutes. Her mother went on talking to me and let her cry. It was the first time I had seen her mother do this. Eventually she fetched Katie, who looked blotchy and had tears in her eyes. Her mother tried to comfort her; Katie went on sobbing. Then she stopped crying and made a look her mother described as 'her hungry look'. Katie gave an enchanting smile. But then nothing seemed to feel right to Katie. Her mother sat down with Katie on her lap. Katie looked around at her mother, at me, the window, the fire. She looked unhappy and discontented. Her mother kept talking to me and paid no attention to Katie. Katie started twisting and kicking. Her mother offered the breast to Katie (still talking to me) but Katie would not turn her head towards it. Her mother said, 'She isn't really hungry,' went on talking, then asked me to hold Katie. I held her for a time, she smiled, then got restless. After asking her mother if it was all right I put Katie down on a rug on the floor. Her mother said, 'She won't like that,' and indeed the corners of Katie's mouth turned down and she looked as if she was about to cry. She looked at her mother. I said that I'd put Katie in that position but it looked as if her mother was getting blamed for it. 'I think she feels everything she feels is my doing,' said her mother.

Katie began to cry hard again. Her mother picked her up and slowly unbuttoned her blouse, still talking to me. Katie went on crying. 'I think she is so annoyed she can't take it yet,' her mother said. Her mother waited, silent for a moment, then went on talking to me. After a minute Katie took the nipple and sucked steadily for several minutes. The telephone rang, Katie jumped and gave a sudden cry. (I answered the telephone and took a message.) Katie let go of the breast and her mother sat her up. After a minute her mother put her back to the breast, Katie gave three sucks, let go and screamed. This time her mother did nothing in particular for a moment and then stopped talking completely. Katie turned her head away from her mother for several moments; her face seemed to relax, then she turned her head back and took hold of the nipple again. Throughout the sucking this time she looked at her mother's face, the first time I had noticed her doing this so continuously. Once she glanced at me. Towards the end of the feed she looked in at the breast and looked dozy. I had to leave. As I went Katie dropped the nipple, then turned back to it.

What can one conjecture about what was going on? First, the mother. Why did she let Katie cry like that when usually she went to her at the first whimper? Esther Bick (1964, 1968), who was supervising these observations, thought the mother was giving Katie what she called 'the double dose'. What she meant was that by putting her in her own room away from her parents the mother felt that she was depriving Katie and shutting her out. Bick thought that the mother felt Katie would feel badly, which made the mother feel guilty. So Katie became persecuting to her mother, reproachful and accusing, and had to be punished a second time by being allowed to cry. And punished a third time by her mother incessantly talking to me and paying very little attention at first to Katie, though I think it possible that talking to me was caused not only by the mother's need to shut out the persecuting Katie, but also by her need to get my comfort and support.

Bick thought that Katie herself was having a phantasy of a bad mother and a bad breast. She had suffered not only the separation in the night but also the rejection of being allowed to wait and sob; then her mother kept talking to me, and Katie might have been hungry as well. Katie had to get her mother to accept the fact of Katie's turning away before she could establish a good relationship with her mother and the breast once more. Once the mother did nothing for a few moments, which perhaps registered her awareness of Katie's rejection of her, Katie turned to the breast and sucked reasonably steadily. My guess is that in turning away Katie was projecting her bad, painful feelings into her mother (or rather into her phantasy of her mother) and, by avoiding her mother was wiping her out. It was not until her external mother showed, by silently doing nothing in an attentive manner, that she accepted the bad feelings that Katie could once again develop a phantasy of a good breast and a good mother. Each interruption brought back the bad breast and mother, and the good breast and good mother had to be found again by another turning away.

This observation made me aware of how much sense of loss Katie might be feeling and of how much we, as parents and adults, take for granted such minor episodes of separation and reunion. Of course not all Katie's experiences involved loss – on the whole she was a happy, well-cared for baby. Cumulatively a baby's and small child's so frequently encountered experiences of loss and gratification soon build up a picture of attachment, temporary loss, reunion and, I assume, an understanding of adults' separateness, their power and the child's separateness and relative but not total helplessness.

Linda: separation/reunion

Linda was brought to analysis because she would not talk (note: another episode in Linda's analysis is discussed in Chapter 9, pp. 192–94). She had in fact begun to talk a bit when she was 18 months years old. Then she and her parents were temporarily housed in a one-room flat while waiting to be rehoused. A brother was born when Linda was just over 2 and since then Linda had not spoken. It seemed likely that Linda was upset not only by jealousy of her brother but also by repeated witnessing of parental intercourse, though it was not clear why her reaction took the form of not talking. Perhaps, I thought later, because she somehow knew that this would get through to her parents, both of whom were keen for her to do well.

After a bit of reluctance, on the first day Linda came to the playroom and played vigorously with the little toys while I tried to keep up with what she was doing as best I could. It seemed clear that she easily understood what I was saying. After our five sessions of this first week of analysis came the first weekend, which Donald Meltzer, who was supervising Linda's analysis, used to describe as 'the wolf in the fold'.

When I came to fetch her from the waiting room on the Monday following the first weekend, Linda looked up from the little toy she had brought with her and gave me a look of deep reproach. 'How could you!' it seemed to say. Tears rolled down her face. Her mother told her to be a good girl and go with the lady to the play room. Linda wasn't having it. She sat watching me accusingly and went on crying. Her mother said she could not understand it. She had been so eager to come that she had pulled her mother along the street, and now this. I said to Linda that she felt terrible because I had left her. She had got very angry with me and now felt I was all bad. Presumably, I thought to myself, she was separating the 'good' analyst she was hurrying to meet from the 'bad' one she encountered as soon as she arrived in the waiting room.

Linda, so much older and tougher than Katie, had no trouble expressing her view about separations. She 'knew' that it was quite wrong of me to have left her for the weekend like that, and she knew how to make me realize what a wrong I had committed. She abandoned me in the same way I had abandoned her. She spent the whole session in the waiting room accusing me silently with angry tears.

But Linda also had a powerful wish to be understood. In later sessions which I have described in Chapter 9, which deals with technique, she skilfully showed me that it was the primal scene that was bothering her, and when I could put that into words she started to talk, first at home, then gradually in the sessions.

An adult patient, Mrs P, returning from a holiday break

Mrs P had been in analysis for three years and was returning from a holiday break. She greeted me as usual with a slight smile as if to mark the fact that we were meeting after not seeing each other for longer than usual. Once she had lain down on the couch she said she had had a good time and described the holiday in some detail, and in a way that gave me the feeling she was full of energy, very much in command of herself, taking me for granted though not unpleasantly. Having described the holiday in some detail, she told me a dream.

'You were coming to give me a session at my country cottage, but it wasn't a cottage, it was a magnificent house. The doorbell rang. I thought it would be you, but it wasn't; it was my brother's friends, great louts who were going to take our hospitality for granted. I said there wasn't room and they weren't to come in. They left. After they left one of my children said, "Don't you realize they're desperate for somewhere to stay?" I said, "Quick, run after them and tell them they can stay in the attic." I wanted to give each of them £10 but doubted if I'd have enough money.'

Omitting her associations and the to-and-fro in the session, my eventual formulation was as follows: Mrs P had put me in the position she was in that day. In reality she was coming to my house but in the dream I was coming to hers. I was in her position and she had become me, or rather her idea of me. In her role as me she was living in a magnificent house, not the cottage-like house I actually live in.

205

In the dream she had attributed her own greedy loutish feelings to her brother's friends, but they were perhaps a substitute for me. She, in her incarnation as me, would not let these greedy loutish feelings in. Did I not realize what every child would know, that she gets loutish and takes me for granted because I deprive her? She had not actually felt badly during the holiday, it emerged, but was feeling uncertain of her mood now, and not at all sure that she wanted to come back to analysis. It slowly became clear that she thought, without being explicitly aware of it, that I should pay her for the sessions I took away from her in the holiday, just as she would have had to pay me for sessions she booked but did not use (£10 was her fee at the time).

In all three of these accounts involving separation, each individual objected to the separation in some fashion, although it was expressed and perhaps also felt not during the actual separation but during the reunion. Katie slept quietly at night but the next day she was restless and discontented and did not easily take the breast. Linda was all right during the weekend (the parents told me this later on), but found a way to express her complaint when she returned. The adult patient appeared to have felt quite all right during the actual break, but told me a dream when she came back in which she reversed our roles. Perhaps this dream expressed at least part of the basis of Mrs P having felt fine during the break: unconsciously she had become me and I had become her, or at least the desperate loutish aspects of her.

Provided the individual or patient is not too disturbed and not in a crisis, I think that this sort of reaction is typical. The actual separation is not experienced as particularly difficult, and usually the first session back in analysis is a sort of 'hello' session. The difficulties are more likely to come in the second session, or sometimes in the second week. It is then that there are likely to be complaints, or an assertion that the patient is now so well that really it is time to stop the analysis, or some similar declaration often involving some sort of reversal of roles between analyst and patient – the patient will leave, the analyst will be the abandoned one. Katie and Linda were more open, they were discontented right at the start, they had not as yet fully built up their defensive systems. Even Mrs P's first day back didn't follow quite the usual pattern, for she brought in reversal of roles in the first session, not the second. But there was something of the usual pattern, for she spent the beginning of her first session telling me her news, in

206

effect saying a slightly protracted 'hello', and the 'attack' came later on, in the second half of the session.

Perhaps the reactions of these three individuals, Katie, Linda and Mrs P, were envious, but I think that if this were indeed so, it was the sort of 'ordinary' envy that I described in Chapter 7. I thought that Katie was probably unhappy about sleeping alone, but not so much that she couldn't turn to the breast after some protest. Linda, I thought, even after just one week of analysis, was actually starting to feel quite relieved to be having her sessions but didn't want me or anyone else to take her for granted and leave her so arbitrarily. And the adult patient, Mrs P, quickly understood her reversal of roles and the element of attack in it. In different ways all were reacting to separation and otherness. All felt somewhat attacked by the separation, or felt that loss was being imposed on them whether they wanted it or not. All made some sort of attack in return, more disguised and defended against in the case of the adult.

Mrs Lewis: three episodes of separation/reunion

I want now to examine three episodes of separation/reunion in the analysis of a patient where it was possible to examine what was going on consciously and unconsciously in more detail.

Mrs Lewis was 37 years old at the time of the three holiday breaks in her analysis I will describe. I will give the sessions in considerable detail.

The first break

These sessions occurred about two years after Mrs Lewis's analysis had begun. She had come to England from a Commonwealth country to do a higher degree in English after which she had started slowly, and with many ups and downs, to work as a writer, critic and journalist. In the midst of this process of getting started in a career she had married in this country and decided to stay. She came to analysis primarily because of difficulties in her career and her relationships, particularly at work. People complained, she said, that in spite of her gifts and intelligence her thinking and writing were at times confused. It also appeared that she could make herself oblivious to things she did

207

not want to know, to the point where she sometimes became controlling and even attacking without realizing it. She got very upset when she realized she had behaved badly.

There is a 'minor' fact of considerable importance to the sessions before the first break I shall describe. Not long before these sessions I had moved house and consulting room. A prominent feature of the new consulting room was that two of its walls were fitted with hand-made mahogany cupboards and bookcases, which were directly in the patient's line of vision as she lay on the couch. Most patients made some sort of comment about these bookcases. Mrs Lewis did not. It was difficult to know whether there was any particular significance in her ignoring the bookcases. In any case she had other things on her mind.

At this period of her analysis Mrs Lewis maintained a friendly, even-tempered stance towards me, including the sessions before breaks. While other patients were sometimes likely to complain about my self-centredness and arbitrariness in having a break and had phantasies about what I might be doing, Mrs Lewis mostly ignored approaching breaks or talked about them in a perfunctory, dutiful way as if she thought I expected it. When I tried to point this out she listened politely, but did not react much one way or the other. I felt I was making bookish interpretations.

On the Monday of a week before a long summer break, Mrs Lewis said she no longer felt as depressed as she had been feeling, though she didn't know why. On Tuesday she talked about an episode of what she called 'echolalia'. She had telephoned a particular woman critic and asked to speak to her husband, an editor with whom she worked. The wife had said, 'Can you hang on a minute?' and Mrs Lewis found herself also saying, 'Can you hang on a minute?' to the wife. In her session she explained that the husband, once he came to the telephone, had agreed to continue working with her on a particular project, but said that she would have to wait. She then told me about a dream she had had the night before the present session.

In the dream the editor was being very friendly and attractive, virtually sexually seductive. But his wife was there. Mrs Lewis couldn't remember exactly what happened. I said her feelings for the editor were similar to her feelings for me. She felt we both tantalized her, apparently offering her something – sessions, a project of working together – and then made her wait. And the editor's wife was there in the dream. I thought Mrs Lewis felt I was leaving her during the holiday to be with someone else, my own editor, whoever that might be.

She agreed with this easily and went back to talk about the echolalia. I said that in the echolalia she had become the wife. 'Can you hang on a minute,' she had said to the wife, meaning that she herself was the one in control and was not the one who was having to do the waiting and the hanging on. In the echolalia the wife had been got rid of, so there remained only Mrs Lewis herself and the man, the editor.

She agreed with this, again rather easily, and described two recent instances in which she had actually made people wait for her. There was a pause. Then she said it was a good thing that she had found a really nice cleaning woman.

After a slight pause because of the apparent non sequitur I said the good cleaning woman was perhaps a substitute for her bad analyst, who wasn't going to be doing cleaning for her during the holiday. There was a pause. Then she said she had decided to redecorate her loo ('loo' is an everyday, slightly euphemistic word for lavatory or toilet in British English). She described in considerable detail how she thought she would buy a mahogany loo seat.

I said: 'The loo here does not have a mahogany seat. But there is one room here in which there is a lot of mahogany.'

'Oh,' she said, 'You mean here, in this room.' She looked carefully around the room. 'Yes', she said, 'this room is full of mahogany.'

I said: 'When you stress that your loo seat is to be made of mahogany, it's as if you are shifting the mahogany from the consulting room into the loo.'

'Oh,' she said. (I felt as if I was spelling things out to an interested but rather bewildered child. Was she really so unaware of what she was saying, I wondered to myself, or had I confronted her too brusquely? It was one of the few occasions up to this time that I was aware of the 'obliviousness' that she said other people sometimes complained of.)

'And so' I went on, 'you are putting the consulting room into the loo, flushing me and your analysis away. I'm the much valued cleaner, but when it's the last week of our sessions, I'm flushed away. It's not a case of my leaving you, it's a case of your flushing me away.'

There was a very long pause. I felt that at last, perhaps, she had some conscious inkling of the feelings that were getting stirred up by my arbitrarily dismissing her at the time of the holiday.

Then she said: 'I wish my mother had been more like you.'

I was silent for a bit, somewhat disconcerted. It sounded like a non sequitur, but clearly was not. Was this, I wondered, a way of getting rid of possible bad feeling between us? Not quite, I thought. What I actually said was: 'I think that at the moment I recognized that you were really being quite attacking and told you so, you felt relieved.' She murmured agreement. I went on to say that if I could see her attack and yet continue to be reasonably well-disposed towards her, it must mean that it wasn't so dreadful after all. 'Yes,' she said, 'that's right.' After a pause I said it was time to stop.

In the next two sessions of the week, Wednesday and Thursday, she went around this material again, adding that at such times she got a feeling that she desperately wanted something and was going to have it, come what may. No waiting. 'I want it NOW,' she said, imitating her small son.

On Friday she told me that she felt sad and flat about her sessions ending, and then told me about two difficult colleagues. While telling me about the colleagues, her feet in their sandals – not absolutely clean – left their customary position on the little carpet at the end of the couch, and began walking all over the couch cover itself, ending up with her feet flat on the couch cover and her knees slanting to one side. I pointed this out. She said, with much embarrassment, that she felt she had got into a sort of foetal position, and that being on the couch was like sitting on my lap. After considerable to-ing and fro-ing about this, including an association about her son jumping up and down on her bed, I said I thought she found it very difficult to put together two views of herself: herself as an innocent baby sitting on my lap, a baby whose feet could do whatever they liked, and herself as a more grown-up person, who, evidently without her being aware of it, could walk all over me, could take advantage of her supposed innocence to do something quite aggressive and spoiling to me and to the partner she felt I would be with in the summer.

I felt that in this week of sessions she was beginning to have some awareness of the ancient feelings of attachment, jealousy and hatred that can get stirred up by separations, by enforced recognition of separateness. She was beginning to be aware of separation and separateness, both mine and hers, though she was fighting against it. I had mainly interpreted her denigration of me and her jealous attack, perhaps partly because I might have been more irritated about the loo seat and the couch cover than I realized at the time. In retrospect, her possessiveness, expressed through her echolalia and her sitting on me, was equally important. I think she was evading awareness of jealousy and exclusion as much as she could by a phantasy of becoming me through a form of projective identification or, even if she did not actually become me, she was getting rid of rivals by sitting on my lap.

The second break

It was Monday, the first session of the week before the second break, which occurred a few months after the first break which I have described above. Mrs Lewis was becoming increasingly aware of being a bit upset in sessions before weekends and breaks, but it was difficult for her to realize that she got rather angry and aggressive rather than just upset. She still reported instances of people telling her things about herself that she hadn't been aware of. She was becoming somewhat more aware in herself of what she called 'wiping people out', which had painful consequences for herself as well as for the targets of the wiping out.

She began Monday's session by telling me more details about a very difficult work situation with her immediate boss, a Mrs K. Then she returned to describe a feeling she had had the preceding Friday that was just awful, though it had not lasted long. She had felt quite 'wiped out' (her words) on Friday, and what had set it off was Mrs K's threatening to make far-reaching changes in the arrangements at work. That had made my patient feel utterly helpless and in despair. I said I thought those feelings were also linked with the coming analytic holiday: I change the arrangement from sessions to no sessions and she feels wiped out.

She said that when Mrs K threatens to change the arrangements she feels that she is trying to make Mrs Lewis ineffectual. Does she (Mrs Lewis) feel like that because she wiped her father out? (We had been talking about her relationship with her father in earlier sessions; I wondered to myself who was making whom ineffectual now, but decided not to tackle the role of her father and the father aspect of me at that moment, for I knew that her feelings towards her father were much easier for her to deal with than her feelings for her mother. Some time later when I was thinking about these sessions again, I felt that this jump Mrs Lewis made to thinking about her father was important, for it slowly became clear as the years of analysis continued that she turned to her father in her mind when the particular

211

difficulties she had with her mother were getting stirred up. But I did not fully see this at the time of the session I am describing.)

What I actually said in the session was that what Mrs Lewis had said sounded right, but I went on to say that she gave the impression that her feelings about her mother might also be involved in this situation. It was as if Mrs K had virtually become a stand-in for her mother. She (Mrs Lewis) was terrified of offending Mrs K, just as she used to be afraid of offending her mother. But when she offended Mrs K, she clung to her, just as she used to cling to her mother. And that, apparently, irritated Mrs K even more, just as it used to irritate her mother.

She was silent, then agreed quite suddenly and with real interest in her voice, as if she had never thought of the similarity in her relationships with these two women. She was then silent for quite a long time, evidently thinking. Then she asked, 'How does it connect with the holiday? And with how I try to manage Mrs K?'

I said she had often described the way she felt her mother wiped her out, was preoccupied or worried about something and did not have time to attend to her. She began to feel this about me as well, especially before a holiday when she felt I turned away from her and didn't attend to her. She felt it about Mrs K, too. I said I thought she tried to manage this experience by becoming like her mother and like me. She wiped me out, as she wiped out Mrs K. She said: 'That really is exactly what I do to Mrs K. I treat her as if she hardly exists.'

Then there was a very long silence. Up to this point I had thought we were working on a more or less surface level, as if accumulating evidence. Then, through her initiative, things deepened.

She said: 'When I'm away from Will [her husband], most of the time he is present somehow or other in my mind. I don't mean I think about him all the time, but he is just there. I feel all right then. But every now and then I just feel he isn't there, and I get in a panic. I find it difficult to describe. It's as if I myself don't exist. Something is going on that just wipes me out. It doesn't correspond at all to what he is really like or to what you're like either – it happens with you too. I know you continue to exist and that I'll be coming back to analysis, but I don't believe it. I go through something awful and I don't know how to describe it. Everything hangs by a thread. Once I'm in this mood I can't get out of it. It's self-perpetuating. The only thing that stops it is when I actually see him or see you. Or when I see Mrs K and she's not as bad as I expect.' She went over this two or three times, as if feeling she could not describe it properly or that I would not understand it.

I said, finally: 'So you have to see and to cling to this actual external me, or Will, or Mrs K to disprove this terrible thing that you've got inside your mind. You can't bear the thought of my leaving you for fear I'll turn into this awful, terrifying person who "unmakes" you (I could not think of a better word), this awful presence who takes your self away, who puts you into terror.'

'That's right,' she said, and her voice was full of relief. 'Being unmade means that I don't have that active presence of you or Will inside me at all.' She paused. 'There's something more. Can't you do a bit more, can't you push it on a bit?'

I said, 'I think you want me actually to do something now, in the session, so that you won't have the awful me inside you, the one who unmakes you.'

She laughed slightly. 'You mean it's happening now? I suppose it is. I think you're right, it's what I do to Mrs K.' (This time I thought that she'd moved to Mrs K to get away from what she thought was happening between her and me. Now, in a small way, she was enacting it, not just describing it.)

'It's not only Mrs K,' I said, 'it's happening now. You're trying to avoid my wiping you out by wiping me out first. You're doing it by moving away to Mrs K. You do it by taking the significance out of my leaving, by making yourself unaware of it. But that's what makes it happen. Unawareness is the real attack. That's what you think I do to you when I leave, and that's what you do to me – you switch me off. But then you get a kind of no-me, a minus-me in your mind, a wiped out/wiping out me that unmakes you from inside.'

'Hmm,' she said. But it was time to stop.

In this set of sessions I think Mrs Lewis was allowing herself to be more aware of what separations could do to her. If she really cared about her object and felt her object cared about her, it was possible that the break would be all right. But if there was discord she was in danger. I think she responded to this feeling of danger by wiping the offending object out of her mind, out of her awareness. But then the particular form of retaliation that she imagined would come from the wiped out bad object was that it would invade her with wiping out, and she would be reduced to a wiped out state in which she would feel serious panic and distress.

When I thought about it later I realized that something else was

213

evident in these sessions around the two breaks I have described. Unlike most patients, Mrs Lewis's disturbance about the separation was expressed more acutely *before* the break, not primarily after it, though she was somewhat upset after breaks as well. Although I did not take note of this at the time, I think now that her disturbance in anticipation of the break probably happened because she was already sensing more tension and strain between us than either of us had consciously noticed.

Sessions of the week after the third break

This break came soon after the second one I have just described, and those sessions were still very much in Mrs Lewis's mind. There were also additional reasons that made this a difficult time for her – 'not a good time for you to be having another one of your breaks', as she put it.

For some time I had noticed a particular pattern in Mrs Lewis's behaviour in the first week after breaks. She fell prey to feelings of contradiction and chaos. She would telephone people to tell them she had no time to telephone them; she double-booked appointments; she scheduled a meeting and forgot to go to it; while racing to answer the telephone she tripped over a chair and sprained her ankle. I think these actions were indications of the state of Mrs Lewis's internal world, which she expressed not only in the actions themselves but also in the way she described them to me, arousing my concern and curiosity. She conveyed in her sessions that she felt very agitated about the way she was feeling and acting and was almost desperate that I should do something to make it better.

It gradually emerged that this first week after breaks expressed much of what she had felt during the break, usually without her being very much aware of it. I had said this to her on numerous occasions, and it seemed right, but something was missing.

On the first day back after the third break Mrs Lewis described what the break had been like – more or less all right. On the second day back she was quite agitated. Everything seemed to be going wrong. In particular, she was desperately worried about money. She hadn't done the sums exactly, but she was sure she couldn't afford to go on with the analysis. Then suddenly she said to herself, 'No! Stop this!', and went on to say that she knew it was because of her upset about my holiday, adding that there was a real problem about money, but that didn't mean she had to get in such a state over it. 'What I can't understand is why I get in such a panic,' she said. But it was the end of the session.

In the next session the panic continued. Several things had upset her at work and she felt she had behaved badly and stupidly, and things between herself and her husband and child were strained as well. I found it difficult to get a sense of what was happening between us. I made a few desultory descriptions of the atmosphere of the session, and she agreed, but continued in an increasingly anxious and chaotic vein. This response was not a validation or a contradiction of my remarks, but rather a confirmation that I could not conceptualize what was going on. In so far as I could understand it at all, I thought she felt rather battered and confused, and so did I. I had a feeling that my inability to think was in part being evoked by my patient, but I could not understand what particular phantasy of projective identification was involved.

In the next session, as I mused about my inability to understand the transference/countertransference situation, there drifted into my mind one of what I called to myself her 'personal stories'. These were stories of things that had happened in her childhood, and she often thought of them when reflecting on herself and her life. Some of them she remembered, some she had been told. This one she had been told by her mother. It concerned the first week of her life; my personal name for it was 'the first week story'. Her mother had tried to breastfeed her, but apparently did not have enough milk and so had given up after a week, and had put her onto the bottle. Mrs Lewis deeply wished that her mother had kept on trying to breastfeed her. She had several attitudes to her mother over this failure in breastfeeding. On some occasions when she had told me the first week story she had sounded sad for herself. On other occasions she seemed to feel sad for her mother, as though her mother might well have felt she had nothing good to offer. On other occasions Mrs Lewis sounded resentful and angry with her mother for having failed her.

On an earlier occasion in her analysis I had drawn Mrs Lewis's attention to the parallel between the first week of her life and the first week after breaks, but had felt it was too much of a mechanical formula and that neither she nor I could do much with it. As I pondered on the first week story this time, I remembered that, characteristically, Mrs Lewis had never put together her contradictory feelings of anger and sadness about her mother's failure to feed her. I had a dim feeling that this lack of putting together opposing feelings had something to do with the chaos she was in at the moment, and perhaps also with the feeling of incomprehensibility that I was having.

Without quite knowing what I was doing I started thinking out loud. Even though she had not mentioned her first week story this time, I reminded her that she often had a tough time during the first week after breaks and that she felt she'd had a tough time in the first week of her life as well. I said, as I had said before, that we had no way of knowing what had really happened at the time, no way of knowing what she had felt or what her mother had felt. (I knew that this story had become a significant part of her internal world, but exactly how the internal version was related to the historical events of the first week of her life I thought I could not know, although I did not say all of this to my patient.) I said I thought that perhaps she imagined that her mother had not been able to stand the pain and sense of loss over not being able to feed her baby, and that perhaps she had dealt with it by convincing herself that bottle was as good as breast – 'all for the best' – that the pain and loss of the breastfeeding had to be minimized, even wiped out. (I knew that my patient thought such 'sensible' attitudes were typical of her mother from later periods in her life when she could actually remember how her mother had behaved, and I knew too that she also expected such sensible no-nonsense attitudes from me. As I said all this about her mother's possible denial of loss, I began to feel things coming together in my mind: perhaps Mrs Lewis thought that I, too, felt there was no loss, that bottle was as good as breast.)

'You mean,' she replied slowly, 'that there is a difference between saying it doesn't matter, bottle is the same as breast, and saying that it is too bad, breast is best, but as I can't have breast, bottle it will have to be.'

'Yes,' I said. (I was struck that she had not only grasped what I had tried to express, but had described it much more clearly than I had. There was no panic or confusion in this formulation.)

She was silent for quite a long time. I said: 'I think you do that too, but even more to the point, you worry that *I* do it. When I have a break, you think that my actual behaviour, whatever I may say in words, says that no sessions are just as good as sessions, bottle is the same as breast. There is no loss, and that's a lie.'

'Ha,' she said, and her voice was full of relief. 'I think the panic is going.' She was silent for quite a long time, and then she said: 'It must link up with the way everything gets so awful, but I don't quite get it. I know that I attack you and the analysis.'

I said: 'You have come to know that your analysis matters to you, and it's a serious thing when I take it away. No sessions are not the same as sessions. Without your quite realizing it, I think you have thought that I was implicitly lying to myself and to you about this, the way you've lied to yourself and the way you thought your mother may have lied to herself too. That's what's always been missing in your idea about the first week of your life, your implicit belief that your mother denied that the loss of the breastfeeding mattered. You expect me to think this too, and it makes you frantic without your knowing why. You attack me, your analysis and yourself. Especially yourself. It's as if you're saying, "Look what you've done to me!" without even knowing that that's what you're saying.' She was silent, but not agitated, I thought.

This was all reasonable enough, but something was missing. Then I had another thought, and this time thought to myself 'Ha! I've got it', though to be accurate it felt as if the thought had got me.

What I said was: 'Actually this time you know that I chose to leave you. I didn't have to, I chose to. But I think you also know that I'm aware that my leaving is hard on you. The fact that I leave doesn't mean that I'm claiming that it's good for you. I think you know that two contradictory things are true at the same time: that I chose to leave, and that I know it's not good for you.'

She said, 'I never thought of it that way.' (I thought of Freud's paper 'Negation', 1925, in which he says that some such form of words is often the first reaction to an effort to uncover the unconscious.) I thought that this set of interpretations was too long and didactic, contrary to what I had been taught and believe about clinical procedure, the precedence of the here-and-now, the role of reconstruction, the harmfulness of intellectualization – and yet I had a sense that I had got hold of something that mattered to both of us.

In the remaining sessions of the week she continued on the same theme, expanding it and adding her own ways of expressing it. She thought it helped to understand why she often felt uncertain about whether she had anything really good to offer her child, her husband, her readers, for what she offered might contain some deadly denial at its core. Or she might have to claim that she and only she was right, because if she listened to the contradiction, the denied opposing thought, she would collapse in confusion – hence her occasional obliviousness. She began to feel she might cope better with the inevitable contradictions and conflicts of everyday life, and that she might be more able to sort out priorities. She said it had been a revelation that she could see the loss of the thing she had wanted without having to deny the goodness of what she did have. 'The important thing,' she said, 'was when you said that you chose to leave, yet you knew what it meant to me. You didn't pretend that it was good for me. You left because you wanted to, but you knew what it meant. Actually you've never claimed it was for my own good, but I think I thought that way. I suppose you've said this before, but I've never got it. It just makes a difference that you know it's a real pig when you leave, even when I make out that it's all right. Whereas if you pretend that it's all for my own good, it's like those Truby King babies being starved for their own good – that's when things go wrong.'

Gradually, between the two of us (and it was hard even at the time to know exactly who contributed what), it became possible to link this material with the fact that she so frequently couldn't hold on to two opposite ideas or feelings at the same time without becoming confused and chaotic. If she opted for one, she had to deny the other. If she recognized both, she got confused, or she got in a panic and acted out the contradiction – such as her telephoning people up to tell them she had no time to telephone them (phone/don't phone), or her rushing to the telephone and tripping over a chair (answer/ don't answer), or double-booking appointments (see two/see neither).

In the course of listening to this material I remembered, among other examples, the earlier session when she had said, 'I wish my mother had been more like you', and realized now that the particular thing that had probably impressed her was that I could have two contradictory feelings at the same time without being confused or in a panic. I could see how denigrating she was being, and I think she thought I must have been at least a bit angry myself, but she also felt that I was reasonably well-disposed towards her. On that occasion, too, in other words, the coexistence of apparent opposites was important.

In these sessions after the third break I think that it had become clear that Mrs Lewis had a particular difficulty in accepting incompatibilities and contradictions both within herself and between herself and her objects. Not all differences between herself and her objects caused her difficulties, however. It was a relief to her, for example, that I could tolerate contradictory attitudes within myself and between her and myself, whereas the differences between herself and Mrs K were deeply disturbing to her. And there were occasions when similarities between herself and her objects caused her difficulties too, as in the case of her relationship with her mother, for it seems likely that Mrs Lewis's mother might also have had a similar sort of trouble with contradictions and incompatibilities. Neither Mrs Lewis nor I developed a firm idea of how her trouble over contradictions had developed. She was too intelligent and too fair-minded to blame her mother, and although the idea occurred to me that perhaps she had identified with her mother, I do not believe that this sort of hypothetical reconstruction can be demonstrated in analysis. It is perhaps useful to think with, but not to be convinced of.

In conclusion

All the individuals I have described recognized at least to some extent that their objects were separate from themselves, although all of them had different sorts of abilities and problems in recognizing fully the nature of the differences and similarities between their objects and themselves, and all made some sort of aggressive statement about separations.

Katie, the 8-week-old baby was near the beginning of a long process of recognizing that she and her mother were separate, and that her mother could do things that Katie did not like. But she was also aware that she could express her discontent in a way that her object might pay attention to. Much appeared to have happened in eight weeks.

Linda used not talking to send a powerful message to her parents. 'Something is wrong with me! And it's your fault!' Whether she was saying precisely this I of course do not know, but that is the message that I think her parents heard. I think that Linda recognized her parents' separateness from her, that she thought they were doing something highly dangerous and exciting with each other at night, that they excluded her from it and subjected her to it at the same time, and that she hated it. In the first week of her analysis she showed considerable enthusiasm about getting into her sessions, and then came the first weekend. If I excluded her like that, she would exclude me. She wasn't going to have yet another person shutting her out and yet being present again and making her feel helpless.

Mrs P, the first adult patient I described, had no trouble in recognizing her separateness from other people, but did not at first realize that she minded separations. It was comparatively easy for her, however, to recognize her defence of reversing our roles, first in the explicit content of her dream, and then in her general approach to separations, not only with me but also with other people who were close to her.

Mrs Lewis recognized her objects' and her own separateness, but had difficulty in accepting some of the differences and similarities between her objects and herself. Gradually her analysis showed both her and me that she had difficulties in tolerating contradictions both within herself and between herself and her objects, and that this difficulty was the basis of her trouble over separations from her analyst and over certain difficulties involving similarities to her objects and differences from them.

My colleague Ronald Britton thinks that individuals vary in degree of what he calls 'psychic atopia', that is, allergy to otherness, allergy to difference between oneself and one's object. As he puts it:

So is there something in *the temperament* of some individuals that *predisposes* them to this particular development or response to trauma? Is there anything in the endowment of the individual that might encourage the individual to believe that an independently existing object will destructively misunderstand him or her? Is there *an innate factor* in the infant that increases the risk of a *failure of maternal containment*, and, if so, what might it be? I believe there is and I have come to think of it as a kind of *psychic atopia*, a hypersensitivity to psychic difference, an allergy to the products of other minds . . .

. . . In analysis this sensitivity applies not only to minute variations in the analyst but also to approximations in understanding. Where this sensitivity is considerable what is required in the way of understanding is perfect understanding. Less than *perfect understanding* might therefore be perceived as *misunderstanding*.

. . . I find Bion's equation of −K with envy less helpful than regarding −K as a variable factor that joins together with other factors to produce envy. This may seem to some like splitting hairs, but I have a suggestion as to what −K might be, namely that which

underlies what I have called psychic atopia – an antipathy to knowing anything that is different. I believe this variable in the individual
constitution, the psychic counterpart to the tolerance and intolerance of the somatic immune system, may contribute to difficulties
in infantile containment.

(1998a: 57–8)

I find Britton's idea of allergy to otherness, 'psychic atopia', both
compelling and at the same time not quite satisfying. In my view the
allergy depends on the content of the otherness. Although I think he
is right that most people are tacitly on the lookout for otherness and
often do not like it, some forms of otherness are deeply desirable –
sexual difference, for example. And milder forms of otherness can be
valued too. Mrs Lewis, for example, welcomed in me certain differences from her own way of being, especially difference from her
difficulty over contradictions. And certain forms of similarity to
others were very difficult for her, especially if the similarity had to do
with intolerance of contradictions.

What I think analysis aims to create is an atmosphere of exploration
where the nature of otherness, separateness, similarities and contradictions can be explored and known, seen more realistically, more as
things one can take responsibility for and not so much as sources of
panic, blame and persecutory guilt. Such exploration, painful as it may
sometimes be, is likely to foster curiosity and an awareness that other
people are separate from oneself but have minds fundamentally similar
to one's own, even though they may have thoughts and feelings
whose contents are different from one's own.

References

Abraham, K. (1919) A particular form of neurotic resistance against the psycho-analytic method, *Selected Papers on Psychoanalysis*, London: Hogarth Press and the Institute of Psychoanalysis, 1965, pp. 303–11.

Abraham, K. (1924) A short study of the development of the libido viewed in the light of mental disorders, in *Selected Papers on Psychoanalysis*. London: Hogarth Press, 1927, pp. 418–501.

Anzieu, D. (1989) *The Skin Ego*. New Haven, CT: Yale University Press.

Arlow, J. (1969a) Unconscious fantasy and disturbances of conscious experience, *Psychoanalytic Quarterly*, 38: 1–27.

Arlow, J. (1969b) Fantasy, memory and reality testing, *Psychoanalytic Quarterly*, 38: 28–51.

Arlow, J. (1995) Unconscious fantasy, in B.E. Moore and B.D. Fine (eds) *Psychoanalysis: The Major Concepts*. New Haven, CT: Yale University Press, pp. 155–62.

Asch, S.S. (1976) Varieties of negative therapeutic reaction and problems of technique, *Journal of the American Psychoanalytic Association*, 24: 383–407.

Baranger, W. (1974) Discussion of a paper by H.B. Vianna, 'A peculiar form of resistance to psychoanalytical treatment', *International Journal of Psychoanalysis*, 55: 445–7.

Barnes, J. (1954) Class and committees in a Norwegian island parish, *Human Relations*, 7: 39–58.

Bell, D. (2001) Projective identification, in C. Bronstein (ed.) *Kleinian Theory: A Contemporary Perspective*. London: Whurr, pp. 125–47.

Beres, D. (1962) The unconscious fantasy, *Psychoanalytic Quarterly*, 31: 309–28.

Berke, J.H. (1986) *The Tyranny of Malice*. London: Summit Books.

Bernstein, I. (1957) The role of narcissism in moral masochism, *Psychoanalytic Quarterly*, 26: 358–77.

Bibring, E. (1947) The so-called English school of psychoanalysis, *Psychoanalytic Quarterly*, 16: 69–93.

Bick, E. (1964) Notes on infant observation in psychoanalytic training, *International Journal of Psychoanalysis*, 45: 558–66.

Bick, E. (1968) The experience of the skin in early object relations, *International Journal of Psychoanalysis*, 49: 484–6.

Bick, E. (1986) Further considerations on the function of the skin in early object relations: findings from infant observation integrated into child and adult analysis, *British Journal of Psychotherapy*, 2: 292–9.

Bion, W.R. (1952) Group dynamics: a review, in M. Klein, P. Heimann and R. Money-Kyrle (eds) *New Directions in Psychoanalysis*. London: Tavistock, 1955, pp. 440–77.

Bion, W.R. (1953) Notes on the theory of schizophrenia, in *Second Thoughts*. London: Heinemann, 1967, pp. 23–35.

Bion, W.R. (1955) Language and the schizophrenic, in M. Klein, P. Heimann and R. Money-Kyrle (eds) *New Directions in Psychoanalysis*. London: Tavistock, pp. 220–39.

Bion, W.R. (1959) Attacks on linking, *International Journal of Psychoanalysis*, 40: 308–15.

Bion, W.R. (1961) *Experiences in Groups and Other Papers*. London: Tavistock.

Bion, W.R. (1962a) *Learning from Experience*. London: Heinemann.

Bion, W.R. (1962b) A theory of thinking, *International Journal of Psychoanalysis*, 43: 306–10.

Bion, W.R. (1963) *Elements of Psychoanalysis*. London: Heinemann.

Bion, W.R. (1965) *Transformations*. London: Heinemann.

Bion, W.R. (1967a) *Second Thoughts: Selected Papers on Psychoanalysis*. London: Heinemann.

Bion, W.R. (1967b) Notes on memory and desire, *The Psychoanalysis Forum*, 2: 272–3, 279–80.

Bion, W.R. (1970) *Attention and Interpretation*. London: Tavistock.

Bion, W.R. (1975) Brasilia, first published in 1987 by Fleetwood Press, later published in 1994 in *Clinical Seminars and Other Works*. London: Karnac.

Bion, W.R. (1978) *Four Discussions with W.R. Bion*. Strath Tay: Clunie Press.

Bion, W.R. (1994) *Clinical Seminars and Other Works*. London: Karnac.

Birksted-Breen, D. (2003) Time and the après-coup, *International Journal of Psychoanalysis*, 84: 1501–15.

Blass, R.B. and Blatt, S.J. (1992) Attachment and separateness – a theoretical context for the integration of object relations theory with self psychology, *The Psychoanalytic Study of the Child*, 47: 189–203.

Blass, R.B. and Blatt, S.J. (1996) Attachment and separateness in the experience of symbiotic relatedness, *Psychoanalytic Quarterly*, 65: 711–46.

Blatt, S.J. and Blass, R.B. (1990) Attachment and separateness – a dialectic model of the products and processes of development throughout the life cycle, *The Psychoanalytic Study of the Child*, 45: 107–27.

Blum, H.P. (1983) The position and value of extratransference interpretation, *Journal of the American Psychoanalytic Association*, 34: 309–28.

Bollas, C. (1987) *The Shadow of the Object: Psychoanalysis of the Unthought Known.* London: Free Association Books.

Botella, C. (ed.) (2002) *Penser les Limites: Écrits en l'honneur d'André Green.* Paris: Delachaux et Niestlé.

Bott, E. (1957) *Family and Social Network.* London: Tavistock.

Bowlby, J. (1944) Forty-four juvenile thieves, *International Journal of Psychoanalysis*, 25: 19–52, 107–27.

Bowlby, J. (1951) *Maternal Care and Mental Health.* Geneva: World Health Organization.

Brenman, E. (1980) The value of reconstruction in adult psychoanalysis, *International Journal of Psychoanalysis*, 61: 53–60.

Brenman Pick, I. (1985) Working through in the counter-transference, *International Journal of Psychoanalysis*, 66: 157–66.

Brenner, C. (1959) The masochistic character: genesis and treatment, *Journal of the American Psychoanalytic Association*, 7: 197–225.

Brierley, M. (1945) Further notes on the implications of psycho-analysis: metapsychology and personology, *International Journal of Psychoanalysis*, 26: 89–114.

Brierley, M. (1947) Notes on psycho-analysis and integrative living, *International Journal of Psychoanalysis*, 28: 57–105.

Britton, R. (1989) The missing link: parental sexuality in the Oedipus complex, in J. Steiner (ed.) *The Oedipus Complex Today.* London: Karnac, pp. 83–101.

Britton, R. (1992a) The Oedipus situation and the depressive position, in R. Anderson (ed.) *Clinical Lectures on Klein and Bion.* London: Routledge, pp. 34–45.

Britton, R. (1992b) Keeping things in mind, in R. Anderson (ed.) *Clinical Lectures on Klein and Bion.* London: Routledge, pp. 102–13.

Britton, R. (1995) Reality and unreality in phantasy and fiction, in E.S. Person, P. Fonagy and S.A. Figueira (eds) *On Freud's 'Creative Writers Day-Dreaming'.* New Haven, CT: Yale University Press.

Britton, R. (1998a) *Belief and Imagination.* London: Routledge.

Britton, R. (1998b) Introduction to *Belief and Imagination.* London: Routledge, pp. 1–7.

Britton, R. (1998c) Contribution to panel discussion, 'The Controversial Discussions Fifty Years Later'. New York: Fall Meeting of the American Psychoanalytical Association.

Britton, R. (2001) Beyond the depressive position, in C. Bronstein (ed.) *Kleinian Theory: A Contemporary Perspective*. London: Whurr, pp. 63–76.

Canestri, J. (2002) Projective identification: the fate of the concept in Italy and Spain, *Psychoanalysis in Europe*, Bulletin 56: 130–9.

Caper, R. (1988) *Immaterial Facts*. Northvale, NJ: Jason Aronson.

Carpy, D. (undated) Fantasy vs. reality in childhood trauma: who's to blame?' Unpublished paper.

Cooper, A. (1987) Changes in psychoanalytic ideas: transference interpretation, *Journal of the American Psychoanalytic Association*, 53: 77–98.

Couch, A. (1995) Anna Freud's psychoanalytic technique: a defence of classical analysis, *International Journal of Psychoanalysis*, 76: 153–71.

Douglas, M. (1966) *Purity and Danger*. London: Routledge & Kegan Paul.

Durkheim, E. (1915) *Elementary Forms of the Religious Life*. Glencoe, IL: The Free Press.

Eidelberg, L. (1948) A contribution to the study of masochism, in *Studies in Psychoanalysis*. New York: Nervous and Mental Disease Monographs, pp. 31–40.

Eigen, M. (1985) Towards Bion's starting point: between catastrophe and faith' *International Journal of Psychoanalysis*, 66: 321–30.

Eisler, M.J. (1922) Pleasure in sleep and the disturbed capacity to sleep, *International Journal of Psychoanalysis*, 3: 30–42.

Etchegoyen, O.R.H., Lopez, B.M. and Rabih, M. (1987) On envy and how to interpret it, *International Journal of Psychoanalysis*, 68: 49–61.

Fairbairn, W.R.D. (1941) A revised psychopathology of the psychoses and psychoneuroses, in *Psychoanalytic Studies of the Personality*. London: Tavistock and Routledge & Kegan Paul, 1952, pp. 28–58.

Fairbairn, W.R.D. (1944) Endopsychic structure considered in terms of object-relationships, in *Psychoanalytic Studies of the Personality*. London: Tavistock and Routledge & Kegan Paul, pp. 82–136.

Fairbairn, W.R.D. (1952) *Psychoanalytic Studies of the Personality*. London: Tavistock and Routledge & Kegan Paul.

Fairbairn, W.R.D. (1963) Synopsis of an object relations theory of the personality, *International Journal of Psychoanalysis*, 44: 224–5.

Feigenbaum, D. (1934) Laughter betraying a negative therapeutic reaction, *Psychoanalytic Quarterly*, 3: 367–70.

Feldman, E. and De Paola, H. (1994) An investigation into the psychoanalytic concept of envy, *International Journal of Psychoanalysis*, 75: 217–34.

Feldman, M. (1992) Splitting and projective identification, in R. Anderson (ed.) *Clinical Lectures on Klein and Bion*. London: Routledge, pp. 74–88.

Feldman, M. (1994) Projective identification in phantasy and enactment, *Psychoanalytic Inquiry*, 14: 423–40.

Feldman, M. (1997) Projective identification: the analyst's involvement, *International Journal of Psychoanalysis*, 78: 227–41.

Feldman, M. (undated) Unpublished paper on grievance.

Feldman, M. (undated) Unpublished paper, The illumination of history.

Ferenczi, S. (1985) *The Clinical Diary of Sandor Ferenczi*, ed. J. Dupont, trans. M. Balint and N.Z. Jackson. Cambridge, MA: Harvard University Press, 1988.

Ferenczi, S. and Rank, O. (1924) The Development of Psycho-Analysis published in English in 1925, New York: Nervous and Mental Disease Publishing Company.

Fonagy, P. (1991) Thinking about thinking: some clinical and theoretical considerations in the treatment of a borderline patient, *International Journal of Psychoanalysis*, 72: 639–56.

Frank, C. (2000) *Melanie Kleins erste Kinderanalysen: Die Entdeckung des Kindes als Objekt sui generis von Heilen und Forschen*. Stuttgart: Fromann-Holzboog.

Freud, A. (1927) Four lectures on child analysis, in *The Writings of Anna Freud*, 1. New York: International Universities Press, 1974, pp. 3–69.

Freud, S. (1900) *The Interpretation of Dreams, Standard Edition*, vol. 4 and vol. 5. London: Hogarth Press.

Freud, S. (1905a) *A Fragment of an Analysis of a Case of Hysteria, Standard Edition*, vol. 7. London: Hogarth Press, pp. 3–122.

Freud, S. (1905b) *Three Essays on the Theory of Sexuality, Standard Edition*, vol. 7. London: Hogarth Press, pp. 125–245.

Freud, S. (1908) Hysterical phantasies and their relation to bisexuality, *Standard Edition*, vol. 9. London: Hogarth Press, pp. 155–66.

Freud, S. (1909) *Analysis of a Phobia in a Five-Year-Old Boy, Standard Edition*, vol. 10. London: Hogarth Press, pp. 3–147.

Freud, S. (1910) The future prospects of psycho-analytic therapy, *Standard Edition*, vol. 11. London: Hogarth Press, pp. 139–51.

Freud, S. (1911) Formulations on the two principles of mental functioning, *Standard Edition*, vol. 12. London: Hogarth Press, pp. 213–26.

Freud, S. (1911–15) Papers on technique, *Standard Edition*, vol. 12. London: Hogarth Press, pp. 85–173.

Freud, S. (1912) Recommendations to physicians practising psychoanalysis, *Standard Edition*, vol. 12. London: Hogarth Press, pp. 109–20.

Freud, S. (1913) *Totem and Taboo, Standard Edition*, vol. 12. London: Hogarth Press.

Freud, S. (1915a) Instincts and their vicissitudes, *Standard Edition*, vol. 14. London: Hogarth Press, pp. 105–40.

Freud, S. (1915b) Repression, *Standard Edition*, vol. 14. London: Hogarth Press, pp. 141–58.

Freud, S. (1915c) The unconscious, *Standard Edition*, vol. 14, pp. 161–215.

Freud, S. (1916) Some character-types met with in psycho-analytic work, I: The exceptions, II: Those wrecked by success, *Standard Edition*, vol. 14. London: Hogarth Press, pp. 311–33.

Freud, S. (1916–17) The paths to the formation of symptoms, Lecture XXIII of *Introductory Lectures on Psychoanalysis, Standard Edition*, vol. 16. London: Hogarth Press, pp. 358–77.

Freud, S. (1918) *From the History of an Infantile Neurosis, Standard Edition*, vol. 17. London: Hogarth Press, pp. 3–122.

Freud, S. (1920) *Beyond the Pleasure Principle, Standard Edition*, vol. 18. London: Hogarth Press, pp. 3–143.

Freud, S. (1921) *Group Psychology and the Analysis of the Ego, Standard Edition*, vol. 21. London: Hogarth Press, pp. 67–143.

Freud, S. (1923) *The Ego and the Id, Standard Edition*, vol. 19. London: Hogarth Press, pp. 3–66.

Freud, S. (1924) The economic problem of masochism, *Standard Edition*, vol. 19. London: Hogarth Press, pp. 157–70.

Freud, S. (1925) Negation, *Standard Edition*, vol. 19. London: Hogarth Press, pp. 233–6.

Freud, S. (1926) Inhibitions, symptoms and anxiety, *Standard Edition*, vol. 20. London: Hogarth Press, pp. 77–174.

Freud, S. (1930) *Civilization and its Discontents, Standard Edition*, vol. 21. London: Hogarth Press, pp. 59–145.

Freud, S. (1937) Analysis terminable and interminable, *Standard Edition*, vol. 23. London: Hogarth Press, pp. 209–53.

Gammill, J. (1989) Some personal reflections on Melanie Klein, *Melanie Klein and Object Relations*, 7: 1–15.

Gero, G. (1936) The construction of depression, *International Journal of Psychoanalysis*, 17: 423–61.

Gill, M. (1982) *Analysis of Transference*, vol. 1, *Theory and Technique. Psychological Issues*, Monograph 53. New York: International Universities Press.

Glover, E. (1945) Examination of the Klein system of child psychology, *The Psychoanalytic Study of the Child*, 1: 75–118.

Green, A. (1990) On the nature of the psychical: some comments on the triadic structure in the analytical exchange, paper presented before Division 39 of the American Psychological Association, April.

Green, A. (2000) *The Chains of Eros*, trans. Luke Thurston. London: Rebus Press.

Greenberg, J. and Mitchell, S. (1983) *Object Relations in Psychoanalytic Theory*. Cambridge, MA: Harvard University Press.

Greenson, R. (1974) Transference: Freud or Klein, *International Journal of Psychoanalysis*, 55: 37–48.

Guntrip, H. (1961) *Personality Structure and Human Interaction*. London: Hogarth Press and the Institute of Psychoanalysis.

Hart, C. (1916) *The Student's Catholic Doctrine*. London: Burns Oates & Washbourne.

Hayman, A. (1989) What do we mean by 'phantasy'?, *International Journal of Psychoanalysis*, 70: 105–14.

Heimann, P. (1950) On counter-transference, *International Journal of Psychoanalysis*, 31: 81–4.

Hinshelwood, R. (1991) *A Dictionary of Kleinian Thought*. London: Free Association Press.

Hinz, H. (2002) Projective identification: the fate of the concept in Germany, *Psychoanalysis in Europe*, European Psychoanalytical Federation, Bulletin 56: 118–29.

Hopper, E. (1992) Unpublished contribution to a discussion of E. Spillius's paper 'Varieties of envious experience' at the British Psychoanalytical Society, 18 November.

Horney, K. (1936) The problem of the negative therapeutic reaction, *Psychoanalytic Quarterly*, 5: 29–44.

Hugh-Jones, S. and Laidlaw, J. (eds) (2001) *The Essential Edmund Leach*, vol. 1, *Anthropology and Society*, vol. 2, *Culture and Human Nature*. New Haven, CT: Yale University Press.

Inderbitzen, L.B. and Levy, S.T. (1990) Unconscious fantasy: a reconsideration of the concept, *Journal of the American Psychoanalytic Association*, 38: 113–30.

Isaacs, S. (1952) The nature and function of phantasy, first version given in 1943 during the Controversial Discussions of the British Society and published in King and Steiner (eds) (1991), pp. 264–321. Revised version published in 1948 in the *International Journal of Psychoanalysis*, 29: 73–97, and finally in M. Klein, P. Heimann, S. Isaacs and J. Riviere (1952) *Developments in Psychoanalysis*. London: Hogarth Press, pp. 6–121.

Jaques, E. (1969) Contribution to a discussion of envy. Unpublished paper contributed to the Symposium of the British Psychoanalytical Society on Envy and Jealousy.

Jarast, G. (in press) Projective identification: projections in Latin America.

Joffe, W.G. (1969) A critical survey of the status of the envy concept, *International Journal of Psychoanalysis*, 50: 533–45.

Joseph, B. (1981) Defence mechanisms and phantasy in the psychoanalytical process, *Bulletin of the European Psychoanalytical Federation*, 17: 11–24.

Joseph, B. (1982) Addiction to near-death, *International Journal of Psychoanalysis*, 63: 449–56.

Joseph, B. (1985) Transference: the total situation, *International Journal of Psychoanalysis*, 66: 447–54.

Joseph, B (1986) Envy in everyday life, *Psychoanalytic Psychotherapy*, 2: 13–22.

Joseph, B. (1987) Projective identification: clinical aspects, in J. Sandler (ed.) *Projection, Identification, Projective Identification*. London: Karnac, 1988, pp. 65–76.

Joseph, B. (1989) *Psychic Equilibrium and Psychic Change: Selected Papers of Betty Joseph*, ed. M. Feldman and E.B. Spillius. London: Tavistock/Routledge.

Joseph, B. (1996) The uses of the past, unpublished paper.

Jung, C.G. (1956) Two kinds of thinking, in *The Collected Works*, vol. 5, *Symbols of Transformation*, II. London: Routledge & Kegan Paul, pp. 29–33.

Jung, C.G. (1961) Sensitiveness and regression, in *The Collected Works*, vol. 4, *Freud and Psychoanalysis*. London: Routledge & Kegan Paul, pp. 182–4.

Kernberg, O. (1969) A contribution to the ego-psychological critique of the Kleinian school, *International Journal of Psychoanalysis*, 50: 317–33.

Kernberg, O. (1984) *Severe Personality Disorders*. New Haven, CT: Yale University Press.

Kernberg, O. (1989) The narcissistic personality disorder and the differential diagnosis of antisocial behavior, *Psychiatric Clinics of North America*, 12: 553–70.

King, P. and Steiner, R. (eds) (1991) *The Freud-Klein Controversies, 1941–1945*. London: Routledge.

Klein, M. (1923) Early analysis, *Writings*, vol. 1, pp. 77–105. London: Hogarth Press.

Klein, M. (1927a) Symposium on child analysis, *International Journal of Psychoanalysis*, 8: 339–70.

Klein, M. (1927b) Criminal tendencies in normal children, *Writings*, vol. 1, pp. 170–85. London: Hogarth Press.

Klein, M. (1928) Early stages of the Oedipus conflict, *Writings*, vol. 1, pp. 186–98. London: Hogarth Press.

Klein, M. (1929a) Personification in the play of children, *Writings*, vol. 1, pp. 199–209. London: Hogarth Press.

Klein, M. (1929b) Infantile anxiety situations reflected in a work of art and in the creative impulse, *Writings*, vol. 1, pp. 210–18. London: Hogarth Press.

Klein, M. (1930) The importance of symbol-formation in the development of the ego, *Writings*, vol. 1, pp. 219–32. London: Hogarth Press.

Klein, M. (1932a) *The Psychoanalysis of Children, Writings*, vol 2. London: Hogarth Press.

Klein, M. (1932b) An obsessional neurosis in a six-year-old girl, Chapter 3 of *The Psychoanalysis of Children*, vol. 2 of *Writings*, pp. 35–57. London: Hogarth Press.

Klein, M. (1935) A contribution to the psychogenesis of manic-depressive states, *Writings*, vol. 1, pp. 236–89. London: Hogarth Press.

Klein, M. (1940) Mourning and its relation to manic-depressive states, *Writings*, vol. 1, pp. 344–69. London: Hogarth Press.

Klein, M. (1945) The Oedipus complex in the light of early anxieties, *Writings*, vol. 1, pp. 370–419. London: Hogarth Press.

Klein, M. (1946) Notes on some schizoid mechanisms, *International Journal of Psychoanalysis*, 27: 99–110.

Klein, M. (1948) On the theory of anxiety and guilt, *International Journal of Psychoanalysis*, 29: 114–23; also in *Writings*, vol. 1, pp. 25–42.

Klein, M. (1952a) The origins of transference, *International Journal of Psychoanalysis*, 33: 433–8.

Klein, M. (1952b) The mutual influences in the development of ego and id, *Writings*, vol. 3, pp. 57–60. London: Hogarth Press.

Klein, M. (1952c) Some theoretical conclusions regarding the emotional life of the infant, *Writings*, vol. 3, pp. 61–93. London: Hogarth Press.

Klein, M. (1952d) On observing the behaviour of young infants, *Writings*, vol. 3, pp. 94–121. London: Hogarth Press.

Klein, M. (1955a) The psycho-analytic play technique: its history and significance, in M. Klein, P. Heimann and R. Money-Kyrle (eds) *New Directions in Psychoanalysis*. London: Tavistock, pp. 3–22.

Klein, M. (1955b) On identification, in M. Klein, P. Heimann and R. Money-Kyrle (eds) *New Directions in Psychoanalysis*. London: Tavistock, pp. 309–45.

Klein, M. (1957) *Envy and Gratitude*. London: Tavistock.

Klein, M. (1958) On the development of mental functioning, *Writings*, vol. 3, pp. 236–46. London: Hogarth Press.

Klein, M. (1959) Our adult world and its roots in infancy, *Writings*, vol. 3, pp. 247–63. London: Hogarth Press.

Klein, M. (1960) A note on depression in the schizophrenic, *Writings*, vol. 3, pp. 264–7. London: Hogarth Press.

Klein, M. (1961) *Narrative of a Child Analysis*. London: Tavistock.

Klein, M. (1963) On the sense of loneliness, *Writings*, vol. 3, pp. 300–13. London: Hogarth Press.

Klein, M. (1975, 1980) *The Writings of Melanie Klein*, vol. 1, *Love, Guilt and Reparation*, vol. 2, *The Psychoanalysis of Children*, vol. 3, *Envy and Gratitude and Other Works*, vol. 4, *The Narrative of a Child Analysis*. London: Hogarth Press and the Institute of Psychoanalysis.

Klein, M., Heimann, R., Isaac, S. and Riviere, J. (1952) *Developments in Psycho-Analysis*, edited by J. Riviere, London: Hogarth Press and the Institute of Psychoanalysis.

Kohon, G. (2000) Dreams, acting out and symbolic impoverishment, in *No Lost Certainties to be Recovered*. London: Karnac Books, pp. 73–86.

Langs, R. (1976) The negative therapeutic interaction, in *The Therapeutic Interaction*. New York: Jason Aronson, pp. 136–9.

Laplanche, J. (1999) *Essays on Otherness*, trans. P. Slotkin, L. Thurston and L. Hill. London: Rebus Press.

Laplanche, J. and Pontalis, J.-B. (1973) 'Phantasy', in *The Language of Psychoanalysis*. London: Hogarth Press, pp. 314–19.

Leach, E.R. (1954) *Political Systems of Highland Burma*. London: London School of Economics and Political Science.

Leach, E.R. (1955/1961) Time and false noses, in S. Hugh-Jones and J. Laidlaw (eds) (2001) *The Essential Edmund Leach*. New Haven, CT: Yale University Press.

Leach, E.R. (1977) Anthropos, in S. Hugh-Jones and J. Laidlaw (eds) (2001) *The Essential Edmund Leach*. New Haven, CT: Yale University Press, pp. 324–79.

Leach, E.R. (1981) Once a knight is quite enough, in S. Hugh-Jones and J. Laidlaw (eds) (2001) *The Essential Edmund Leach*. New Haven, CT: Yale University Press, pp. 194–209.

Leach, E.R. (1986) The big fish in the Biblical wilderness, *International Review of Psychoanalysis*, 13: 129–41.

Likierman, N.M. (2004) *Melanie Klein: Her Work in Context*. London: Continuum.

Loewald, H.W. (1972) Freud's conception of the negative therapeutic reaction, with comments on instinct theory, *Journal of the American Psychoanalytic Association*, 20: 235–45.

Lussana, P. (1992) Envy, *Rivista di Psicoanalisi*, 38: 122–53.

Mahler, M., Pine, F. and Bergman, A. (1975) *The Psychological Birth of the Human Infant*. London: Karnac Books.

Malinowski, B. (1929) *The Sexual Life of Savages*. New York: Eugenics Publishing Co.

Mason, A. (in press) Vicissitudes of projective identification.

Massidda, G.B. (1999) Shall we ever know the whole truth about projective identification? *International Journal of Psychoanalysis*, 80: 365–67.

McLaughlin, J.T. (1993) Work with patients: the impetus for self analysis, *Psychoanalytic Inquiry*, 13: 365–89.

Meltzer, D. (1975) Adhesive identification, *Contemporary Psychoanalysis*, 11: 289–10.

Meltzer, D. (1978) *The Kleinian Development*. Strath Tay: Clunie Press.

Meltzer, D., Bremner, J., Hoxter, S., Weddell, D. and Wittenberg, I. (1975) *Explorations in Autism*. Strath Tay: Clunie Press.

Middlemore, M.P. (1941) *The Nursing Couple*. London: Hamish Hamilton.

Money-Kyrle, R. (1956) Normal counter-transference and some of its deviations, *International Journal of Psychoanalysis*, 37: 360–6.

Money-Kyrle, R. (1968) Cognitive development, *International Journal of Psychoanalysis*, 49: 691–8.

O'Shaughnessy, E. (1981a) W.R. Bion's theory of thinking and new techniques in child analysis, in E.B. Spillius (ed.) *Melanie Klein Today*, vol. 2. London: Routledge, 1988, pp. 177–90.

O'Shaughnessy, E. (1981b) A clinical study of a defensive organization, *International Journal of Psychoanalysis*, 62: 359–69.

O'Shaughnessy, E. (1989) The invisible Oedipus complex, in J. Steiner (ed.) *The Oedipus Complex Today*, London: Karnac, pp. 129–50.

O'Shaughnessy, E. (1992a) Psychosis: not thinking in a bizarre world, in R. Anderson (ed.) *Clinical Lectures on Klein and Bion*. London: Routledge, pp. 89–101.

O'Shaughnessy, E. (1992b) Enclaves and excursions, *International Journal of Psychoanalysis*, 73: 603–11.

O'Shaughnessy, E. (in press a) Three patterns of identification.

O'Shaughnessy, E. (in press b) Contemporary Freudians, independents and Kleinians: the concept of projective identification and the British Society.

Ogden, T. (1990) On the structure of experience, in L.D. Boyer and P. Giovacchini (eds) *Master Clinicians on Treating the Regressed Patient*. Northvale, NJ: Jason Aronson, pp. 69–95.

Olinick, S.L. (1964) The negative therapeutic reaction, *International Journal of Psychoanalysis*, 45: 540–8.

Olinick, S.L. (1970) The negative therapeutic reaction: report on scientific proceedings, *Journal of the American Psychoanalytic Association*, 18: 655–72.

Petot, J-M. (1990, 1991) *Melanie Klein*, vol. 1 (1990) *First Discoveries and First System, 1919–1932*, vol. 2 (1991) *The Ego and the Good Object*, trans. C. Trollope. Madison, WI: International University Press.

Pine, F. (1992) Some refinements of the separation–individuation concept in light of research on infants, *The Psychoanalytic Study of the Child*, 47: 103–16.

Quinodoz, J-M. (1991) *La Solitude Apprivoisée*. Paris: Presses Universitaires de France.

Quinodoz, J.-M. (2002) Projective identification: what do French-speaking analysts think? *Psychoanalysis in Europe*, European Psychoanalytical Federation Bulletin, 56: 139–47.

Quinodoz, J-M. (in press) Projective identification in contemporary French-language psychoanalysis.

Racker, H. (1953) A contribution to the problem of counter-transference, *International Journal of Psychoanalysis*, 34: 313–24.

Racker, H. (1957) The meaning and uses of countertransference, *Psychoanalytic Quarterly*, 26: 303–57.

Racker, H. (1958) Counter-resistance and interpretation, *International Journal of Psychoanalysis*, 6: 215–21.

Racker, H. (1968) *Transference and Countertransference*. London: Hogarth Press.

Radcliffe-Brown, A.R. (1933) *The Andaman Islanders*. Cambridge: Cambridge University Press.

Radcliffe-Brown, A.R. (1952) *Structure and Function in Primitive Society*. London: Cohen & West.

Rayner, E. (1991) *The Independent Mind in British Psychoanalysis*. London: Free Association Books.

Reich, W. (1933) *Character Analysis*, trans. Theodore Wolfe. London: Vision Press, 1950.

Rickman, J. (1951) Reflections on the function and organization of a psycho-analytic society, *International Journal of Psychoanalysis*, 32: 218–37.

Riesenberg-Malcolm, R. (1981) Melanie Klein: achievements and problems, in R. Langs (ed.) *The Yearbook of Psychoanalysis and Psychotherapy*. New York: Gardner Press, 1986.

Riesenberg-Malcolm, R. (1986) Interpretation: the past in the present, *International Review of Psychoanalysis*, 13: 433–43.

Riesenberg-Malcolm, R. (1994) Conceptualisation of clinical facts in the analytic process, *International Journal of Psychoanalysis*, 75: 1031–40.

Riviere, J. (1932) Jealousy as a mechanism of defence, *International Journal of Psychoanalysis*, 13: 414–24.

Riviere, J. (1936) A contribution to the analysis of the negative therapeutic reaction, *International Journal of Psychoanalysis*, 17: 304–20.

Riviere, J. (1956) Unpublished letter to Melanie Klein in the Melanie Klein Archive, C18. Wellcome Institute for the History of Medicine.

Rodman, F.R. (ed.) (1987) *The Spontaneous Gesture: Selected Letters of D.W. Winnicott*. London: Harvard University Press.

Rosenfeld, H.R. (1947) Analysis of a schizophrenic state with depersonalization, in *Psychotic States*, London: Hogarth Press, 1965, pp.13–33.

Rosenfeld, H.R. (1950) Notes on the psychopathology of confusional states in chronic schizophrenia, *International Journal of Psychoanalysis*, 31: 132–7.

Rosenfeld, H.R. (1964) On the psychopathology of narcissism: a clinical approach, *International Journal of Psychoanalysis*, 45: 332–7.

Rosenfeld, H.R. (1965) *Psychotic States*. London: Hogarth Press.

Rosenfeld, H.R. (1969) Unpublished contribution to the discussion at the Symposium of the British Psychoanalytic Society on Envy and Jealousy.

Rosenfeld, H.R. (1971a) A clinical approach to the psychoanalytical theory of the life and death instincts: an investigation into the aggressive aspects of narcissism, *International Journal of Psychoanalysis*, 52: 169–78.

Rosenfeld, H.R. (1971b) Contribution to the psychopathology of psychotic states: the importance of projective identification in the ego structure and object relations of the psychotic patient, in E.B. Spillius (ed.) (1988) *Melanie Klein Today*, vol. 1, *Mainly Theory*. London: Routledge, pp.117–37.

Rosenfeld, H.R. (1975) Negative therapeutic reaction, in P. Giovacchini (ed.) *Tactics and Techniques in Psychoanalytic Therapy*. New York: Jason Aronson, pp. 217–28.

Rosenfeld, H.R. (1983) Primitive object relations and mechanisms, *International Journal of Psychoanalysis*, 64: 261–7.

Rosenfeld, H.R. (1986) Transference-countertransference distortions and other problems in the analysis of traumatized patients. Unpublished talk given to the Kleinian analysts of the British Psychoanalytical Society.

Rosenfeld, H.R. (1987) *Impasse and Interpretation*. London: Routledge.

Roth, P. (2001) The paranoid-schizoid position, in C. Bronstein (ed.) *Kleinian Theory: A Contemporary Perspective*. London: Whurr, pp. 32–46.

Roussillon, R. (1998) Historical reference, *après-coup* and the primal scene, Standing Conference on Psychoanalytical Intracultural and Intercultural Dialogue. Paris: International Psychoanalytical Association.

Rycroft, C. (1968) Phantasy, in *A Critical Dictionary of Psychoanalysis*. London: Nelson, p. 118.

Salzman, L. (1960) The negative therapeutic reaction, in J.H. Masserman (ed.) *Psychoanalysis and Human Values*. New York: Grune & Stratton.

Sandler, J. (1976a) Dreams, unconscious fantasies and identity of perception, *International Review of Psychoanalysis*, 3: 33–42.

Sandler, J. (1976b) Countertransference and role responsiveness, *International Review of Psychoanalysis*, 3: 43–7.

Sandler, J. (1986) Reality and the stabilising function of unconscious phantasy, *Bulletin of the Anna Freud Centre*, 9: 177–94.

Sandler, J. (ed.) (1987a) *Projection, Identification, Projective Identification*. Madison, WI: International Universities Press.

Sandler, J. (1987b) The concept of projective identification, in J. Sandler (ed.) *Projection, Identification, Projective Identification*. Madison, WI: International Universities Press, pp. 13–26.

Sandler, J. and Nagera, H. (1963) Aspects of the metapsychology of fantasy, *The Psychoanalytic Study of the Child*, 18: 159–94.

Sandler, J. and Sandler, A.M. (1978) On the development of object relationships and affects, *International Journal of Psychoanalysis*, 59: 285–96.

Sandler, J. and Sandler, A.M. (1983) The 'second censorship', the 'three box model', and some technical implications, *International Journal of Psychoanalysis*, 64: 413–26.

Sandler, J. and Sandler, A.M. (1984) The past unconscious, the present unconscious, and interpretation of the transference, *Psychoanalytic Inquiry*, 4: 367–99.

Sandler, J. and Sandler, A.M. (1986) The gyroscopic function of unconscious fantasy, in D. Feinsilver (ed.) *Towards a Comprehensive Model for Schizophrenic Disorders*. New York: Analytic Press, pp. 109–23.

Sandler, J. and Sandler, A.M. (1987) The past unconscious, the present unconscious and the vicissitudes of guilt, *International Journal of Psychoanalysis*, 68: 331–41.

Sandler, J. and Sandler, A.M. (1994) Phantasy and its transformations: a contemporary Freudian view', *International Journal of Psychoanalysis*, 75: 387–94.

Sandler, J. and Sandler, A.M. (1995) Unconscious phantasy, identification, and projection in the creative writer, in E.S. Person *et al.* (eds) *On Freud's 'Creative Writers and Daydreaming'*. New Haven, CT: Yale University Press.

Sandler, J., Dare, C. and Holder, A. (1970) The negative therapeutic reaction, in *The Patient and the Analyst*. London: George Allen & Unwin, pp. 84–93.

Sandler, J., Dare, C., Holder, A. and Dreher, A.U. (1997) *Freud's Models of the Mind: An Introduction*. London: Karnac.

Schafer, R. (1997) *The Contemporary Kleinians of London*. Madison, CT: International Universities Press.

Schoeck, H. (1969) *Envy: a Theory of Social Behaviour*, trans. M. Glenny and B. Ross. London: Secker and Warburg.

Segal, H. (1952) A psycho-analytical approach to aesthetics, *International Journal of Psychoanalysis*, 33: 196–207.

Segal, H. (1956) Depression in the schizophrenic, *International Journal of Psychoanalysis*, 37: 339–43.

Segal, H. (1957) Notes on symbol formation, *International Journal of Psychoanalysis*, 38: 391–7.

Segal, H. (1964a) *An Introduction to the work of Melanie Klein*. London: Heinemann.

Segal, H. (1964b) Phantasy and other processes, in *The Work of Hanna Segal*. New York: Jason Aronson, 1981, pp. 41–7.

Segal, H. (1967) Melanie Klein's technique, in B.B. Wolman (ed.) *Psychoanalytic Techniques*. New York: Basic Books.

Segal, H. (1969) Unpublished contribution to the discussion of the Symposium of the British Psychoanalytical Society on envy and jealousy.

Segal, H. (1972) A delusional system as a defence against the re-emergence of a catastrophic situation, *International Journal of Psychoanalysis*, 53: 393–401.

Segal, H. (1982) Mrs Klein as I knew her, unpublished paper read at the Tavistock Clinic.

Segal, H. (1989) Interview with Hanna Segal, in V. Hunter (ed.) *Psychoanalysts Talk*. New York: Guilford Press, 1994, pp. 41–80.

Segal, H. (1991) *Dream, Phantasy and Art*. London: Routledge.

Segal, H. (1997) *Psychoanalysis, Literature and War*, ed. J. Steiner. London: Routledge.

Shane, M. and Shane, E. (1990) Unconscious fantasy: developmental and self-psychological considerations, *Journal of the American Psychoanalytic Association*, 38: 75–92.

Shapiro, T. (1990) Unconscious fantasy: introduction, *Journal of the American Psychoanalytic Association*, 38: 39–46.

Sharpe, E.F. (1930–1) Papers on technique in the *International Journal of Psycho-analysis*; reprinted in *Collected Papers on Psycho-Analysis*. London: Hogarth Press and the Institute of Psychoanalysis, 1950.

Sodré, I. (2004) Who's Who? Notes on pathological identifications, in E. Hargreaves and A. Varchevker (eds) (2004) *In Pursuit of Psychic Change: the Betty Joseph Workshop*. London: Brunner-Routledge, pp. 53–68.

Sohn, L. (1985) Narcissistic organization, projective identification, and the formation of the identificate, *International Journal of Psychoanalysis*, 66: 201–13.

Spiegel, L.A. (1978) Moral masochism, *Psychoanalytic Quarterly*, 47: 209–36.

Spillius, E. Bott (1980) On the negative therapeutic reaction, *Bulletin of the European Psychoanalytic Federation*, 15: 31–9.

Spillius, E. Bott, (1983) Some developments from the work of Melanie Klein, *International Journal of Psychoanalysis*, 64: 321–32.

Spillius, E. Bott (ed.) (1988) *Melanie Klein Today*, vol. 1, *Mainly Theory*, vol. 2, *Mainly Practice*. London: Routledge.

Spillius, E. Bott (1989) On Kleinian language, *Free Associations*, 18: 90–110.

Spillius, E. Bott (1992) Clinical experiences of projective identification, in R. Anderson (ed.) *Clinical Lectures on Klein and Bion*. London: Routledge, pp. 59–73.

Spillius, E. Bott (1993) Varieties of envious experience, *International Journal of Psychoanalysis*, 74: 1199–212.

Spillius, E. Bott (1994a) Developments in Kleinian thought: overview and personal view, *Psychoanalytic Inquiry*, 14: 324–64.

Spillius, E. Bott (1994b) On formulating clinical fact to a patient, *International Journal of Psychoanalysis*, 75: 1121–32.

Spillius, E. Bott (2002) On the otherness of the other, in C. Botella (ed.) *Penser les Limites: Écrits en l'honneur d'André Green*. Paris: Delachaux et Neistlé.

Spillius, E. Bott (in press) Projective identification in the United States.

Steiner, J. (1982) Perverse relationships between parts of the self: a clinical illustration, *International Journal of Psychoanalysis*, 63: 241–51.

Steiner, J. (1984) Some reflections on the analysis of transference: a Kleinian view, *Psychoanalytic Inquiry*, 4: 443–63.

Steiner, J. (1987) The interplay between pathological organizations and the paranoid-schizoid and depressive positions, *International Journal of Psychoanalysis*, 68: 69–80.

Steiner, J. (1989) (ed.) *The Oedipus Complex Today*. London: Karnac.

Steiner, J. (1992a) The equilibrium between the paranoid-schizoid and the depressive positions, in R. Anderson (ed.) *Clinical Lectures on Klein and Bion*. London: Routledge, pp. 46–58.

Steiner, J. (1992b) Unpublished opening of the discussion of an earlier version of 'Varieties of envious experience' by E.B. Spillius at the British Psychoanalytic Society.

Steiner, J. (1993a) *Psychic Retreats: Pathological Organizations in Psychotic, Neurotic and Borderline Patients*. London: Routledge.

Steiner, J. (1993b) Problems of psychoanalytic technique: patient-centred and analyst-centred interpretation, in *Psychic Retreats*. London: Routledge.

Steiner, R. (1988) Paths to Xanadu . . . Some notes on the development of dream displacement and condensation in Sigmund Freud's *Interpretation of Dreams, International Review of Psychoanalysis*, 15: 415–54.

Steiner, R. (1991) Some scattered notes on *Die Zeitgeist* (spirit of the age) and *Die Ortgeist* (spirit of the place) and their relevance in the cultural background of the Controversial Discussions 1941–1944. Unpublished lecture given to Conference on the Freud-Klein Controversies, March 1991.

Steiner, R. (1999) Who influenced whom? And how? *International Journal of Psychoanalysis*, 80: 367–75.

Steiner, R. (2004) Susan Isaacs (1995–1948) yesterday or today? A short reminder of her work, *Bulletin of the British Psychoanalytical Society*, 40: 1–12.

Stern, D. (1977) *The First Relationship*. Cambridge, MA: Harvard University Press.

Stern, D. (1983) The early development of schemas of self, of other and of various experiences of 'self with other', in S. Lichtenberg and S. Kaplan (eds) *Reflections on Self Psychology*. Hillsdale, NJ: Analytic Press, pp. 49–84.

Stern, D. (1985) *The Interpersonal World of the Infant: A View from Psychoanalysis and Developmental Psychology*. New York: Basic Books.

Stern, D. (1988) Affect in the context of the infant's experience, *International Journal of Psychoanalysis*, 69: 233–8.

Stewart, H. (1992a) *Psychic Experience and Problems of Technique*. London: Routledge.

Stewart, H. (1992b) The process of therapy and theory of technique. Unpublished paper given at a Colloquium in London on Self-Psychological and British Independent Technique in Psychoanalysis.

Strachey, J. (1934) The nature of the therapeutic action of psychoanalysis, *International Journal of Psychoanalysis*, 15: 127–59.

Trosman, H. (1990) Transformations of unconscious fantasy in art, *Journal of the American Psychoanalytic Association*, 38: 47–59.

Turner, V.W. (1969) *The Ritual Process*. London: Routledge.

Tustin, F. (1972) *Autism and Childhood Psychosis*. London: Hogarth Press and the Institute of Psychoanalysis.

Tustin, F. (1981) *Autistic States in Children*. London: Routledge.

Tustin, F. (1990) *The Protective Shell in Children and Adults*. London: Karnac Books.

Valenstein, A. F. (1973) On attachment to painful feelings and the negative therapeutic reaction, *Psychoanalytic Study of the Child*, 28: 365–92.

Van Gennep, A. (1908–9) *The Rites of Passage*. London.

Weber, M. (1947) *Max Weber: The Theory of Social and Economic Organization*, trans. by A.M. Henderson and T. Parsons, ed. by T. Parsons. New York: Oxford University Press.

Whelan, M. (2000) *Mistress of her Own Thoughts: Ella Freeman Sharpe and the Practice of Psychoanalysis*. London: Rebus Press.

Weiss, E. (1925) Über eine noch nicht beschriebene Phase der Entwicklung zur heterosexuellen Liebe, *Int. Z. Psychoanal.*, 11: 429–43.

Winnicott, D.W. (1945) Primitive emotional development, *International Journal of Psychoanalysis*, 36: 137–43.

Winnicott, D.W. (1952) Psychoses and child care, *British Journal of Medical Psychology*, 26: 68–74.

Winnicott, D.W. (1953) Transitional objects and transitional phenomena, *International Journal of Psychoanalysis*, 34: 89–97.

Winnicott, D.W. (1956a) Primary maternal preoccupation, in *Through Paediatrics to Psychoanalysis*. London: Hogarth Press and The Institute of Psychoanalysis, 1975, pp. 300–5.

Winnicott, D.W. (1956b) Letter of 3 February, 1956 to Joan Riviere, in F.R. Rodman (ed.) *The Spontaneous Gesture: Selected Letters of D.W. Winnicott*. Cambridge, MA: Harvard University Press.

Winnicott, D.W. (1958) The capacity to be alone, *International Journal of Psychoanalysis*, 39: 416–20.

Winnicott, D.W. (1962) Ego integration in child development, in *Maturational Processes and the Facilitating Environment*. London: Hogarth Press, 1965, pp. 56–63.

Winnicott, D.W. (1965) A personal view of the Kleinian contribution, in *The Maturational Process and the Facilitating Environment*. London: Hogarth Press, pp. 171–9.

Winnicott, D.W. (1969) The use of an object, *International Journal of Psychoanalysis*, 50: 711–16.

Winnicott, D.W. (1974) Fear of breakdown, *International Review of Psychoanalysis*, 1: 103–7.

Yorke, C. (1971) Some suggestions for a critique of Kleinian psychology, *Psychoanalytic Study of the Child*, 26: 129–55.

Zetzel, E. (1956) An approach to the relation between concept and content in psychoanalytic theory (with special reference to the work of Melanie Klein and her followers), *The Psychoanalytic Study of the Child*, 11: 99–121.

Zetzel, E. (1958) Review of Klein's *Envy and Gratitude, Psychoanalytic Quarterly*, 27: 409–12.

INDEX

Page entries for headings with subheadings refer to general aspects of that topic

acquisitive projective identification (Britton) 117–18, 121
actualization (Sandler) 41, 54, 112, 120; *see also* enactment
aggression 29, 34, 81
alpha function (Bion) 44
American Psychoanalytic Association 180
American schools 180
analytic attitude 71, 72
analytic relationship: anthropological perspective 14–15, 18, 19; contemporary Kleinian perspective 187–90, 191, 192; subjective/objective aspects 85
anatomical language *see* language of interpretation
annihilation fears *see* death instinct; persecutory anxiety
anthropological perspective 2, 11–12, 196–7; functionalism 8, 9; ideal-types 8; London families study 9; methodology/causality 15–20, 23; nature/nurture debate 18; need-satisfying approach 8; participant observation 8, 13–14; past influences 20, 21; and psychoanalysis 12, 20–22; research perspectives 13–15, 21; social anthropology 7, 8; social networks 10;

structural-functionalism 9, 10, 11, 20; structuralism 8, 11, 17; and therapeutic relationship 14–15, 18, 19; Tonga study 11, 17, 19; wilderness 21–2, 23
anxiety: depressive 38; interpretation of 77; persecutory 35, 37, 88; psychotic 29–30; response 33; role in development 26
après-coup 20, 104
archive, Klein's 65–66; use of the past described 89–93; projective identification 66, 106, 108–11, 121–6
atopia, psychic (Britton) 147, 148, 220–1
attachment 199–200; *see also* separateness and otherness
'Attacks on linking' (Bion) 80, 114
attributive projective identification (Britton) 117, 121

Beyond the Pleasure Principle (Freud) 29
binary opposites 21; *see also* paranoid-schizoid position
Bion, Wilfred 80; on container/contained 43–5; on countertransference 54, 84; on need/wish to know 61; on phantasy 166, 175; on projective identification

241

42–3, 51, 53, 114–16, 120, 187–8;
psychoanalytical theory/models 18,
19
Birksted-Breen, Dana 104
blame, culture of 18
bodily/anatomical language *see*
language of interpretation
bodily concreteness, children's phantasy
166–7, 170–1, 175, 181, 183, 185
Brierley, Marjorie 106–7
Britain, Klein's influence in *see* Kleinian
psychoanalysis, contemporary
British Psychoanalytical Society 1, 2, 68
Britton, Ronald 117–18, 121, 147,
220–1

catharsis 74
Catholic religious doctrine 157
causality 15–20, 23
child/ren: analysis 69; development 167,
174–5; *see also* infant/s
clinical material: impenitent envy
153–9; Klein's methodology with
children 183–4; negative therapeutic
reaction 133–7; ordinary envy 151–3;
effect of the past
95–9 99–102, 105; phantasy 171–2,
175–8; primal scene enactment
192–4; projective identification 111,
118–20, 121, 123; schizoid
mechanisms 82–3;
separation/reunion 201–7, 219–21;
technique 82–3, 97–9; *see also* Mrs
Lewis
concrete phantasies 167, 170, 171, 175,
181, 183, 185
consciousness-dystonic envy 148, 149,
157, 161
container/contained model of thinking
43–5, 47, 116, 175
containment 220—1
contemporary Kleinian psychoanalysis
see Kleinian psychoanalysis
continental/French school 179
'A contribution to the psychogenesis of
manic-depressive states' (Klein) 33
Controversial Discussions 58; archive

notes 66, 81; on phantasy 163, 165,
168, 169, 173, 185
countertransference 110, 112, 114, 118,
120–1; contemporary Kleinian
perspectives 53–5, 61, 187–90, 197;
Klein's discussion with young
colleagues 78–81; redefining 114;
technique 72, 77, 84
creativity 47

death instinct 30, 34, 50–1, 74, 88; and
envy 141, 143, 146; and negative
therapeutic reaction 130
defence/s 38, 47–8, 49; against envy
150–1, 157; negative therapeutic
reaction as 130, 131, 132, 138;
phantasy as 167, 173–4; projective
identification as 42
deferred action 20, 104
denial, of feelings towards analyst 71–2
depression, role in negative therapeutic
reaction 131, 135, 138
depressive position 8, 21, 26, 33–5, 37–9;
and envy 146, 158, 159; past/present
influences 88, 91, 102–4; and
pathological organization 46–8; and
phantasy 167, 173, 175; and
separateness and otherness 201; and
symbolic thought/creativity 47
destructiveness 50–1, 74; *see also* death
instinct
development: phases 31; psychic model
86; role of phantasy in 167, 175;
sexual/gender 30–1; *see also* ideal-
typical model
The Development of Psychoanalysis
(Ferenczi/Rank) 74
dogma, psychoanalytic 48, 52, 68, 190–2
drive/s: derivatives 178;
Freudian/Kleinian conceptions 27
drive-structure theory 61
Durkheim, Emile 7, 8, 9, 11

echolalia 208–9
The Ego and the Id (Freud) 32, 129
ego: dystonic envy 148, 149, 157, 161;
and self 33

Elementary Forms of the Religious Life (Durkheim) 7
enactment: phantasy 175; transference as 169, 189, 191, 194
environmental influences *see* nature/nurture debate
envy: Catholic doctrine 157; clinical material 142, 151–3, 153–9; 167; constitutional basis 142–3, 144–5, 161; critique of Kleinian conception 143–5; and death instinct 141, 143, 146; defences against 150–1, 157; definitions 141, 146–7; and depressive position 146, 158, 159; giving/receiving models 159–61; and greed 141; and grievance 142, 148–50, 155, 156; and guilt 148, 149; impenitent 147–51; infant 145–6; and jealousy 140, 141; Kleinian conception 81, 140–1; and narcissism 149, 150; ordinary/impenitent 147–51; ordinary, clinical example 151–3; and paranoid-schizoid position 146, 158, 159; penis 140
Envy and Gratitude (Klein) 33, 34, 37, 50, 108, 140, 142
Envy and Jealousy Symposium 143, 150
epistemophilic instinct, the 'wish to know' 30, 45, 84
experiences of external reality 72

Family and Social Network (Spillius) 10
'Formulations on the two principles of mental functioning' (Freud) 163
free association 25
French school 179
Freud, Anna 16, 25, 81
Freud, Sigmund/Freudian theory 11, 16, 25, 32–3; drives 27; and Klein's work 25; on negative therapeutic reaction 129–33; on phantasy 163–7, 179; topographical model of mind 164, 171, 179; on transference 186
Fritz (Klein's 5-year-old patient/son) 167
frustration model of thinking 43
functionalism 8, 9

G (Klein's clinical material) 95–99
Gammill, James 67, 81
gender development 30–1
giving/receiving models of envy 159–61
good object 38
greed 141; *see also* envy
grievance 73, 142, 148–50, 155, 156, 161; *see also* impenitent envy
'groups' British Psychoanalytical Society 2, 23–4
guilt: and envy 148, 149; and negative therapeutic reaction 130–3, 137–9

hate 27, 34, 45, 76, 142
here-and-now: contemporary emphasis on 55–7, 60, 190, 197; and the past 76, 102–5
hypothetical infant *see* ideal-typical model of infancy

ideal self 158
ideal-typical model of infancy 8, 57–60, 76, 85–6, 88, 91, 102; notes on 76–7; *see also* depressive position; infant cognition; paranoid-schizoid position
Impasse and Interpretation (Rosenfeld) 113
impenitent envy 147–51; clinical example 153–9; *see also* grievance
Independent Group 179
infant/s: cognition xiii, 16, 18, 57–8, 146, 199; ego/object relations 200–1; innate knowledge 28, 43, 166; inferring/deducing infants' thoughts 168, 199–200; *see also* development; ideal-typical model
'Infantile anxiety situations reflected in a work of art and in the creative impulse' (Klein) 38
innate/inherent knowledge 28, 43, 166
insight, patient's 74–5
internal objects 26, 28, 72, 170
interpersonal perspectives, analytical 180
The Interpersonal World of the Infant (Stern) 200

interpretation: destructiveness 50–1; Klein on 72, 73, 77; mutative 186, 197; transference 91–3, 97–9; *see also* language of interpretation
Introductory Lectures in Psychoanalysis (Freud) 163
introjection/introjective identification 106, 113, 118–20, 122, 123, 124–5
Isaacs, Susan 36; conception of phantasy 163, 168–9

jargon, psychoanalytic 2
jealousy 140, 141; *see also* envy
Joseph, Betty: on destructiveness/death instinct 51; on total situation 103, 189; on transference/past 87, 103; on unconscious phantasy 175, 189–90
Jung, C. G. 20

K (Bion) 45, 220; *see also* epistemophilic instinct
Kachin people 9
Katie (8-week-old baby observation) 201–4, 219; *see also* separateness and otherness
Klein, Melanie: as clinician 67–8, 92; countertransference discussions 78–81;; lecture presentation style 69–70; methodology with children 183–4; published papers on technique 67; on secrecy 69–70; technique 83–6; technique notes 74–7; as theorist 86, 92, 144; unpublished lectures 65, 68–74; *see also below*
Kleinian thought, development of 25–6, 61; anxiety 26, 33, 35, 36, 38; depressive position 26, 33–5, 37–9; drives 27; early infancy, ego/object relations 200–1; early period (1920–1935) 26–33; epistemophilic instinct/the wish to know 30; infantile innate knowledge 28, 43; later period (1935–1960) 33–5; mourning 38; object relations theory 28, 35, 34; Oedipus complex 28, 39; paranoid-schizoid position 26, 33,

35–7, 39; parental influences 31–2; phases 31; play technique 25–6; projective identification 36–7, 106–8, 118; reparation 26, 38; sadism 29–30, 31, 32; sexual/gender development 30–1; superego in children 28–9; symbol-formation 30; transference 25; *see also* phantasy
Kleinian psychoanalysis, contemporary 39–40; 50, 61; analyst-patient relationship 187–90, 191, 192; depressive position 46; destructiveness 50–1; environmental influences 44; here-and-now emphasis 55–7, 60, 190, 197; infant cognition xiii, 16, 18, 57–8, 146, 199–200; infant developmental framework 59–60; interpretation 52–3, 60, 185, 197; K/epistemophilic instinct 30, 45, 84; maternal reverie 43, 44, 47; models of thinking 42–6, 47; paranoid-schizoid position 46; Ps–D fluctuations 45, 46; pathology 40, 46–8; phantasy 174–8; projective identification 40–2, 53–5, 61, 187–90, 197; reintrojection 43; separateness and otherness 201; Spillius approaches on technique 192–7; states of mind framework 60; stereotypes/variation 190–2, 197–8; symbolic equation/symbolization 40, 42–4; technique 48–57, 83–6, 183–5, 197–8; transference 48, 53–5, 61; unconscious phantasy 49, 52–3; *see also* ideal-typical model of infant development; language of interpretation; transference
knowledge, innate/inherent 28, 43, 166

Lacan, J. 17
language of interpretation/part-object anatomical 61; and phantasy interpretations 52–3, 175, 181, 185, 189–90, 197
lecturing style, Klein 69–70
Leach, Edmund 9, 10, 12, 21, 22
'Learning from experience' (Bion) 45

Lévi-Strauss, Claude 9, 11, 17
life instinct 34, 147; *see also* love
Linda (Klein's 3½-year-old child)
    192–4, 204–5, 219–20
linking 80, 114
London families anthropological study
    9
loneliness 46
love 26, 27, 28, 34, 45

Mahler, M. 16, 200
Malinowski, Bronislaw 7, 8, 11, 13, 14
masochism, moral 130, 131, 135, 137
maternal reverie 43, 44, 47
Melanie Klein Today 40
Melanie Klein Trust 65
memories in feeling 195
Menzies-Lyth, Isabel 9, 70
models: of envy 159–61; of thinking
    42–6, 47, 116, 175; topographical 164,
    171, 179
moral masochism 130, 131, 135, 137
mourning 33, 38
'Mourning and it's relation to manic-
    depressive states' (Klein) 33
Mr B (clinical material) 133–5
Mr C (clinical material) 175–8
Mr X (clinical material) 111, 123
Mrs A (clinical material) 151–3
Mrs B (clinical material) 153–9
Mrs D (clinical material) 135–7
Mrs Lewis (clinical material) 207; first
    break 207–11; second break 211–14;
    third break 214–19;
    transference/countertransference
    situation 215
Mrs P (clinical material) 205–7, 220
Mrs R (clinical material) 118–20
Mrs X (clinical material) 194–7
Mrs Z (clinical material) 99–102, 105
mutative interpretation (Strachey)
    185–6, 197
mutual analysis (Ferenizi) 14
'The mutual influences in the
    development of ego and id' (Klein)
    89
myths 17, 18, 21

narcissism 47; and envy 49, 150
Narrative of a Child Analysis (Klein) 32,
    68
'The nature and function of phantasy'
    (Isaacs) 163, 168
nature/nurture debate 18, 32, 44; and
    envy 142–3, 144–5, 161
negative therapeutic reaction 129–31,
    137–9; as attack on analyst 133;
    backtracking 130, 131; clinical
    definition, Freudian 131–3; clinical
    material 133–7; and depression 131,
    135, 138; and envy/narcissism 130–3,
    127–9, 142; as resistance/defence
    130, 131, 132, 138; and unconscious
    guilt 130–3, 137–9
'Notes on some schizoid mechanisms'
    (Klein) 33, 88, 106; 1952 version
    107–8
'Notes on symbol formation' (Segal)
    113

object relations theory 28, 35, 34, 61;
    and early infancy 200–1
Oedipus complex 28, 39, 47
omnipotence 37
'On the development of mental
    functioning' (Klein) 88
'On identification' (Klein) 108
'On the sense of loneliness' (Klein)
    108
'The origins of transference' (Klein) 67,
    87, 88, 94
otherness *see* separateness and otherness

paranoid-schizoid position 8, 21, 26,
    33–7; and envy 146, 158, 159;
    past/present influences 88, 91, 102,
    103, 104; and pathological
    organization 47–8; and phantasy 167,
    173, 175 and separateness and
    otherness 201; symbolic equation 40,
    42–4
parental influences 32; *see also* nature-
    nurture debate
part-object anatomical language *see*
    language of interpretation

participant observation 8, 13–14, 23, 192

past 76, 102–5; acting out childhood abandonment 99–102; anthropological perspective 20, 21; archive quotations 89–92; clinical material 95–9, 99–102, 105; conscious view 88, 102, 104; and depressive/paranoid schizoid positions 88, 91, 102, 103, 104; developmental time 104; and here-and-now 76, 102–5; ideal-typical model of infant development 88, 91, 102; persecutory anxiety 88; projection 88; projective identification 102, 105; re-signification of 20, 104; and unconscious phantasies 87, 88, 104; *see also* transference/countertransference situation

past unconscious (Sandler and Sandler) 179

penis envy 140

persecutory anxiety 35, 37, 88

Peter (Klein's 3¾-year-old patient, case example) 183–4

phantasy 27–8; American schools 180; clinical material 175–8; and container/contained model 175 contemporary views 174–8; continental/French school 179; Controversial Discussions on 163, 165, 168, 169, 173, 185; definitions 164–7, 168–9, 179, 181; enactment 175; Freud's central usage 164–7, 179; global 174; Independent Group views on 179; interpretations 52–3, 185, 197; Isaacs' conception 163, 168–9; and the past 87, 88, 94–5, 104; play 25–6; primal 166, 179, 181; and primary/secondary process thinking 164, 169, 170, 180, 181; projective identification as 188; and reality 173, 175; thing presentations 169; topographical model of mind 164, 171, 179; and unconscious

mind/system unconscious 164–6, 170–1, 179; as wish-fulfilment 164–5, 181; *see also below*

phantasy, Klein's conception 28, 29, 163–4; bodily concreteness 166, 167, 170–1 175, 181, 185; clinical material (Klein) 167, 171–2; clinical material (Spillius) 175–8; deducing infant 168; defensive 167, 173–4; and depressive/paranoid-schizoid positions 167, 173, 175; and development 167, 174–5; and external reality 173; functions of 167, 168; inhibition 167; internal objects/world 170; interpretations 157, 185; part-object anatomical language 175, 181, 185, 192; as synonymous with unconscious thought/mind 168, 169, 178, 181–2; unconscious 167, 170–2, 174, 181–2

phases of development 31

play technique 25–6

post-Kleinian analysis *see* Kleinian psychoanalysis, contemporary

preconception model of thinking (Bion) 43, 166

present unconscious (Sandler and Sandler) 179

primal: phantasies 166, 179, 181; scene 192–4, 205, 219

primary narcissism 27

primary process thinking 164, 169, 170, 180, 181

projection 84, 88, 108, 111, 120, 122, 126

projective identification 106, 120–1; acquisitive 117, 121; actualization 41, 54, 112, 120; archive notes 66, 106, 108–11, 121–6; attributive 117, 121; Bion 114–16, 121; Britton 117, 121; changing conceptual trends 112; clinical example (Klein's patient) 110–11, 123; clinical example (Spillius' patient) 18–20; concrete/symbolic 117, 118; contemporary Kleinian perspective 40–2, 53–5, 61, 187–90, 197; and

countertransference 109–10, 112, 114, 118–20; definition 108–9, 120; as feature of all relationships 110, 111, 118, 120; intrusive 120; Klein 36–7, 80, 106–8, 118; motivation for 109, 113, 120, 124–5; normal/pathological 42, 115, 116–17; past, influence of 102, 105; role responsiveness 41; Rosenfeld 113, 117, 120; Sandler 118, 120; Segal 113–14; Sodré 117; Spillius 118–20; and transference 53–5, 61; as unconscious phantasy 109, 112, 126
Ps-D fluctuations 45, 46; *see also* depressive position; paranoid-schizoid position
psychic atopia (Britton) 147, 148, 220–1
psychic development model 86
psychoanalysis, anthropological perspective 12, 20–22; aims and differences 13 analogical similarities 23; beliefs/myths 17–18; methodology/causality 15–20 nature/nurture debate 18; influences of the past 20, 23; research perspectives 13–15, 23; scientific approach 16; therapeutic aims 13; therapeutic relationship 14–15, 18, 19; wilderness 20–2
The Psychoanalysis of Children (Klein) 30, 32, 57, 106
'The psycho-analytic play technique' (Klein) 67
psychosis 40
psychotic anxiety 29–30

Radcliffe-Brown, A. R. 7, 8, 11
reintrojection 43
religious doctrine 157
reparation 26, 38
repetition 75
re-signification of the past 20, 104
resistance, negative therapeutic reaction as 130, 131, 132–3, 138
Richard (Klein's 10-year-old patient) 91
rites of passage 21

Riviere, Joan 130, 144–5
Rosenfeld, Herbert 51, 53, 56, 191; on projective identification 113, 117, 120
Ruth (Klein's 4½-year-old) 171–2

sacred and profane 21
sadism 29–30, 31, 32, 34
Sandler, Joseph 41, 54, 112, 118, 120, 179, 192
schizoid mechanisms, case illustration 82–3
secondary process thinking 164, 169, 170, 180, 181
Segal, Hanna 51, 56, 113–14, 142, 150, 175, 191
self 33
separateness and otherness 199–201; and attachment 199; critique of Mahler's approach 200; and depressive position 201; early infancy, ego/object relations 200–1; inferring infant thoughts 199; Katie (8 week old baby) 201–4, 219; Linda (Klein's 3½-year-old child) 204–5, 219–20; objection to separation 206–7; and paranoid-schizoid position 201; symbiotic attachment 200; *see also* Mrs Lewis
sexual/gender development 30–1
Sharpe, Ella Freeman 70
social anthropology 7, 8
social networks 10
Sodré, Ignês 112, 117
'Some theoretical conclusions regarding the emotional life of the infant' (Klein) 108
Spillius, Elizabeth: on projective identification 118–20; technique, analytic 192–7, 197–8
splitting *see* paranoid-schizoid position
states of mind, positions as 60
Steiner, John 146–7
Stern, Daniel 59, 200
Strachey, J. 73, 185–6
structural-functionalism 9, 10, 11, 20
structural model of personality 32

structuralism 8, 11, 17
superego in children 26, 28
symbiotic attachment 200
symbol-formation 30
symbolic equation 42
symbolic thought 47
symbolization 42, 44
'Symposium on child analysis' 67

Tavistock Institute of Human Relations
9, 10, 11
technique *see* Kleinian psychoanalysis
'The importance of symbol-formation
in the development of the ego'
(Klein) 30
theory of mind 60
'A theory of thinking' (Bion) 45
therapeutic relationship *see* analytic
relationship
thing presentations 169
thinking/thought: development of 175;
models 42–6, 116 175;
primary/secondary process 164, 169,
170, 180, 181
Tonga study 11, 17, 19
topographical model 32, 164, 171,
179
total situation, Klein's view 87, 94–5;
and transference 186–7; Joseph's view
103, 189

transference: analysis in/of 191;
contemporary role 49, 85, 187–90,
189–97; as enactment 185, 189, 191,
194; Freud on 186; interpretations
91–3, 97–9; Klein on 25, 64–5, 85; as
living past 104, 105; negative 25, 184;
notes on technique 92–3; positive 25;
and projective identification 53–5,
61; situation 87, 89–92, 97–9, 215; as
total situation 87, 94–5, 103, 186–7,
189, 197; and the unconscious 75,
76
transitional objects (Winnicott) 21

unconscious: guilt 130–3, 137–9; Klein
on 64, 74; knowledge 28, 43, 166;
past/present 179; system unconscious
32, 164–6, 169, 170, 179, 182;
transference as royal road to 75, 76; *see
also* phantasy

Weber, Max 8
Weiss, E. 106
wilderness 21–2, 23
Winnicott, D. W. 16, 21
wish: fulfilment 164–5, 181; to know 30,
45, 84
The Writings of Melanie Klein 27

Zetzel, Elizabeth 144